FLASHBACKS

The Flashback series is sponsored by the
European Ethnological Research Centre,
c/o the Royal Museums of Scotland,
Chambers Street, Edinburgh EH1 1JF.

General Editor: Alexander Fenton

Other titles in the Flashback series include:

Bondagers: Eight Scots Woman Farm Workers
Ian MacDougall

'Hard Work, Ye Ken': Midlothian Women Farmworkers
Ian MacDougall

'Look After the Bairns': A Childhood in East Lothian
Patrick McVeigh

*Monkeys, Bears and Gutta Percha:
Memories of Manse, Hospital and War*
Colin MacLean

*'Oh, Ye Had Tae Be Careful': Personal Recollections
by Roslin Gunpowder Mill and Bomb Factory Workers*
Ian MacDougall

Scottish Midwives: Twentieth-Century Voices
Lindsay Reid

Your Father and I: A Family's Story
Colin MacLean

Andrew Purves, 1931

A SHEPHERD REMEMBERS

Reminiscences of a Border Shepherd

Andrew Purves

TUCKWELL PRESS
in association with
The European Ethnological Research Centre

First published in Great Britain in 2001 by
Tuckwell Press
The Mill House
Phantassie
East Linton
East Lothian EH40 3DG
Scotland

Copyright © Andrew Purves, 2001

ISBN 1 86232 157 4

British Library Cataloguing in Publication Data
A catalogue record for this book is available
on request from the British Library

The right of Andrew Purves to be identified as the author
of this work has been asserted by him in accordance
with the Copyright, Designs and Patent Act 1988.

Typeset by Hewer Text Ltd, Edinburgh
Printed and bound by
The Cromwell Press, Trowbridge, Wiltshire

To My Wife Jean

CONTENTS

Prologue   1

PART I. CHILDHOOD TO MANHOOD

1. Linton   7
2. Roxburgh   42
3. Fogo   74
4. Glendale   106
5. Wartime   138
6. Gala Water   153

PART II. BORDER FARM LIFE BETWEEN THE WARS

7. Shepherding   167
8. Droving   191
9. The Sheep Sales   203
10. Rural Frolics   216
11. The Farm Workers   229
12. Rural Housing   250
13. The Farmers   258
14. Craftsmen and Lairds   268

Epilogue   276
Glossary   277

PROLOGUE

For a long while I have had it in mind to write about Border farm workers and their past way of life. I have spent all of my years as a shepherd on Border farms and, having thought over the idea for such a book for some considerable time, I have now set down my crook and taken up the pen. For me, this act of writing is an act of remembrance for a dying community – a community which once sustained a way of life and in which I shared a part.

Others have written about the farm folk of Scotland but these, with few exceptions, were journalists or sociologists writing 'from the outside' as it were. Such writings have in any case been mostly concerned with the North East. By contrast, this book is about the farm system in the Border area and it is that system as seen from the inside; as seen, that is, from the point of view of a shepherd at work within it.

Books about the Borders have usually been topographical or have been about the fairly distant past. Sometimes they have been just plain whimsical. Such books contain few uncoloured allusions to the lives of ordinary people. Powerful lairds like Buccleuch, Home and Ker ride roughshod across the Border hills and through such books. Celebrities like Sir Walter Scott and John Buchan people their pages. Only the occasional 'character' like 'Edie Ochiltree' or 'Rob o' the Trows' emerges from the obscurity of ordinary lives to add 'local colour' to the literature of semi-fictional romance and fond reminiscence.

Despite their often expensive education, local lairds and farmers of the recent past have produced but few accounts of life in the Borders (and few accounts of little else besides for that matter). Ministers of the Church, that other well-educated section of the rural community, have likewise made little literary mark in recent times. Such writings as have emerged from this quarter characteristically pay little attention to farm workers and others of a similar station in life. We farm workers seem to have acquired a facility for merging harmoniously into the background of their recollections.

This account of Border farm life and the place of the shepherd in it tries to redress what is a great and increasing loss. What is being lost is the experience of a group of people whose habit it is to take their story unrecorded to the grave. The life and work of the people about whom I am concerned to write lives on only in the memory, and what is now being forgotten by the few of us who remain will soon be lost for ever and to all. No one has yet spoken for these, the men and women of the Border farm touns. I will try to speak clearly for one of them at least.

Like any autobiographer, I rely on my memory. I have not gleaned any second-hand facts or anecdotes from other people. I have not undertaken research into any documents or records of the times. My object is simple: it is to record a way of life which has disappeared for ever. I find that things we accounted commonplace less than 30 years ago have now been virtually forgotten. As for the life before the Second World War, that now seems like another world altogether.

In recalling the past and in looking back to childhood and youth, one has to avoid the temptation to go to extremes of either nostalgia or revulsion. On the one hand, one might see the past through the kind of rose-coloured glasses which make 'the good old days' seem much better than those of today. On the other hand, one might hold forth with embittered indignation to the 'bad old days', emphasising all the worst aspects of life in the past. It is all too easy to see our past in such simple but misleading ways. I will try to avoid these temptations. I will try simply to record life as it was and I will do so as exactly as I can.

The fact is that the general quality of life for workers on the farm is much improved and the labour easier than ever it was. But neither was the past a state of unrelieved misery. In spite of the daily grind, people found time to laugh and to love, to dance and to sing. With progress and material improvement, with the ending of old evils and injustices, it is, however, inevitable that much that is worthwhile gets lost besides. Today's relative affluence and leisure have replaced poverty and drudgery on the arm. At the same time, however, a great deal has vanished, particularly from the social and cultural lives of farm workers.

To a man of my generation who once saw the fields, lanes and steadings of the Borders alive with people going about their business, the countryside today has a dead and empty look. It is an emptiness which the noise of modern traffic fails to dispel. The great farm touns are now all but deserted of working people. The remaining population of a sadly de-pleted Borders is now largely urbanised. These town-dwellers – some of whom have come straight from the farm and many of whom are only a generation or two away from it – appear to have cut completely their social and cultural ties with the land around them. Affection for the land and the spirit of mutual help and camaraderie which prevailed at the farm touns has to a great extent disappeared.

When I see how farm production has increased out of all knowledge since my boyhood, it saddens me to note how few people are left on the land to share directly in its benefits. In the countryside one is constantly struck by the complete absence of people in the fields. With only the odd tractor and its driver aboard even in the rich farming landscape of Tweedside, the overall impression is one of the utter empti-ness and loneliness of upland moors.

Would to God the policies responsible for the high output and living standards of today had gone hand-in-hand with policies for maintaining a vigorous and actively employed rural society.

PART I

Childhood to Manhood

I

LINTON

In the south-east corner of Roxburghshire close to the English border, among the Cheviot foothills, is the parish of Linton. It was in a farm cottage at Burnfoot in that parish that I was born, a couple of years before the Great War.

Linton is a parish without a village. The original village must have disappeared during the Agricultural Improvements in the late eighteenth century. All that remain today are the kirk, the mill house, a farmstead, the school, smith and joiner's shop. Those remnants are in three separate clusters about half a mile apart. The school and joiner's shop have been closed for many years now.

Burnfoot, like all farms in the locality, has steep fields and stony ground, except for the bog and the flat haughs that formed part of an ancient lake, which stretched for five or six miles from Primside to Caverton Mill.

The steepness of the ground is well illustrated by a story I once heard of an English farmer, who came up from the south to view a farm, which was to let in the neighbourhood of Yetholm. 'Well, I have seen fields which lay from north to south and from east to west', said he, 'but never before did I see fields that stood on end!'

My father was an 'inbye' shepherd, which means field herding as distinct from hill herding. In hill herding the sheep are kept on the open hill all the year round, whereas inbye sheep are confined to fields. The two systems differ widely and require separate skills, although shepherds often engaged in both systems during their careers. My father never herded on the hills, and except for two brief intervals neither did I.

My parents occupied a cottage on the farm but not in the

hinds' row. At Burnfoot the houses of the shepherd and steward stood together, semi-detached style, apart from those of the other men.

Father was always a shepherd from his youth up, though his father was not a shepherd, being a farm grieve or steward. He got the notion of being a shepherd from an uncle – a brother of his father – who was a shepherd. Both our father and mother were incomers to the Borders. Father was a native of East Lothian, while mother hailed from Midlothian. They met and married in Yarrow in the early years of this century, when father was shepherding there, and mother was in service as a housemaid in one of the mansion houses.

As a family we were very well versed regarding our antecedents, both parents being able to trace their forebears for a couple of generations, with all the permutations of uncles, aunts, cousins, brothers and sisters and in-laws.

Father's father was East Lothian born and bred, a farm grieve (as the stewards are called in most districts of Scotland outwith the Borders), who took great pride in East Lothian, and in its high farming reputation. He is said to have boasted, 'Aye, yince ye cross Dungless Brig, ye leave fermin ahint!', Dunglas Bridge being on the county boundary between East Lothian and Berwickshire. Yet his wife (our granny) told us that his father – my great grandfather – had been born at Swinton in the Merse, and had been taken to East Lothian as an infant, when his parents had moved there from Swinton. My grandfather was born about 1840, so it follows that the Swinton-born bairn who was to become his father could have appeared on the scene about the time of Waterloo.

I was named after my grandfather, in the time-honoured fashion followed by most Scots families. The rule was as follows: eldest son named after father's father; second son after mother's father; third son after father or father's elder brother; fourth son after mother's eldest brother; fifth son after father's next brother and so on. Of course if names of relatives clashed, other alternatives would be used.

The girls were named after the same manner thus: eldest

daughter after the mother's mother; second girl after her father's mother; third girl after mother or mother's elder sister; fourth girl after father's eldest sister and so forth. So strictly was this rule adhered to that one could almost trace a person's place in the family by his or her name and antecedents.

But to return to the family tree: father's mother was actually a native of Peeblesshire, her father having been a grieve in Newlands parish and for a good few years at Kingside near Leadburn.

Our mother was brought up in Midlothian near Glencorse, where her father, also a farm grieve, had settled after moving about some in his earlier life. She herself was born at Newbiggin near Carnwath in Lanarkshire, but her real calf country was Glencorse and the Pentlands. Her father's folk had long connections with Peeblesshire, notably Tweedsmuir and Drumelzier. She was named after father's grandmother Grace Laidlaw, who, it was claimed, was sib to the same Laidlaw family of whom the Ettrick Shepherd's mother was a member. Mother always said she ought to have been christened Veronica after her father's mother, Veronica Watson, but that her parents did not fancy Veronica as a name!

My mother's grandfather was a ploughman on various farms in Peeblesshire, and then Stanhope where her father was born. He also spent some years as coachman at the Crook Inn, Tweedsmuir.

Mother's mother was a Lanarkshire woman. She was of small farmers' stock from the Carluke area. She died before mother was married, so we bairns never knew her. She had been a dairymaid at Hamilton Palace, when she met and married our grandfather, who would be a single ploughman on the estate at that time. To go further back, mother's maternal grandmother was a Buchanan from Stirlingshire, so my sisters and I could scarcely be called native Borderers! We were not the only ones at Burnfoot who were not of pure Border stock, but the difference between us and them was that they had one parent who was really a native. So we might be described as being in the Borders but not of it. This coloured our early lives to a certain extent but of that more anon. Unlike our mates who had grannies, grandfathers, uncles, aunties etc. living nearby, all our relatives were far away except for a sister of my father, whose husband tenanted a small farm at Ednam for some years, before they went over to the Lothians.

As I have already said, the houses of the steward and the shepherd stood together at Burnfoot some distance from the hinds' row and nearer the steading. It was not the general practice, all over the area, for the steward and shepherd to be housed side by side: in some cases both lived in the row; at other places they would occupy detached cottages on their own. The shepherd sometimes was housed at what had been an off farm, some distance from the main steading. The sheep buchts (pens) at Burnfoot were situated just behind our house, which was very convenient for father, and there was also a disused sheep shed – formerly used to house Border Leicester tups – where sheep feeding boxes etc. were stored, in which we played on wet days.

Shepherds and stewards occupied a special position on Border Farms, a privileged position some might say. Both were independent of each other and responsible only to their employer, the farmer. The steward, under the farmer, ran the day-to-day work on the farm, giving orders to the hinds and other workers, and had the responsibility of seeing that everything went according to plan. The farmer and he would discuss and plan the farm work on a daily basis. As far as I can recollect, the farmer never interfered with the work or consulted with the other men. At the period of which I write, most large farmers just assumed a managerial role, doing little or no manual work. I speak of farms of 300 to 400 acres and upwards, the prevailing size in the Borders.

The shepherd, on the other hand, had charge of the sheep flock, and was directly responsible to the farmer and flockmaster. In all the years that I can remember, the shepherds wielded a great deal of power on Border farms. This was because the sheep were the linchpin of the farming practice, the farm work and crop rotation revolving round them as it were. The turnip crop, grown for wintering and fattening of sheep and cattle, formed an important part of the rotation, and entailed a large amount of work: sowing, singling, shawing, storing in pits or clamps, and carting out to live-stock in spring. The usual rotation of crops was oats, turnips, barley, two or three years ley, with part of the grass cut for hay, and a small acreage of potatoes for the use of the farmers and the workers. The proportion of arable ground, including leys, to older or permanent grass varied according to the quality of the land. On the whole, not a lot of cattle were summer grazed on the farms of the Scots border at that time. There were exceptions to this, of course.

Shepherds and stewards were sometimes at variance, because sheep were so central to the business of the farm, and because each maintained a degree of independence from the other in his work. Unlike the hinds, each had fairly constant and direct access to the master, who sometimes had to intervene if too much friction occurred. Sources of friction between the two were usually in the form of pin pricks if they took a dislike to each other. The steward would be suspected of dragging his feet in meeting a request from the shepherd to have sheep, handling gear shifted, turnips laid out or feeding-stuff taken out to bins in the fields.

The term 'hinds' raw' as described above is not used in a derogatory sense, for this was the usual term applied to the ploughmen's cottages. We would say 'doon tae the raw' or 'at the raw', and once you were there it was 'on the doors' or 'alang the doors'. At Burnfoot there were five cottages facing the road, with flower gardens at the front and the main vegetable gardens running up from the backs. They had doors front and back, unlike ours which had no back doors then. The cottages were not occupied in any specific pattern by certain workers, and one was even tenanted by the blacksmith's son from Linton Downs, who worked alongside his father in the blacksmith's shop.

The use of the word 'hind' for a ploughman lingered on right down to the post-war tractor age. The women were called 'bondagers' in my boyhood, a relic of the bygone age, but it was giving way gradually to 'weemen workers'. On the Border farms the male workers were referred to as 'the men'. 'What's yer men busy wi the noo?' was a typical query heard from one farmer to another when they met on market days.

My father herded at Burnfoot for twelve years; in fact he did not move around a great deal during his working life. Herds did not move from place to place as much as did some of the other workers. His stay at Burnfoot, where I and my youngest sister were born, was a lengthy one since the place was handy for the school at Linton, and the kirk at More-battle. My parents were great kirk folk, brought up in the Free Kirk tradition, which is why they were members of the United Free Kirk, at Morebattle, rather than the Parish Kirk at Linton. All of us bairns attended the kirk and Sunday school from an early age.

When my father came to Burnfoot in 1911, a family called Hogarth were farming the place, but they gave up the tenancy the following year. Tenancies were usually on a 19-year lease with a break at five years, and six months' notice was required for a change by either side. I'm not sure whether the Hogarths' lease had expired or not, but I believe they gave up for financial reasons. 1911 was a very bad year for Border farmers: there was a prolonged drought, and returns from both crops and stock were poor.

Mr Small, a member of the Berwick publishing family, became tenant in 1912. He was an able young man who had come into farming from the outside, and I can remember my parents speaking highly of him both as a farmer and employer. Being a captain in the Territorial Army, a company of the Northumberland Fusiliers, he was called up with his unit in 1914, and subsequently died of wounds in France. During his absence on active service the farm was managed on his behalf by a neighbouring farmer. Mr Small's trustees gave up the tenancy at the May term in 1917. The new tenant was Mr Fraser from Tynehead in Midlothian, an established farmer. There was a farm sale at Burnfoot that year, though I can't remember anything about it. Mr Fraser brought his plenishings with him, i.e. his livestock and implements and household furniture. Those were brought by rail to Kelso Station, the livestock were driven on the hoof home to Burnfoot, and the implements and other effects were brought from the station by steam waggon.

Mr Fraser brought one of the Tynehead hinds with him, but the steward, father and some others of the Burnfoot staff he hired to stay on with him.

Burnfoot was essentially a stock-rearing farm, carrying about 20 score of ewes but not many cattle. Up till 1917 it carried a hirsel of Half Bred ewes, a type of sheep kept almost exclusively on inbye hirsels on both sides of the Border. This popular whitefaced sheep was a crossbred based on Cheviot ewes from the hills and upland farms, and sired by Border Leicester rams, a lowland breed evolved in the North of England and Scotland, from the famous Dishley Leicesters established by Robert Bakewell in the eighteenth century. The Half Bred ewes were again crossed for fat lamb production with rams of the English Down breeds, the Oxford Down being prime favourite then.

The sheep brought from Tynehead were Cheviot ewes with Half Bred lambs at foot, that farm being in the upland country, where production of Half Bred ewe lambs was specialised in. Gradually the Half Bred ewe stock was reintroduced at Burnfoot, but a nucleus of Cheviot ewes was retained for the breeding of replacement Half Bred ewe lambs.

Father had a few sheep of his own. This was a custom widespread on Border farms both hill and inbye. The shepherd's sheep were called the shepherd's 'pack'. There are quite a few herds who still have a pack at the present day. I have no idea what was the maximum or minimum number of sheep allowed in a pack on inbye farms; all I know is that father had 10 ewes plus 3 ewe hoggs as replacements. They ran along with the farmer's sheep and were kept in regular ages, one crop, two crop and three crop, at which age they were sold as draft ewes, the same as those of the farm flock. If father lost a sheep by death during the winter and spring, he would purchase a replacement, usually at one of the May sales, when the ewes had lambs at foot. Any ewe lost during the summer would be replaced by a purchase at the autumn sales. Father was very pernickety about keeping his pack up to strength, for he was aware that it was an important part of his wage. In addition to his pack, he had a certain amount of cash, plus the keep of a cow, a free house and forty stones of oatmeal. The latter was largely used as dog feed. In common with the other workers he had potatoes as a perquisite, a practice which prevailed on the majority of farms. The usual custom right up until the 1930s was that each householder was allowed to plant several hundred years of potato drills in the farmer's field: I believe 1600 yards was around the average amount. The worker had to provide his own seed. The lifting of the crop was done either by the worker himself aided by his family, or by the farm staff at the same time as the employer's crop, according to the usage of the particular farm. The former custom, which caused some hardship to the householder who had no grown-up family, prevailed for a time at Burnfoot. This was brought about by one of the hinds complaining that he did not get the full complement of potatoes off his drills, when they were lifted by the staff, and opted to dig his own. The changeover to the do-it-yourself method was all very well for him who had a grown-up son and daughter to help. I can remember helping my schoolgirl sisters to lift our quota of drills, dug laboriously by father with a graip.

I don't know what other perquisites the steward and other workers had besides their potatoes, house and cow.

Eventually the 'potatoes by the drill' custom died out, and workers were given two tons per household (or more or less as bargained for) of undressed potatoes straight from the field, and latterly one ton per house of dressed potatoes.

The charge fixed by farmers for the keep of a cow, deductible from a man's wage, was five to seven shillings a week. This was exorbitant, considering that for most of the period between the wars the return from a bullock beast grazed and fattened in a year might be in the region of ten pound or even less. One old hand once remarked ruefully, 'If the fermers cud stock their ferms wi hindses kye they'd be on tae a richt guid thing!'

Workers who bargained for a cow but could not afford one of their own were supplied with a 'putten on coo', that is, a cow owned by the farmer but the use and produce of which was enjoyed by the worker, except that the calf was retained by the employer. The man's wage would be adjusted accordingly.

I had three sisters but no brothers; two of my sisters were older than I, so I was the one in the middle. We had a fairly happy childhood with plenty of free scope around our country home. There were always plenty of other bairns to share our games and adventures. The two main families beside ourselves were the steward's three boys, and the blacksmith's three boys, one about my age and two younger. Of girls there were my three sisters and one or two girls who lived in the rows at different times.

Many were the ploys the other boys and myself got involved in. We were keen bird nesters and bird watchers of a sort. We collected eggs of the various species, blew them and kept them in boxes, but except for jackdaws' nests in holes of three trunks were not guilty of 'herrying' nests and pulling them to bits. For some reason we regarded the 'jecks' as fair game, and on occasions we caught young 'jecks' and kept them as pets. The water hens came in for attention too; commonly we robbed their nests, if accessible, and took the eggs home for frying. We treated the peesweeps' eggs in the same way, though my parents frowned on my taking full clutches. One would think that given the almost total absence of small boys from our Border country scene at the present day, the place would be 'fair hotchin' with bird life. But alas! this is not so; much more drastic agents have been at work decimating our bird life than the bands of nest-harrying schoolboys. There was an abundance of birds in my boyhood, many species then common being now extinct or rarely seen.

Game birds' eggs were of course strictly taboo. I remember another boy and I came on a partridge nest, lifted the eggs, divided them between us and took them home. My parents were horrified and sent me straight back to the nest with them, giving me a good smacking into the bargain. The enormity of my crime was conveyed by my father's stricken look, and his remark of, 'D'ye want me putt in the jail?' A staunch kirk man, he had no wish to tangle with the game-keeper and the law. I never heard of what came of that other clutch of eggs. It is possible the other boy's parents were less tender of conscience.

At times when the spirit moved us we kept lists of all the birds seen. For the first few days the numbers would mount whilst we noted all the most familiar birds, such as craw, jecks, blackies, mavises, spuggs, stiddies, and the like. As time went on our daily lists grew shorter, and great was our excitement when a rarer species was sighted, such as the kingfisher or the bullfinch. In spring and early summer we hailed the arrival of swallows, swifts and martins, but two we rarely ever saw were the cuckoo and the corncrake. The latter was very common in the hay fields and sedges in those days, and kept up its eternal 'aik-aik' cry day and night, yet we seldom got a glimpse of it. The cuckoo was the one which teased us most, being heard mostly in the distance. The fieldfares or felty-flee'ers were our chief winter visitors.

Our games varied with the seasons and the whims and fashions of the school playground, for those would be repeated in the evenings or on Saturdays. We kept girds or hoops of iron, which we steered before us with a metal cleek, a piece of wire with a hook on the end. This implement or toy, call it what you will, was made for boys by the local

blacksmith, and accompanied us on the road on most occasions.

The girls played at ball games, stotting the ball on the
ground or against a wall. Those games and the skipping ropes
were played at certain times of the year, but they played at
'hoosies' at all times. Sometimes we boys joined in as well,
but I was a dud at skipping ropes. Sometimes too we took
part in the hoosies game, and acted as husbands or sons. It
always intrigued me how the girls 'putt on the English' when
they played 'hoosies'. We would join in with the girls at
playing 'schools' as well, when the main activity of the
'teacher' was wielding the tawse!

One game we never played was hopscotch, or 'pickie beds'
as it is called in Scotland. I never saw this game played during
my schooldays, and my youngest sister only came across it
during her brief period at a Berwickshire school.

We played at the bools usually in spring and early summer,
and when this craze was in vogue we went at it like fanatics
both at home and at school. I can't recall now the various
games of bools we played; some were for three or more
players and some for two players only. The bigger games
were generally played at school. Our bools were mostly
obtained from a shop in Morebattle, but also on the very
occasional visits to Kelso. 'Glassies', the glass bools with
coloured centres, were greatly prized but dear to buy.

Another popular game shared by both boys and girls was
'hoose ba', a form of rounders, in which we used a hand to hit
the ball instead of a bat.

Cricket was unknown to us, but I remember two boys who
came from Selkirk to spend their holidays with an aunt in the
row, who used to rave about Selkirk Cricket Club, and tried
with little success to teach us the rudiments of the game.
Football was another game we knew nothing about at Linton
school, at least it never was played there.

The time-honoured game of hide-and-seek was a prime
favourite, of course, all the more thrilling because there was a
variety of hiding places. The seeker would be obliged to count

up to a hundred, either by single figures, fives or tens, depending on how long a space was allowed for those hiding. Both sexes joined in, of course, and playing in the evenings might extend until well after dusk.

Tig was another game we played with relish. There was high tig and low tig; the latter was ordinary tig but in high tig one was immune from being 'tig' as long as one's feet were off the ground.

When autumn came we played at 'cheggies', our name for conkers. There were several good horse chestnut trees at Burnfoot, and in the season (often before they were quite ripe enough) we spent a lot of time trying to knock down the nuts from the trees. When really ripe the nuts fell off by themselves and could be easily gathered off the ground. A gale in mid or late September was considered a windfall by us. We played the old game of matching each others' cheggies in combat, engaged in by generations of boys before us and since.

With the coming of winter, with its spells of frost and snow, we took to sledging and sliding. Our sledges were home-made affairs of deals nailed together, two stout sideboards to which were fixed iron runners obtained from the smith, with a few boards across the top with holes in the front one, to which was attached a rope or string for hauling the sledge about. Some sledges were just single seaters, but others were long enough to hold two or three bairns seated one behind the other.

The local term for sliding on the ice was 'slying'. At Burnfoot there was a curling pond, used occasionally for the roaring game by the farmer and his friends, which made an ideal playground on ice for us bairns in hard frosty weather. As far as I can recollect, the curlers were very tolerant of us, and we never seemed to clash with them. This was maybe because they used it so seldom, and then mostly in daytime, and we slyers frequented the pond in the evenings. We used to have some rare fun on moonlit evenings when the young men and women would come and join in as well. None of us possessed skates: they were a luxury enjoyed only by the well-to-do.

Linton

I used to wander off on my own should there be no others at hand to play with. I could be a bit of a loner at times, and enjoyed playing private games of make-believe on my own, blethering away to myself and letting my imagination run riot. When surprised by an intruder I'd be covered with sheepish confusion.

Once I was able to read and enjoy story books, I became very fond of history. We had books of many sorts in our house, some of them religious and some on other various subjects, but most were children's books given by relatives, or gained as prizes at school or Sunday school by my sisters and myself. The household's books had been acquired over the years, though neither of our parents were bookworms. Mother, like most of her housewife contemporaries, had little time for reading, though she was very literate and had a good fund of stories. Father didn't read many books, but was a keen reader of the newspapers; he didn't take a daily paper but got the *Scotsman* handed down from the farmhouse a day old, and in those days it was very full of reading matter indeed. We got *The Southern Reporter*, sent every week by post from the Selkirk office, and after reading it we swopped it with our next-door neighbour for *The Kelso Chronicle*. Both of these were solid, meaty papers at that time, unlike the sketchy ghosts they have become in this day and age. Father also got the *North British Agriculturist*, a weekly farming journal defunct long ago.

Thus it was, with imagination fired by history, my favourite reading matter, I devised and played games of make-believe. I would pretend I was Wallace or Bruce, some Border reiver or Highland clansman or chief. I didn't admit the other boys into my world of fantasy, but my little sister was often used as an accomplice.

The land at Burnfoot sloping up to the hilltop is divided by two glens, or 'deans' as the locals called them, the near glen just above the steading, and the far glen a few field breadths further east. The near glen is the larger of the two, and at that time the tumbling burn running through it – giving the farm

A Shepherd Remembers

its name – fed three ponds throughout its course. These served the purpose of collecting water for the water wheel, which operated the threshing mill and corn grinder. Water power was still in use when I was a boy. The lower pond, which was the largest, was equipped with a sluice to divert the water into the underground mill race leading to the water wheel in the steading. The other two ponds, the little pond midway up the glen, and the upper pond near to the burn head, were feeding ponds.

Many a time we bairns played around those ponds and looking back I often think of what fears and agonies our respective mothers must have endured, wondering whether some of us might get drowned. Our mothers forbade us to go near the ponds alone, but we went nevertheless. Luckily none of us fell into the water or came to any harm.

I remember having an eerie experience on one of my lone trips up the glen, rapt as usual in some imaginary game. It was a cold, grey, gurly day in late spring, the sky overcast and forbidding. Suddenly as I neared the glen head a hawk flew up from a dead thorn tree uttering its piercing cry. Awakened from my reverie, I suddenly felt an uncanny feeling of being very much alone, and menaced by some unseen presence. I was assailed by a feeling of blind terror and took off home as fast as my legs could carry me.

The feeling of fear for wild nature was shared by other country bairns. In the gloaming we would be engaged in some game around the houses when suddenly an owl would hoot from a nearby tree, followed by an answering 'kee-ee'wik' from another. The sounds, so close and unexpected, had a chill effect even on the bravest of us, our game lost its ardour and we slunk off indoors.

At the same time none of us were really afraid to venture out in the dark, though we preferred not to be alone. I can remember walking to and from Morebattle – just over a mile each way – on dark Saturday nights in company with the others. We used to sing lustily on the homeward journey probably to frighten off the bogles!

Linton

We used to play in the dark too in either of the small woods beside the hinds' row. Quite often too we went down to the row and played tricks on the householders in the dark, knocking on doors, then running away and such like. One of our favourite ploys was to make up a brown-paper parcel to which we attached a long piece of string. One of us knocked on a door while the rest huddled sniggering out of sight holding the end of the string. When the door was opened, the parcel was handed over with the tale, 'Here's a parcel that Dawson the baker left for ye' or something to that effect. When the helpless recipient had the parcel in his or her hands, the string was pulled by the hidden jokers and it was whisked away. We soon made a quick getaway followed by angry threats from our victim.

Now and then we would have mishaps such as falling into burns and such like. The first occasion this happened to me seems like yesterday, though it took place before I went to school. I was mortally afraid of a dog the farmer had then which was a surly brute; I happened to be crossing a plank bridge over a burn when the animal appeared at the other end in a distinctly unfriendly mood. To avoid the dog I tried to jump to the burn's bank from the middle of the plank, but fell woefully short and into the water. Fear of the dog, the fall and the ducking, made it a very miserable little boy who trotted home that day, only to incur his mother's wrath.

Then there was the time when the much more serious accident befell me, which might have cost me my life. It was on a hot summer day during the school holidays that we were playing 'Follow my leader' in and out of one of the cattle courts, the half-open sliding door of which gave access to a field. It so happened that a sheep had come into the court to shelter from the sun and flies, and when the leading bairns in the line of players entered, the animal panicked and bumped violently against the sliding door, knocking it off the groove, just as I, being last in the line, was coming in. As the door fell, it struck me a glancing blow on the head, knocking me to the ground. I can still remember making my way home, with my little sister crying by my side, and recall my mother's horror when I stumbled into the house, face covered with blood from a deep cut in my forehead. Our companions had disappeared and left us to it, for they well knew we had been playing on forbidden territory and feared reprisals. Our parents continually warned us not to play about the steading. The farmer himself ordered us off at times, but would tolerate our presence when accompanied by an adult.

Occasionally mother organized picnics when pals of my elder sisters chanced to call. Usually I went along as well, also one or two of my playmates. A favourite haunt was on the banks of the Kale Water, where the kettle was boiled on a fire of sticks, and tea and eatables were served on a cloth spread on the ground. We played games, paddled in the water and had a good time in general. On one such occasion we were all set to go on a picnic, and as we waited for mother and the girls, myself and the two blacksmith's boys were playing on a swing just outside our door, when the elder boy fell off and cut his head badly on a stone. Mother picked him up in her arms, and carried him down to his mother's house in the row, with his small brother trotting tearfully by her side. After she returned and had changed her bloodstained blouse, we set off for our picnic. The picnic and ensuing games proved to be less than enjoyable to me, as I thought of my wounded pal who ought to have been with us.

On Saturdays and during school holidays, if the weather was really warm, we would repair in a group to the River Kale to wade, dook and catch baggies. The pools in the Kale were not too deep so our visits there were not forbidden. Some of the village bairns from Morebattle came there as well, one or two of the bigger ones being able to swim, an accomplishment we others envied but never attained. We were content to frolic about in the water pretending to swim and dive. The baggies we caught were carried home in glass jars, and kept in larger containers where they often survived quite a while. Pieces of water plants were put in beside them to eat. We also tried our hand at gumping and girning trout with little success.

None of us Burnfoot boys joined the Boy Scouts or Boys' Brigade. I'm not even sure if there were any troops of these except in Kelso. A company of Girl Guides was formed in Morebattle; my elder sisters joined and went on weekly parades. The Girl Guide captain was Miss Cowan Douglas of Corbet Tower. My sisters went to camp with the Guides, and us younger ones learned all the guide songs from them.

On Sundays, a day on which all games were frowned on, and whistling forbidden, we used to go for afternoon rambles up on to Linton Hill or Primside Hill, weather permitting. The far glen was another favourite spot; there we used to pace our eggs at Eastertide. Easter Monday was the traditional day and was included in the school holidays. The far glen was a great place for primroses as well as a haunt for birds' nests among the whin bushes. During the summer it was a well-known habitat for wild flowers. My elder sisters collected specimens of wild flowers and pressed them in books, a trick they were shown at school. They had many varieties and I was always on the look-out for the new specimens to take home to them. Flowers in the cornfields were much more common than they are now; poppies, sow thistle, madder, cranesbill were found everywhere, and in the leys and permanent pastures were found plantain, yarrow, self heal and chicory, just to name a few.

A place with sinister associations which we were forbidden to frequent was the Bog. This marshy tract, divided between the farms of Burnfoot and Morebattle Tofts, was partly drained by a ditch called the Cut. It contained some spots where cattle could lair, and several pools of water surrounded by bulrushes were reputed to be bottomless. We were regaled with stories of such pools having been measured for depths with a weight tied to a cart rope, without reaching the bottom. Although it was an innocent enough place in appearance in summer when the sedges and marsh flowers were in bloom, I used to dream of it at nights sometimes, and had nightmares in which I found myself sinking in the ooze. The Bog was the only place where I have ever seen bulrushes growing.

My first school was the parish school at Linton, which was about a mile distant from my home. For most of the six years I attended Linton School there were eight or nine scholars from Burnfoot. At school we had the company of our 40 other pupils. The school, which has long since been closed, had two teachers then. The schoolroom was all one really but was divided by a sliding partition into the 'big end' and the 'little end'.

Mr Lumsden the headmaster taught in the big end, and a lady teacher had charge of the infant classes, I'd say up to nine years old. The headmaster was a strict disciplinarian, but a good teacher. I don't recall that he made excessive use of the tawse, but he had a thundering voice which sufficed to strike terror into the most recalcitrant pupils. Everyone stood in awe of him, though we could call him names behind his back. His favourite subject was music and he certainly plugged it strongly, and was able to arouse enthusiasm among his pupils. Even before I went to school I had learned from my sisters singing such songs as 'The lass of Richmond Hill', 'Early One Morning', 'John Peel' and 'A Wet Sheet and a Flowing Sea'.

My first teacher in the little end was Mrs Cobban who lived in Morebattle and cycled across every morning. She was succeeded by Miss Storrar, who also stayed in Morebattle in lodgings, but she walked to Linton.

I was in the headmaster's room and was taught by him for at least a couple of years before we left Linton parish, and I certainly received a good grounding in the three R's, history and geography, along with a deep appreciation of music and song. Even yet I have only to whistle or hum to myself any of the song tunes I learned at Linton, and I find myself transported back more than 60 years.

Although boys and girls played together on their home ground at the farms, in the school playground they always played separately. We boys played hoose ba', tig, bools and cheggies in season, and two games for which sides were picked called Base and King's Coffee respectively. I cannot recall the rules and intricacies of those two games, which were played with much enthusiasm and which sometimes gave rise to violent arguments leading to blows in some cases, regarding breaches of the rules. Cheating of course was never far from the surface if a side found it was being beaten.

The girls played their own colourful singing games which, I have discovered since, were played by girls everywhere with local variations. To quote a few examples there was, 'The Wind, the Wind, the Wind Blows High', 'Fair Mary Sits a Weeping', 'Water Water Wallflower', 'Around Around goes the Galley Galley Ship', and half-a-dozen others.

On the way to and from school there was often teasing and bullying. One of the very few occasions when I got the tawse arose out of an incident which took place on the way home from school. I clouted a girl who had been taunting and teasing me, her mother sent a note of complaint to the headmaster next day, and I was duly punished. This system of giving pupils the tawse for extra-mural misdemeanours was not uncommon. I can remember three or four boys much older than I, who were called out to the master's desk, and strapped for stealing and eating turnips out of a farmer's field on their way home. Another instance was of a big boy getting the tawse for being rude to Mrs Cobban, the lady teacher. As she passed the group of boys on the road riding her bike, one of them called out 'Ca' yer gird, Katie!' Needless to say he got his deserts next morning.

Our parents were, as we say, well doing and thrifty like most of the Border farm workers. We enjoyed few luxuries, and everything we used had to be made to go as far as possible. Yet we always had enough to eat and were comfortably clad, thanks to our mothers who had to make do and mend a great deal. Hand-me-downs were the order of the day. When older children outgrew clothes and footwear the younger ones got them to wear out. We ran barefoot most of the summer, though in most cases this was done through choice rather than necessity. Indeed I'd go as far as to say that running barefoot was as much a tradition as anything else among bairns of my generation. We enjoyed doing it and looked forward each year to a warm spell in May, when we could discard our boots again. Many of the mothers made their own bairns' clothes out of remnants, or discarded adult wear. Our mother obtained a soldier's khaki great coat from some source, from which she made two or three pairs of short trousers (no boys wore long trousers then till they left school).

Although my khaki shorts were well enough made, they attracted jibes and ridicule from my schoolmates, much to my mortification. Both boys and girls wore hobnailed boots at home and at school; on Sundays they were lighter boots; the girls had buttoning boots or shoes for Sundays. The bairns' fathers cobbled their boots in most families. Families were smaller in my day than they had been in our fathers' time, five or six children or seven at the most, though families of eight or ten were occasionally met with.

As far as I can recollect there was little sign of the grinding poverty and hopeless misery, which was then rampant among the working folk in the towns and cities, to be found in country places. Our infant teacher Miss Storrar, who had taught in city schools, used to tell us how well off we were compared with the bairns she had taught there.

The better fed lot of the farm bairns may be attributed to the fact that many farm workers kept a cow, and thus had milk and butter in plenty for the families. Milk and eggs were not usually allowed as perquisites on Border farms, but these could be had cheaply and in good supply from the farmhouses by those households who had no cow or hens of their own. The keeping of hens was not encouraged in the hinds' rows, as their presence often give rise to quarrels, should they escape from the hen-runs and trespass in neighbours' gardens. At Burnfoot some folk kept a bantam or two, but only in strict confinement. Our parents never kept poultry, for they always lived beside neighbours.

Nearly all householders kept pigs for which sties called 'cravies' were provided, the row of pigsties referred to as the 'soocrives' being a feature of every farm. A pig was always referred to as the 'soo', irrespective of its sex; other names given were the guffie or the grumphy. The pigs were fed on small potatoes and barley meal, which latter was bought off the grocer, or at the local mills, some of which, including Linton, were still in use in my childhood. Householders were allowed free straw bedding for their pigs.

Pigs were kept by the farmer himself too, and the task of killing and cutting up those swine was by long usage given to the shepherd. I have no idea whence this custom sprung or how long it had been in vogue.

The pig furnished the cottager with meat at killing time, and bacon and ham throughout the year. I shall enlarge on this theme in subsequent chapters.

At Burnfoot the workers' cows were housed from autumn till early summer in a byre of their own, having a few hours out in a field by day. They were fed and tended by the byre woman, who had charge of the farmer's milk cows and all the other cattle in the steading. The milk cows were fed a diet of hay, straw and turnips, plus in some instances a small ration of cattle cake. Their treatment varied from farm to farm, according to the circumstances and character of the employers. Some farmers grudged every bite given to the workers' animals, those in charge of them being under strict orders not to pamper.

After being dried off for a couple of months the cows were calved in spring, so that they would be in full milk when turned out to the grass in May. The farmer himself kept two or three cows, calving at different times, so that he had a year-round milk supply.

The cow's calving was an event eagerly looked forward to in our household when we were bairns, for we had to buy milk from other sources while the cow was dry. The event was a time of anxiety for our parents and their cow-owning neighbours, lest something or other should go wrong. A sick or dead cow was a heavy blow to the farm worker and his family. To mitigate hardship in such an exigency, Cow Clubs existed to which shepherds and other workers paid a monthly subscription, and at which they could apply for assistance in the event of loss.

The approach of the calving date was a busy time for the housewife, for the milk pail and milk dishes had to be prepared and the cream separator got ready for action. The first milk from the cow after calving or colostrum was by us called 'beastings', and what was left over after feeding the calf was made into a curd-like pudding by boiling and was looked upon as a great delicacy.

As soon as she got word that the calf had been safely delivered and all was well, mother would hurry to the byre, even if it were the middle of the night, to milk the cow and feed the calf. The calf was not allowed to suckle, but was put into a little pen by itself, in another part of the byre, where it was fed morning, noon and evening. The reason it was not allowed to suck was because of the belief that a milk cow would not let her milk down properly to the milker, after being suckled.

When we were bairns we liked to accompany mother to the byre, when she went to do the evening milking, the byre being in the steading about 100 yards from our house. Our light was a hurricane lamp, which was hung up on the byre wall. After some preliminaries, such as giving the cow a pailful of bran mash and wiping the udder clean, mother sat in on a stool against the cow's flank. In no time the jets of milk would go pinging into the pitcher, the tune of the raining jets changing to a muffled patter as the pitcher filled and the froth rose on the milk.

When the pail was half full, mother rose from the stool to feed the calf, which had by this time grown restless, knowing full well that feeding time was due. We tried to keep it quiet by fondling it and letting it suck our fingers. The suction was so strong at times that we felt our fingers must be pulled off!

The reason why mother stopped to feed the calf before the

milking was quite done was because the cow herself grew restless when she heard the calf crying, wouldn't stand still and was in danger of upsetting the milk pitcher.

Mother poured some milk into a basin and the calf half drank, half sucked the contents, the process being repeated until it was satisfied. Calves had to be taught at first to drink, out of a vessel, for their instinct was to suck. There was a certain knack in teaching a new-born calf to drink. This was done by inserting some fingers into the calf's mouth and drawing it down among the milk. After some effort on the part of the calf and person, the former managed to imbibe enough milk. In a few days it would be slurping expertly and drinking without the aid of fingers in its mouth.

Our calves were usually sent to market at Kelso when they were about three weeks old, which was an occasion for tears on the part of us young ones.

What memories are evoked of those childhood evenings in the byre with mother: the smell of straw, cows and paraffin; the flickering shadows cast upon the wall by the lantern; the rattling of cow chains and other movements of the cows in their stalls; the gentle humming moos from the cows answering the impatient cries of the calves in their small pens, for there was often more than one calf in the byre at a time. One heard the swishing of the milk into the pitcher, the occasional rustling of mice in the pile of straw which occupied a corner of the byre. Sometimes a farm cat would appear from nowhere, hoping to obtain a sup of milk.

Occasionally a neighbour wife whose cow also had had a calf would come into the byre accompanied by her husband or some of her family. Then the place would take on an atmosphere of comradeship with laughter and gossip.

During the summer and early autumn the cottage folks' cows grazed in a little field of their own called the Cow Gang, just in front of the hinds' row. This was very handy for the women who milked them three times a day when they were in full milk. Milking was done in the open field morning, noon and evening. The amount of milk got from a cow at each milking was called a 'mail', it being said of a high-yielding cow that 'she gies a guid mail o' milk'.

Butter was churned from the cream, which was 'hained' each day until enough for a 'kirnin' from the churning we called 'kirk milk' or 'soor dook'. It was both a good drink and useful to the housewife for baking scones. The skimmed or separated milk was fed to the pig, and used in baking too.

The butter not required for home use was sold to the grocer who called weekly with his van, or maybe I should say it was used as an article of barter for groceries. At the height of the summer, with the cow in full flush of milk, mother often had as much butter for sale as would cover her weekly grocery bill and more.

From the time I could walk I was daft about sheep, and nothing delighted me more than to be allowed at times to accompany father in the fields. I recall how he often used to carry me on his back over the thistly patches, or when my small legs grew tired. Many, many years later I did the same for my own sons when they were small. In those days, of course, right up till very recent years, shepherds did all their travelling on foot. There were no jeeps, tractors or land-rovers, and few men went round the sheep on horseback. The shepherd usually set out about 6 o'clock in the morning, taking roughly two to two-and-a-half hours to complete his rounds depending on the size of his hirsel. Crook in hand and accompanied by one or two dogs, he maintained a pretty sharp pace, pausing only to examine the sheep in each field. Before setting off, he would have a cup of tea or coffee and a bite of bread, having his main breakfast when he returned to the house. The rest of the day, with a break for dinner about midday, was occupied by various tasks relating to the sheep, and about four o'clock in the afternoon he set out on his evening round of the fields.

There was a game I used to play a lot on my own which might have been called sheep farming. Using fir cones as make-believe sheep, I mimicked father's work, laying out fields and miniature sheep pens. I was not unique in this respect, for the other boys played among sand at ploughing, harrowing, sowing and so forth. On tracts of grass they used shears to cut out make-believe hay and corn, binding the latter into little sheaves which were stooked and stacked in mimic harvest fashion.

The highlights of my year as far as the sheep were concerned were lambing time in March and April, clipping time in June, and the summer and autumn dippings in July and September respectively. On the occasions when father had sheep in the buchts, which were adjacent to our house, there I would be too of course, if it was a Saturday or in the school holidays, to see what was going on.

As I grew older I was able to help more and more with the lambs at lambing time. What excitement I experienced when father told me that the first lamb had been born. Lambing time on the inbye border farms has always been a 24-hour job, it being customary to shut the ewes in at night. The night lambing was done in the steading at Burnfoot, the ewes being housed in one of the cattle courts. In daytime they occupied a field nearby. Father and the farmer's sons sat up night about with the ewes, using the harness room, which was only a few yards from the lambing shed, as a bothy.

At shearing time I could run with the 'buist', as the marking iron was called, which was blacksmith-made with a handle and a letter on the end representing the initial of the farm of the owner. At Burnfoot it was F for Fraser. Each sheep as it was shorn was marked with the farm brand dipped in hot tar, the tar pot being hung over a fire near the shearing shed. When a shearer had shorn his sheep and was ready to release it he cried 'Buister!', and whoever was available fetched him the buister. It was a favourite job for us boys, when we happened to be about on Saturdays or after school. The buist was applied to the nearside (left) of the sheep's body, the gimmers were branded on the hip and the ewes on the rib, except for the draft ewes which were left unbranded, since they were due to be sold in the autumn.

Shearing was done in the cartshed, emptied and rigged up

with pens for the purpose, the actual job was done on boards, and a cart load of sawdust was used to keep the pens clean. All clipping was done with hand shears then, though here and there farmers were experimenting with mechanical shearing. At Burnfoot, shearing was done by the farm staff, consisting of father, Mr Fraser jun., the steward and one or more of the hinds who were able to clip. The fleeces were rolled up by the byrewoman, who also barrowed them away in batches to the wool store.

The aroma of hot tar, sawdust and sheep, the swallows twittering around the farm buildings blended with the clank of the shears and the voices of men and sheep, are my fondest memories of clipping time.

Then there were the dipping times, the summer dipping in early July and the autumn dipping in late September. The sheep were dipped in summer to protect them from the maggot fly, and in the back end to rid them of wool parasites before winter.

The dipper at Burnfoot was beyond the steading some distance from our house. On dipping days father didn't come in for his breakfast, but ate it by the dipper along with the men who were detailed to help. Since he had been out at dawn gathering in sheep to the dipping pens, he didn't carry his breakfast with him, but had it brought to the dipping place by one of us bairns before we set off for school. His breakfast consisted of sandwiches of fried ham and a can of tea. When I was old enough, five or six maybe, it was my job to carry his breakfast. How I hated to leave the scene of operations and hie me off to school. I can vaguely remember during my first summer at school, crying for most of the day, because I wished I was at home at the dipping. Mr Fraser, the farmer, did the droving of the various lots to and from the fields and the dipper, but once I was about nine or ten years old, father sometimes planned the dipping for a Saturday, so that I could undertake duty, much to my joy.

Such was my involvement with the sheep and other aspects of farm life in my boyhood, an involvement shared by all the other country boys of my time, whether they were the sons of shepherds, hinds or byremen. The girls, too, took an interest and played a part, when not engrossed in their own games, though the older ones were more often occupied in household duties on behalf of their mothers.

I shared with the other boys the delights of harvest, following the binder round the field, fascinated by the way it cut the corn and threw out the bound sheaves at regular intervals, till there was row upon row of them awaiting the band of stookers. The stookers worked in pairs setting up the sheaves in batches of six or eight. We kept a sharp look-out for any rabbits which might run out of the standing corn. Rabbits were very plentiful at Burnfoot, frequenting the cornfields. As the binders in harvest time finished cutting a field, the rabbits were forced to flee from the ever lessening area of standing corn. Everyone tried to bag as many of them as possible, chasing them and felling them with sticks:

> Rabbits het an rabbits cauld,
> Rabbits in the pot nine days auld;
> Rabbits tough an rabbits tender,
> Rabbits sitting on the fender.

Thus ran the homely rhyme describing the glut of rabbits at harvest time. It was a free-for-all then, but for the rest of the year the taking of rabbits was the prerogative of the rabbit catcher and the gamekeeper.

At harvest time, too, we bairns used to ride in the farm cart, when they returned empty to the cornfield from the stack-yard, to lift another load of stooked sheaves. We were never allowed to ride on top of the loaded carts on their way home from the field. We enjoyed watching the stackers at work, as they built the neat round stacks of oats and barley sheaf by sheaf. Wheat was not grown on Burnfoot, and seldom on any farm in the parish as far as I know.

Once the harvest was over and the grain crop stacked, the stacks were thatched to stand the winter. Threshing of oats was done at intervals, as the grain and straw were required throughout the winter and spring, by means of the water powered threshing mill in the steading.

To thresh the barley crop the travelling mill was hired in maybe twice a year. The 'traveller', owned by a contractor, was moved from farm to farm by a steam engine, which also provided the power to drive the threshing mill. The rare occasions when the travelling mill came to the farm were exciting events for us bairns. We could hear it approaching while it was still a good way off, for it moved slowly, engine and mill trundling along the quiet country road like some juggernaut. It usually arrived just after nightfall, having completed a day's threshing at some other farm in the neighbourhood. It was set up in our stackyard ready to start work the next day, the mill men staying in a mobile hut for the night. We rose betimes in the morning to see it at work, before it was time to leave for school. Just as I was reluctant to tear myself away from the sheep dipping, so were the other boys drawn to watch the travelling mill.

To get as many stacks of barley put through the mill as was possible in one day, the farmers used to help each other out, when they had the travelling mill in, and workers would be loaned from neighbouring farms. Two other farms, Linton and Bankhead, banded together with Burnfoot in what was called 'neighbouring'. The barley when threshed was bagged and sorted in the granary until it could be sold, for it was essentially a cash crop. The straw was bunched by a trusser attached to the mill, and built into a long stack called a soo stack.

We country boys were so closely identified with the farm and its cycle of work from an early age that the upshot was we developed a pride in and a dedication to our work in later years. These qualities were grossly exploited by our employ-ers, it being taken for granted that farm men would give of their best, which in most instances they did. Many farmers of the present day and the last two decades who have to put up with half-baked, slovenly staff many of whom have no farm roots whatsoever, would welcome men of the calibre commonly met with on the farms in my youth. Yet those fine workers were not appreciated at the time, by employers who girned and grat, and held them down with low wages, never being satisfied that they did enough.

As I said earlier, our parents were staunch kirk folk, the kirk and religion playing a prominent part in our lives. I never ever heard my father swear, and he invariably said grace before meals. The *Christian Herald* came into our house every week and father would read parts of it aloud to us on Sunday evenings. We attended the United Free Kirk at Morebattle and were pupils of the Sunday school attached to it. There was a strong secession tradition at Morebattle and the UF Kirk was well attended. The parish kirks of both Morebattle and Linton occupied second place. From the time I was born there were three successive ministers in the UF Kirk, the Rev Mr Lindsay who christened me, the Rev James Rae and the Rev William Lawrence. While Mr Rae was on war service, the kirk was supplied by two elderly ministers, Mr Shaw and Mr Stockdale, whom I can just faintly recollect. I can remember the great interest aroused during the search for a successor to Mr Rae, after he had left for another charge. There were quite a few candidates, who were 'heard' by the congregation on successive Sundays, and in the subsequent voting Mr Lawrence was elected. The established kirk was always called the Auld Kirk in the days before the reunion in 1929, although by my time the rancour caused by the Disruption had greatly subsided. The Auld Kirk at Morebattle had a change of minister at about the same time as our kirk, when Mr Cowan was succeeded by Mr Pryde.

Our Sunday school had a large roll of pupils, was well staffed with teachers and was run very efficiently by the superintendent Miss Tully. She and her sister were real live wires in the life of the kirk. We got a thorough grounding in the scriptures and had a system of annual examinations, prizes being awarded for both good attendance and proficiency. We walked over to Morebattle on Sunday mornings to attend Sunday school at ten o'clock, and after Sunday school we joined our parents in the family pew for kirk service about 11 am. In spite of its early start, attendance at the Sunday school was good and regular. Looking back, I cannot help but marvel at the dedication of our teachers, who rose on Sunday mornings all the year round, and did their stint in God's work.

Several of the farmers in Linton parish were members of the UF kirk at Morebattle, and besides our parents many of the working folk as well. Some of the latter went on foot from Frogden and Bankhead, an all-round journey of three or four miles. The farmers for the most part travelled in horse-drawn gigs and later by motor car.

The hymns we sang in kirk and Sunday school stayed with me all my life, and still ring fresh in my mind today, even though most of my favourites have been dropped from our present-day hymn book. Being a shepherd's son, the connections between sheep, shepherding and the Bible made an early impression on me.

Through our orientation towards Morebattle on Sundays, we had only tenuous links with the parish kirk at Linton, our own parish. Mr Leishman, the minister, however, never failed to call at every house in the parish. He always had a chat and put up a prayer in the house. He travelled the parish regularly by bicycle or on foot, was a keen antiquarian and was very well versed in the history of Linton. He was a native of the parish, his father, the Right Reverend Thomas Leishman, an erstwhile Moderator of the General Assembly, having been incumbent of Linton before him.

Among the historical events and legends kept alive by Mr Leishman was that of the Worm of Wormieston, a dreadful serpent-like monster, which terrorised the folk of the parish in the twelfth century, until it was eventually slain by a knight called Somerville, who got as his reward the lands of Linton, and whose feat was commemorated by the sculpture above the door of Linton Kirk, where it can be seen to this very day.

The awe and respect with which ministers were regarded

was still pretty strong in my youth, and any levity displayed toward them was considered very improper.

One comical incident was related by a young mother at Burnfoot, in connection with one of Mr Leishman's visits. He, being a rather old gentleman, was uncovered whilst kneeling in prayer in this particular home, when the toddler of the family piped up, 'What a wee pickle hair ee hiv, and ye've got collars on yer airms tae!' – the last remark directed at the minister's starched cuffs. The bairn's mother, telling someone afterwards said, 'Aa wuz black affronted an didna ken where ti look but the minister payed nae attention til um'.

Another story concerned Mrs Cowan, the wife of the Auld Kirk minister at Morebattle. A certain young man in the village was courting the manse's maid. Having trysted to meet her, one evening he lay in wait for her among the bushes in the manse drive intending to play a prank on her in the darkness. Hearing footsteps coming along the drive, which he thought were those of his lass, he waited until she drew abreast of his hiding place, when he sprang out, seized her in his arms and gave her a hearty kiss. To his horror he realised that it was not his lass he had embraced, but the minister's wife! He was horrified at the enormity of his 'crime' and apologised profusely to the lady. She, good woman, took it all in good part, and simply said, 'Oh, it's all right Tom, there's no harm done'.

Apart from my preoccupation with the sheep, home games, playmates and school, there were other rural frolics and diversions.

There were, for instance, the annual Morebattle Games which are still held to this day. Although I never took part in any of the events, I enjoyed the spectacle and shared in the excitement. The games formed a topic of conversation and argument among us youngsters for days after the event.

The hunting season was another major diversion; like our elders, we country boys took a great interest in the 'hounds' as the hunt was called, and when the Buccleuch Hunt met at the Clifton Park, which it did once or twice during the season,

A Shepherd Remembers

we all got caught up in the euphoria that reigned. We were allowed time off school to go down to the Park, to witness the meet and see the hound pack move off, then we returned to school. Some of the older boys, throwing scruples to the wind, set off to follow the hunt, and never returned to school that day, with dire consequences to themselves afterwards. Sometimes the hunt would run over Burnfoot fields after meeting elsewhere, and if it happened on a Saturday we would try to get to some vantage point to follow its progress. Everyone around us was very pro-hunt, so it was little wonder that Border bairns had invented a game called 'Foxy', in which boys and girls took part. It was a version of what the English call 'Hare and Hounds', the only difference being that no trail was laid by the person who assumed the role of 'Fox'. This game was also played at school during playtime and outside the playground, sometimes resulting in us coming into school late after playtime, having ventured too far out of earshot of the school bell.

When the Circus and Menagerie visited Kelso, some of our schoolfellows used to go, but none of our family ever went. It was a long journey on foot, seven miles each way. Our folks were not keen to let us go when they were unable to accompany us themselves. It was not considered right to let bairns go to such places on their own. At time an adult would offer to take a neighbour's bairns along with their own, to some event or other.

On Hogmanay morning the bairns of the parish were always invited by Mr and Mrs Leishman to Linton Manse, to take part in a short service. Mr Leishman was very keen to uphold old customs such as celebrating Hogmanay. After singing the second Paraphrase and a prayer of thanksgiving, we were presented with an apple and an orange each, and a picture postcard of Linton Kirk.

Some of the bairns used to go on from the manse, to the surrounding farmhouses and the mansion at Clifton Park, to 'seek their Hogmanay cakes' in time-honoured style; there they received gifts of sweets, cakes, fruit and the like. We

38

ourselves and some others were forbidden to do this by our parents, who considered that such behaviour savoured of mooching.

We did not celebrate Halloween, but some of the bigger boys from Morebattle used to come guizarting round the doors at Burnfoot. They were all dressed up in disguise, and were invited into the houses where they performed a short play and sang a song or two.

At Linton school an annual concert was nearly always held. It was given by the pupils to raise money for some project or other. Since all country bairns attended the parish school up to the age of fourteen, there was no lack of varied talent. We performed solo or in groups in front of a large, appreciative audience consisting of parents and older brothers and sisters; farmers and their families; the minister and his wife; and last but not least, some of the gentry from Clifton Park. On those occasions, though all keyed up, we did our best under the watchful eyes of our teachers, who must have heaved a sigh of relief when it was all over.

It is worth mentioning that, then as now, scarcely any farmers' bairns attended the village school, being sent to boarding school at an early age. This practice tended to generate a 'them and us' attitude between farmers and farmworkers.

One of the great events of the winter was the annual Sunday school treat (or party as it is now called) given around Christmastide by the ladies of the congregation. Some of the scholars' mothers, including our own, were invited along to help. We enjoyed a good tightener of tea and cakes, followed by a high old time playing party games. Each of us was presented with an apple and an orange as we left for home when the treat was over.

Another treat we looked forward to was that given for all the Burnfoot bairns, by Mrs Fraser and her daughters at the farmhouse. It was quite common in those days for a farmer's womenfolk to entertain the workers' bairns around Christmas or New Year. The young guests were expected to recite poetry or sing the songs learned at school. At New Year, the farmers would present gifts to every householder. This took the form of cuts of beef or mutton, currant loaf or shortbread, and in isolated cases, coals. Early in the New Year columns of the local newspapers, under the heading 'Seasonable Gifts', carried notes of thanks for such gifts. The following is a specimen wording: 'Highside Hill, Mr and Mrs Brown with their usual kindness presented each householder with a prime cut of mutton, also sweets for the children, which were much appreciated by all'.

My recollections of Burnfoot up to the age of eleven are of a full and lively community life. This was overshadowed in my earliest years by the impact and aftermath of the Great War. I can faintly remember how the conversation of my elders was coloured by events: France, Belgium, Gallipoli (pronounced by us Galli-polli), the Dardanelles were household words. One sensation was a Zeppelin raid on the Borders, in which a bomb was dropped at Grahamslaw, a place just a few miles from us. The names of the local men who were 'at the front' were constantly being mentioned, and of those who fell or were wounded or maimed. I can recall seeing one poor chap who had come back shell-shocked and had developed a permanent shaking of the head; another who moped around after returning, a victim of melancholia. The actual Armistice Day on November 11, 1918 I can recall quite distinctly; we boys and girls were playing in the big wood when the church bells rang out at Linton and Morebattle at 11 o'clock, signalling the end of the war. We shouted to each other 'It's peace! It's peace!' and one of the younger ones echoed 'I want a piece!', thinking it was bread and jam that was on offer.

A Victory Picnic was held in the grounds of Clifton Park in the summer of 1919. There was music, speeches, races for bairns and adults, and of course tea and buns. A real carnival spirit prevailed and even the haughty lairds' folk unbent for the occasion.

There followed the holding of parish meetings to discuss the erection of a War Memorial, which most of the adults, including our father, attended. I believe there were some heated arguments ere a site and design were agreed upon. At the unveiling at Linton Downs, father and my elder sisters were among the audience, and it must indeed have been a touching occasion. There are about twenty names of the fallen from Linton parish on that memorial, and it is a sad reflection on the present decay of rural communities that one could scarcely find that number of men of military age in the whole parish today.

The horizons of myself and my mates were very limited, being restricted to the farm, the school, the kirk, a very occasional visit to Kelso, seven miles away, and a day to Yetholm Show. The farm community in which I spent those early years was quite a harmonious one, though there may have been differences and undercurrents of which I was unaware at such an early age. After the turn-up of 1917, with the change of tenancy, there wasn't much flitting among the workers during the subsequent years of our stay.

2

ROXBURGH

When I was eleven years old father decided to leave Burnfoot. He gave notice to his employer just before Christmas, the customary time for stewards and shepherds to be 'spoken to', prior to the onset of the January hirings. We bairns knew nothing about it till we saw his situation advertised in the local press. It came as a shock to us, especially my youngest sister and myself who had known no other home. Father's reason for leaving was not clear to me at the time, but I gathered in later years that Mr Fraser and he had not been hitting it off too well for the past few years. Father alleged that he had tholed the unpleasantness for our sakes, since Burnfoot was handy for the kirk and school. Be that as it may we were now set to leave at the Whitsunday term.

Father heard of a place through Mr Bell of Primside, whose relative Mr Bell of Roxburgh Newtoun required a shepherd. He went over to Primside one evening to a meeting arranged at the farmhouse there between himself and the farmer from Newtoun, and was hired by him there and then. When the 28th of May came, three carts were sent to flit us and our household effects, and we duly landed at Roxburgh Newtoun which was to be our home for four years.

Though it was a mere ten miles away, Roxburgh to me seemed in a different world. I was extremely homesick for Linton at first, and it took me a long time to get hefted to the new place and surroundings. This affection for the Linton/Morebattle area in particular, and the Border country in general, stuck to me all my life. Even as an adult I got homesick for the Borders, and found it difficult to settle anywhere else.

Roxburgh

Roxburgh Newtoun is situated in that tract of land which lies between the rivers Teviot and Tweed a few miles above their confluence at Kelso. The lands of the farm border the river Tweed and slope gently up to Roxburgh Muir, which forms the watershed between the two streams. The farm has always been part of the Roxburghe Estates, property of the Dukes of Roxburghe. As I have already indicated, the tenant of our day was Mr Bell.

The fields are not steep and stony as at Burnfoot, but gently undulating. The stock was roughly twenty score of Half Bred ewes plus ewe hoggs. The staff was much the same as at Burnfoot, although the acreage would be fully a hundred acres less than Burnfoot's six hundred and forty. There was the shepherd, steward, three hinds, byreman, spademan, odd laddie and one or two women workers. Our house and that of the steward were built together and stood quite near to the steading. Their situation was fairly high, commanding a splendid view of the Eildon Hills, but at the same time sorely exposed to the west winds. From our front window we saw some lovely sunsets, which in my youthful fancy conjured up visions of Heaven! The hinds' row of five cottages stood at the foot of a steep brae, beside the Kelso-St Boswells road.

There had once been a water wheel in the steading to provide power to drive the threshing mill and other barn machinery, but it was now superseded by a paraffin engine. The remains of the mill race which led from the empty and overgrown pond, were still to be seen. The burn which had fed the pond came all the way from Fairnington, and flowed through a woody dean just below the farm buildings, which occupied a position on a steep bluff.

By the time we moved to Newtoun there had been some changes at home. My eldest sister had left home two years previously, and had a situation as housemaid at Langlee House near Jedburgh. This was the property then of Captain Scott, a retired soldier. She used to cycle home on her day off, about ten miles each way, a good long ride. I can remember visiting her at her place of work one Saturday, along with mother and my young sister. We walked over to Roxburgh station in the morning to catch the train for Jedburgh, from Jedburgh station we had to walk fully two miles to Langlee. In the evening we made the return journey, having no bother getting a suitable train at Jedburgh for Roxburgh. It involved a lot of walking in one day, but that was the only way to get about for those who had not bicycles.

Girls in service were allowed visits by their parents and friends. We were quite well received in the servants' hall by my sister's workmates, and had a couple of meals there. Mother was shown over parts of the house by the house-keeper, and she, being an ex-housemaid herself, was very interested.

Many farmworkers' daughters preferred to go into private service rather than work in the fields, that is if they were given the option. Private service and farm work were about the only choice of jobs for country girls in those days. Beside mansion houses, girls found work in farmhouses, in the manses or with other small gentry. Then every farmhouse had at least one resident maid, many of the wealthier farmers' wives em-ployed two or even three. The ministers' wives too kept at least one maid.

My sister trained to be a housemaid and made that her career. She started work in Jedwater, and after filling posts in various parts of the country, including London, she even-tually returned to Jedwater and worked there until her marriage to a gamekeeper in the area.

My second sister had started to attend Kelso High School a year before we left Burnfoot. She cycled the seven miles to school every day, except for a few months in the winter, when she and another girl from Linton went into lodgings in the town to avoid the hazards of cycling on wintry roads. After we went to Newtoun, which was only four miles out of Kelso, my sister was able to travel by bike all the year round. Pupils who lived near railway stations travelled by train.

Kelso High School was then a selective school taking pupils from the age of 12. Those who could pay for their bairns' education could send them there from that age, but for those parents both in the town and from the country areas, who had the ambition to give their bairns a higher education, yet were unable to pay for it, there was a bursary available for such pupils as were able to pass an entry examination. I have never been able to ascertain where the money came from for the bursaries, probably from some Endowment Trust or other. Places were limited and pupils in the rural schools were denied the chance even to sit the exam, simply because their parents could not afford to keep bairns at school till they were fifteen or eighteen, the courses being for three and six years. Some families with ambition tried to send at least one bairn to the High School. This was obviously unfair to their other bairns, who had to leave school at fourteen to earn a living. As often as not it was the youngest of a family of three or four, who got the chance of higher education.

My sister completed a three year course, and then went to train as a nurse at Sanderson Hospital, Galashiels. her secondary education certificate was one of the conditions of entry into nursing. She made nursing her career until she got married, then she returned to nursing in later life.

As a family we were well fed, for mother was a good cook. For breakfast we had fried ham and egg; not a whole egg each but a share of a sort of omelette made by whisking egg, flour and milk together. Along with our ham and egg we had lashings of gravy in which to dip our bread or scone, the latter being made of wholemeal or barley meal. We carried a piece to school along with a flask of tea or cocoa, replaced by milk in the summer. On our return from school after four in the afternoon, mother had a hot dinner ready for us of soup, potatoes with Welsh rarebit or some other meat or non-meat dish, followed by a milk pudding. Later in the evening we had a supper of porridge and milk, or porridge with treacle or syrup when the cow was dry. Father always preferred to have his porridge for supper, so of course we had to follow suit.

On Saturdays we had broth, lentil or tattie soup; tatties and boiled meat or ham, followed by a baked milk pudding of

A Shepherd Remembers

rice, or barley, or maybe a plain milk pudding of sago, cornflour or tapioca. On Sunday it was always tatties and mince for dinner, followed by 'Uncle Tom', a species of steam pudding made in a bowl with treacle or syrup. Quite often though we had a dumpling in a clout, the leftovers of which were sliced and fried the next day, a delicious feast! Mother bought steak and minced it herself for the Sunday dinner.

In summer when milk was plentiful we had curds on Sundays. We ate large quantities of stewed rhubarb and stewed apples in season, and of course tarts made with those, blackcurrants and gooseberries. Mother made a great deal of jam of all sorts, also marmalade. Sunday tea was usually very special, starting with cheese on toast, we had the usual bread and jam, a tart made with currants, jam or apples, and to wind up a home baked gingerbread.

When the pig was killed, mother made mealie puddings containing a mixture of oatmeal, minced liver and fat; she also made pork sausages, and from the pig's head and trotters bowls of potted head. For a short while after the killing we partook of fresh pork in the form of collops and spare ribs.

We did not have mutton very often, just on the occasions when father had to butcher a fat lamb that had fallen sick. This carcase mostly went into the farmhouse, father being allowed a leg to himself. In the event of the farmhouse folk not requiring a carcase, it would be sold off to the workers at a cheap rate, and we got our share along with the rest. It was deemed wasteful not to slaughter and use the carcases of lambs which took ill on the turnips, a frequent occurrence than, but shepherds had to be very careful and above board in such circumstances. The least suspicion that a herd had appropriated such a carcase to his own use would be a smirch on his reputation, and looked upon as a betrayal of the trust placed in him by his master.

Some farmers and their households were very fond of mutton, and would from time to time order the slaughter of a sheep for the house.

Roxburgh Newtown's farmland was divided by the railway track which ran between Kelso and St Boswells. This was a double track line and quite important and busy then, being part of the railway system linking the Waverley line at St Boswells with Berwick-on-Tweed.

To us when we first came there, the railway was a great novelty. It was only about a hundred yards from our house, and we used to rush up to the bridge over the railway to see the trains pass. This caused some amusement to the surface men who occasionally worked on that part of the line. One of them must have mentioned our train spotting enthusiasm to his schoolboy son, for that classmate of mine said to me one day, 'Hiv ye nivver seen a train afore? Ma faither says ye rin up tae the line whenever ye see a train comin'. 'Oh aye', I replied, 'Ah've seen trains at Berwick, Dunbar and Edinburry' which was perfectly true, I had been to those places when on visits to relatives in the Lothians, but I'd never seen trains on my own doorstep as it were.

Roxburgh was very much a railway village, being the junction where the single line for Jedburgh branches off. The head porter used to call out the station names in a strident ringing voice, which we used to mimic: 'Roxburry, change for Kirkbank, Nisbet, Jedfoot and Jedburry'.

A good many railway employees were housed in Roxburgh, more than half a dozen households, others lived on neighbouring farms, where a relative would have a house as a hired worker. Some railwaymen even had houses rented off farmers, but were expected to give paid service at harvest in the evenings, or at weekends. The rail people and their families helped to swell the population of the parish.

The station was a bustling place in the evening when folk gathered there to get the evening papers off the train. Those were the *Evening News* and *Evening Dispatch* from Edinburgh, and were read in the village itself and the nearby farms. The station was also a favoured meeting place in the evenings for the boys and girls. I never went there myself, it being a bit too far away, but I used to hear my schoolfellows talk about the fun they had.

A Shepherd Remembers

Newtoun was midway between Roxburgh and Rutherford stations, so we were handy enough for trains, though it meant a two mile walk to either station. If we should be going to St Boswells or beyond we boarded the train at Rutherford, if bound for Kelso or beyond, or to Jedburgh, we caught the train at Roxburgh. There was a good service with half a dozen trains each way daily, plus numerous goods trains.

Roxburgh parish is divided in two by the River Teviot, it consists of three separate communities, the villages of Roxburgh and Heiton on opposite sides of the river, and the hamlet of Fairnington at the western end of the parish. These three parts are served by Roxburgh Parish Kirk, and a school at both Roxburgh and Heiton. At the time of which I write, 1923–1927, there was also a school at Fairnington, and it had a smithy and joiner's shop of its own. The only road link between Heiton and Roxburgh then was a footbridge, built against the beautiful railway viaduct that carried the line towards Kelso. The viaduct has now been converted into a roadway for vehicles. Before the railway was built communication between the two places was by fording the river at Roxburgh Mill or by boat.

There was great rivalry between the two villages, and the school pupils found themselves in separate camps. Both schools catered for pupils up to the age of 14, and from the age of twelve the Heiton scholars came across to Roxburgh on certain mornings of the week, to get instruction in woodwork for boys and cookery for girls, along with the Roxburgh pupils. Fights often broke out between the boys of the two schools, and sometimes among the girls as well. Fighting usually started with name calling and pushing and then blows were struck, the onlookers forming a ring round the combatants.

There was both a blacksmith and a joiner in the village. We boys sometimes went to the smithy in our dinner hour to watch the smiths at work. The smiths then were two brothers called Aitken, both bachelors, and the joiner was a Mr Nichol but he died and Mr Ormiston came in his place. The smith and joiner both had fields adjoining the village, and there were also two or three other villagers who had fields and cows. Their cows were grazed on the common which lay a short distance from the village beside the road to Newtown and Fairnington. The crops grown on those strips of land were oats, turnips, tatties and hay. To harvest the corn, the cotlanders, as they were called, got the use of a reaper from some neighbouring farm and the loan of a horse and cart to lead it home. Those with cows supplied the other villagers with milk and butter. In addition to the smith and joiner, the other cotlanders probably had part time jobs as well.

Roxburgh boasted a shop and a post office. The shop in the centre of the village was part of a railwayman's cottage, and it supplied general items, and of course sweets for those of us schoolbairns who had pennies to spend. The post office was at the station, being run by the stationmaster and his daughter. The village was an official post town not only for its own parish, but for some neighbouring parishes as well, several postmen being employed to distribute the mail by bicycle.

We had many playmates at Newtoun during our first year here, for there was a family of twelve at the row. This family, of whom seven were of school age, contained two sets of twins. Their mother had great credit with them for they were always clean and tidy. When they left at the next May term there was only one girl on the place besides ourselves. Tidiness and respectability were the norm among farm workers' bairns; only a tiny minority of families fell into the category of 'rough' or 'rag-tag'. Such bairns were distinguished by being smelly in their persons and with ragged ill-kept clothes. Patched clothes were not unacceptable, but boys with shirt tails hanging out of trouser behinds, or dirty knickers in the girls were treated with disdain. The girls wore frocks and pinafores reaching just below their knees, and if a girl's knickers showed inadvertently, the boys would call out, 'Ah can see yer breeks!' which invariably brought the tart reply, 'well, thur clean an paid for!' The boys generally were clothed in jerseys and short trousers.

A Shepherd Remembers

During our first year at the farm, there were thirty eight souls on the place all told, a big contrast from the present day when you will be lucky to count half a dozen. During our four years' stay, there was a good deal of coming and going among the workers, apart from our folk and the steward, at each May term, more so than at Burnfoot. We youngsters were vaguely aware of an undercurrent of unrest among the folk at the row, but it was not until years later that I learned that most of the trouble had been caused by the steward, who, in his zeal to please the master, drove the workers a bit hard. One main bone of contention was their being made to work outside on wet days. On most farms, even in those days, it was customary to give the folk an inside job on a really wet day, the men to clean harness and the women to tidy up in the buildings and steading yard. Should they be at work in the fields, and the weather set in really wet they were called in, and after changing out of their wet clothes at home, they reported to the stable for further orders. There was an old saying 'It's a clear rain that droons the plooman', which meant that men working outside were more liable to get wet through by intermittent rain, when they were kept out in the hope of it clearing up, than in a regular downpour from leaden skies when most likely they would be ordered home.

The workers who came and went at Newtoun and other farms in the parish, seemed to move in a different orbit from those we had neighboured in the Linton/Morebattle area. Quite a few families moved in and out from Berwickshire, using Kelso as their central point. When new bairns came to the school after the May term, they would be asked their name. The timid ones would give it readily enough, but some of the more truculent would answer the query, 'What's yer name?' with the pert reply, 'Soo saim!' Again when asked, 'Where did ye come frae?' they would reply, 'Soocriv Mains!' to bamboozle their questioners.

After the initial settling in period my young sister and I came to like Newtoun very much. There were plenty of places to play and we made good use of them. One of those was the

Roxburgh

Law, a tree-crowned eminence situated in a field between the St Boswells road and the River Tweed. This eminence was a source of mystery to everyone about us, but I learned later in life that it was of prehistoric origin. We joined the other bairns in the row to play there quite often. After the first year when there were no other boys on the place to play with, I played together with my sister, but more often I played on my own, letting my imagination run riot as usual with make believe.

One of my chosen playgrounds was the Muir Wood, a conifer plantation at the west end of the farm. There was a lovely green open glade deep in the wood, where we used to roll our eggs at Easter, have picnics and hunt for mushrooms. I used to go there alone at times to play at my sheep games with fir cones. One day I had a very eerie experience at that spot. I was deeply absorbed in my game, conducting a make believe auction sale, blethering away to myself, when I suddenly had a strange feeling I was being watched. All at once I felt very much alone in the silence of the wood, which was broken only by the cooing of pigeons. A sort of fear gripped me, and losing interest in my game I left for home.

I was never able to define what had caused that eerie feeling of being watched. Perhaps a fox or other small animal was gazing at me from cover, or maybe the gamekeeper or rabbit catcher stood hidden among the trees, looking on with amusement at my antics. Needless to say I never returned to play alone at that spot.

Once I resolved to try to follow the burn, which flowed past the place, to its source. I found it very difficult in places owing to the presence of trees and undergrowth. I only managed to follow its course for a short distance beyond the march between Newtown and Rutherford Burnside. I felt a bit apprehensive about pursuing my quest on strange ground. A gamekeeper or farmer might have looked less than kindly on a strange boy wandering on their patch.

Our transfer to Roxburgh school was a bit of an ordeal for my young sister and me. The ways of the school were strange;

one aspect especially, new to me, was having homework to do, which I found to be both a burden and a worry. Our schoolmates too were all strangers, they played games unfamiliar to us and had even a slightly different turn of speech. It is hard to understand today the linguistic contrasts between the various local communities at that time. The people of the foothills spoke differently from those of the Kelso area. For example they said 'than' for 'then', 'enow' for 'the now', and used a whole lot of words borrowed from the Gypsies of Yetholm, such as 'panny' water or rain, 'jugal' a dog, 'gherrie' a hare, 'gadgie' a man or boy and so on. This was most marked in Yetholm itself, once the gypsy capital, and a Yetholm man could be spotted whenever he opened his mouth, for they had a special twang all their own.

The distance we walked to school from Newtoun was two miles, and this we did every day in all weathers. Sometimes it was a sore fight, walking that road in stormy weather for it was a pretty exposed one. We carried a piece in our schoolbags, along with our books. This piece consisted of several slices of bread, with jam, syrup or treacle. We had a tin flask each of tea or cocoa (we preferred the latter), which we were allowed to heat up at the schoolroom fire. The various flasks belonging to pupils were set down in a row before the fire at the morning break, with the corks removed in case the popped out if the flasks became overheated. In addition to our main piece which was eaten at the dinnertime hour about noon, we had a smaller piece, a scone, a bit of gingerbread or some other titbit, called our 'leavie piece', which we ate at the forenoon playtime break or 'leavie time'. In summer we carried a bottle of milk instead of cocoa. The bairns from the village, or from Over Roxburgh and the Mill went home for their dinner, but all those who lived too far out to manage home for dinner, had, like us, to carry pieces then. School dinners lay far, far into the future. Some bairns had as far as us to travel to school, those from the Trows and Roxburgh Barns, but the furthest travelled were the fisherman's children from Daniel's Den, the nickname for Barns Cottage. This fisherman (or ghillie as they are called up north) was employed by the Duke of Roxburghe.

The farms around Roxburgh were all known by shortened names: Over Roxburgh was the Upper Toun, Roxburgh Barns was the Berns, Roxburgh Mains, the Rig, Roxburgh Mill, the Mill and of course Roxburgh Newtoun was Newtoun.

Roxburgh was a larger school than Linton, the big end and the little end being separate rooms. It was also a much older building, having the date 1859 above the door, whereas Linton was dated 1881.

At both schools I attended we had slates and jotters. Slates were for temporary work and slate pencils were used for writing on them. We cleaned our slates by breathing or spitting on them and rubbing them with a duster, but at each day's end water was provided to wash them thoroughly. Most of our writing on jotters was done with a lead pencil, frequent rubbing out being frowned on. Only serious work such as composition and tests were done in ink. Mr Hislop at Roxburgh mixed the ink himself using ink, powder and water. Our inkwells fitted into a hollow in the desks, and were filled each morning. All school books, jotters, slates and accessories had to be provided by parents; the schoolmaster carried a stock of such materials and sold them to us as required.

The schoolmaster was Mr Hislop, a good teacher, strict disciplinarian and pretty handy with the tawse. His worst fault in the schoolroom was his cutting sarcasm, and his habit of ridiculing pupils in front of the class, which could not have had a good effect on the more sensitive pupils. He had a habit also of picking on the backward scholars and thrashing them for their failures and – in his estimation – their laziness. I suppose such practice was the norm in most schools at that time, and it was more than a generation later ere steps were taken to provide remedial schooling for the dunces and the dyslexics.

On the whole he gave us a thorough grounding in the three Rs, geography, history etc. which were then the basics at country schools. He was a keen gardener himself and since there was a school garden, he saw that the older boys got garden work during their last year. Outside school Mr Hislop took a deep and lively interest in the affairs of the village. He had great organising ability and had a hand in every activity. The assistant teachers in the school were Miss McRae at first, followed by Miss Thomson. I had little contact with them except for the very rare occasions when the headmaster was absent. Miss Thomson conducted the school choir, of which more anon.

In the playground football was played by the boys, to the virtual exclusion of any other game. I could never account for why this should be. Until I went to Roxburgh I knew nothing whatever about the game, but willy-nilly became indoctrinated like all the rest. The football fever which prevailed at Roxburgh school may have arisen from the fact that the village had a football team, or it could have been connected with the railway station, at which the evening and sporting papers were readily available. For the first time in my life I heard tell of Hibs, Hearts, Celtic and Rangers.

Our school game was pretty rudimentary, played on a very rough surface in the playground, with a tennis ball or rubber ball about the same size. The public road formed part of the playground, and we frequently had to pause to allow vans or carts to pas through. There were cottage gardens too, which bordered the 'pitch', and when the ball landed in one of them, we had to run the gauntlet of being observed by the owners when we went to retrieve it. Frequently, the ball was confiscated by irate housewives, which was very frustrating. The playground sloped sharply, which gave the side playing down the hill a distinct advantage. Again, since the boys were of all ages and sizes, when sides were picked it only sufficed for a couple of the biggest to be on the same side, for that side to enjoy a walkover.

Rugby football was of course the main sporting interest in the Borders as it is at the present day. We seldom played it at school though, for the ground was really too hard, and injuries could have ensued. All the same, our school gossip was all about the Border teams and their respective merits. It was a curious thing that most of the boys favoured Hawick, which was then the rampant team. They sang, 'Hawick' Queen o' the Borders!' but I can remember one or two of the more patriotic retorting, 'Well, if Hawick's the Queen, Kelsae's King o' the Borders!'

The girls played by themselves, largely ignored by the boys. Any boy who associated with the girls in the playground was jeered at and dubbed 'lassie pot'. In addition to skipping ropes and ball games, the girls played singing games, much the same as those at Linton, but with variations of titles and words. When they were at the 'courting' games, like 'All the Boys of London', or 'Down in the Meadow where the Green Grass Grows', in which some boy or other was named as 'sweetheart' of the girl in the middle of the ring, should the boy be within earshot, he would rush forward and break up the ring in enraged embarrassment. At the same time it was sometimes sham anger, for the boy and girl in question would have a secret admiration for each other. Although nothing of the sort would be openly admitted, schoolfellow 'crushes' were not unknown among the more precocious amongst us.

Notes and conversation sweets were passed furtively below desks. I remember sending a short poem to a girl I secretly admired, and was mortified when her appreciative reply was confiscated by another boy en route, after which I was mercilessly teased for a spell.

Bullying was not rife at Roxburgh school, and no particular boys were picked on regularly. Fights sometimes did arise, but were quickly quashed should the master notice out of the window. Any boys caught fighting were dealt with summarily inside the school, both parties getting a good dose of the tawse.

We got on well at school, not finding the lessons too hard, though the homework was irksome. A new thing to us were the itinerant teachers who came on certain days. Those people came for a forenoon session on their appointed days to teach PT, music, cookery, dressmaking and woodwork. There was a building at the foot of the playground, in which the girls of twelve and over were taught cookery and dressmaking, and the boys of the same age groups were taught woodwork. All the bairns were given PT and those who could sing, singing lessons. Except for Mrs Brown, the music teacher, who was a real nice gentle person, the itinerant teachers were not very popular with us scholars.

I myself hated the woodwork class and the teacher likewise, a sarcastic sneering person, who could make one feel like a worm. I came to dread the Wednesday morning when we got woodwork, for I was ham-fisted at the job, and therefore came in for a large share of the teacher's scorn.

But the visiting teacher we loathed most was the PT teacher. She was a loud voiced, hard faced, upper middle class woman, who spoke with a 'bool-in-the-mouth' accent and who never sought to hide her contempt for us working class bairns. Significantly the sole farmer's son in the school, was the only one she addressed by his own name, the rest of us she would call names such as Green Jersey, Red Head, You with the Pleat, Snub Nose, Roley Poley, Suet Dumpling etc. On occasions she took us into the playground to play outdoor games, but those we did not enjoy, for we were too much regimented. One game chosen, she called by the absurd title of King's Covenanters – I don't know whence it came – which had a faint resemblance to our King's Coffee game played at Linton.

The singing sessions I very much enjoyed, partly because of my natural love of music, and partly from the winning personality of the music teacher, who had the knack of inspiring her pupils to give of their best. Those pupils who had a good ear for music were mustered to form a school choir. Under the guidance of Mrs Brown, and with Miss Thomson the infant teacher as conductor, we gave a good account of ourselves, when we competed at the annual Border Musical Festival held alternately at Galashiels and Hawick.

The songs we sang at the festivals still live on in my

memory, alongside many more which were learned at the singing class at Roxburgh. Even yet, nearly sixty years on, one has only to hum the tunes, to be transported back to the carefree days of boyhood.

The Border Musical Festival was held in the month of May, and lasted several days. It consisted of solo singing, verse speaking, choral and instrumental competitions for both bairns and adults; also included were action songs by school-bairns. The festival survived right down till the 1970s when it was finally discontinued because of dwindling support.

We attended the Roxburgh Parish Kirk, since there was no United Free Kirk nearer than Kelso, four miles off. Our parents switched kirks as a matter of convenience; to them the act of worship was more important than mere sectarianism. In any case many of the causes that had split the kirk at the Disruption had been removed, and reunion was to take place in 1929, a mere six years on. Nevertheless we were aware of a lack of drive and vitality in the Auld Kirk compared with the UF.

The minister at Roxburgh was Dr Mathers DD who spent the greater part of his ministry there right up till his retirement. He was a native of Northern Ireland. He was, to us bairns, a rather gruff formidable person. He was not a very approachable man, but a good preacher in the pulpit; at least my parents thought so, as unhappily I had not much taste for sermons at that age. He was a faithful pastor, visiting his flock regularly and doing all his journeys on foot. At times Mrs Mathers, a quiet lady, accompanied him.

At Roxburgh the seating in the kirk was arranged according to the farms, two or three pews to this place and two or three to that place and so on. The village folk from Roxburgh and Heiton had their respective pews as well.

The Sunday School which we attended regularly had for superintendent a Mr Rogers who travelled from Kelso and doubled up as organist. He was assisted in the Sunday school by one of the young women of the village, Miss Murray, a railwayman's daughter. Sunday school was at 10 am and was held in the school rather than in the kirk as at Morebattle. I believe that this was common usage by the parish kirks. The Sunday school was not so well attended as that we had left, few bairns from the outlying farms caring to make the journey six days in the week. It was not nearly so well run either, having no exams or serious Bible reading. We had to commit to memory the Shorter Catechism and verses from the psalms and paraphrases, and the hymn singing was good, accompanied by a harmonium. The Fairnington children had a Sunday school too, and they joined with us for the annual Sunday school picnic in the manse grounds. Heiton Sunday school did not seem to have close connections with Roxburgh church, being run by private persons, though Heiton itself made a good contribution to church attendance. The Fairnington folk came in fair numbers, considering the distance away, and Mr Rutherfurd, the aged laird, was a regular attender.

One Sunday evening in the autumn of 1923, the choir from St Johns Edenside Church in Kelso, was invited to give a rendering of the cantata 'The Messiah' in our church. I cannot remember how many choristers there would be, but they gave a great performance which was listened to by an audience who filled the church to capacity. Our family and others from Newtoun who attended, took a short cut by walking the railway line. As there were no trains running on Sunday we were quite safe but it was illegal for pedestrians to use the line.

In the kirkyard at Roxburgh is the grave of Andrew Gemmells, a gaberlunzie man, who was the prototype of Sir Walter Scott's character, 'Eddie Ochiltree' in *Old Mortality*. Andrew died in the byre at Newtoun in 1793 and a headstone was erected over his grave by a local farmer. The byre in which he died had still the same door on it in the 1920s, and we were told that, under a clause in the farm lease, the door was never to be altered.

My involvement with the sheep increased at Newtoun. At special times such as the lambing and the clipping I could not get from school quickly enough to see what was going on. At lambing time especially I did quite a few small jobs for father ere I set off for school in the morning. I fed the ewes which were in the 'parricks' with corn and turnips. A parrick was the name given to the small separate pen, in which a ewe and her lambs were put after she lambed at night. There were usually twenty-five to thirty of those pens built into the perimeter of the lambing shed. A row of such pens was also erected in the middle of the lambing field, to hold ewes with new born lambs in bad weather. Another task I carried out was the bottle feeding of hungry or motherless lambs. In the evenings and at weekends I helped generally. Father had no lambing assistant at Newtoun, and the farmer or his son gave him help when required, taking a share of the night work by tending the ewes on alternate nights. During my last spring at school I got exemption from school for a month to help with the lambing.

At other times of the year I helped with sheep work in the faulds on Saturdays or during school holidays. In this way I added to my knowledge of shepherd lore. I learnt to read lugmarks, which are snips taken out of the sheep's ear with a special small instrument. Lugmarks are used for a variety of purposes: as a stockmark to signify what farm it belonged to, to distinguish the various ages of ewes or for some other purpose. A hole might be punched in the centre of the ear to identify a special batch among the ewe lambs bought to carry on the stock. In stockman's parlance no farm animal has a right or left side, but a near and a far side; near signifies left and far is right. This applies to all farm animals as well as sheep, and covers other parts of the body as well as the ears. A sheep's ears are classed fore (top) and back (bottom), thus 'a fore bit o' the near' means a snip out of the top side of the left ear, and 'back bit o' the far' is a snip out of the bottom side of the right ear. A 'fork' is a snip out of the tip of the ear, and a 'hole' of course is a hold punched in the middle of the ear. It all sounds very complicated when written down, but to a shepherd the lugmarks and their significance can be read at a glance.

A Shepherd Remembers

I learned how to handle a sheep and how to carry young lambs – this is done by holding them by their forelegs. Yet this is not permissible when they are newly born on a cold day when they must be wrapped in a sack to conserve what body heat they have. Another must to be learned was how to ascertain if a lamb was full enough. It had to be held up by the forelegs and its belly gently felt. If that was slack the lamb either needed to be suckled, or if its dam was short of milk given some cow milk from a bottle. I also learned how to skin a lamb, put the skin on a live lamb and set it onto the dam of the dead one.

Most years we would have two or three motherless lambs, called pet lambs, which had to be reared by hand. Those were lambs whose mothers had died out in the field after lambing was past, and a foster mother could not be had for them. They were kept in a field nearby our house and fed with cow milk from a bottle until about midsummer. My sisters took part in the task of rearing pets and often got so involved that they cried when the lambs were sent away to the sale.

At clipping time, although I was not strong enough to hold a sheep, I used to get a shot with the shears on a sheep my father was clipping.

I had a special interest in father's pack sheep. I knew them all intimately and was always excited when they were ready to lamb, curious to see what sort of lambs they would have. I was always a good 'kenner' of sheep, though not up to the standard of those shepherds who are reputed to know every sheep in their flock. To 'ken' sheep is to recognise them at sight by 'headmark', that is by their faces, by the shape of their bodies, their gait etc. To be able to know sheep individually is commonplace among shepherds, and nothing to marvel at, for no two sheep any more than any two human beings look exactly alike. Father used to tease me at times, to test my kenning ability, he would argue with me that such and such a sheep was not the one I said it was. After I'd got quite het up and aggrieved on the point, he would give the game

away by bursting out laughing; then I knew he had only been
having me on.

Some of the main lamb sales at St Boswells took place
during our school holidays, so I was able to accompany father
there. There were two auction marts at St Boswells then, the
Southern Central Mart conducted by Messrs Swan & Son,
and the St Boswells Auction Mart of Messrs Davidson and
Sons. Both marts were at Newtown St Boswells beside the
railway station. The Southern Central was the biggest mart of
the two, and our lambs were usually sold there, though
occasionally a waggon load would be sent to Davidsons. A
'waggon of lambs' was 40 to 50, corresponding to the number
that a railway waggon would hold. Waggon loads were in
three grades, large, medium, and small differing in price
according to size. Railway cattle waggons were actually all
of the same size, the several grades being arrived at by putting
a board across the inside, thus reducing the capacity to suit
the required grade. A large waggon, that is a waggon without
partition, held 50 lambs or 30 adult sheep; a medium waggon
45 and 25; and the small waggon forty and twenty.

The lambs were sent by rail from Rutherford station, the
waggons from there being picked up by a special train of
cattle trucks containing lambs already loaded at Kelso,
Roxburgh and stations on the Jedburgh line. Father put
the lambs in a field next to the farm march overnight, thus
shortening their journey to the station in the morning. The
herds and their dogs rode in the guard's van, which was
sometimes a bit crowded, for there could be seven or eight
herds in it.

Very large numbers of lambs were sold at the two St
Boswells marts then, the majority of them arriving by rail.
Lambs from farms within a five or six mile radius were
generally driven to the sale, and the roads leading to Newtown and St Boswells were literally full of sheep, as drove
after drove made their way there on a sale morning. Luckily
there was not a great deal of motor traffic using the road in
those days.

A Shepherd Remembers

It was a great novelty to me to see so many sheep from all over the Borders from places beyond my ken; to see such an array of sheepmen gathered together – farmers, shepherds and their dogs. Now and then fights broke out among the dogs, then sticks and voices would be raised to quell the fracas. I recall one occasion when a shepherd got bitten, as a pair of snarling fighting dogs got entangled among the legs of the bystanders.

Father would get involved in crack with neighbour shepherds and other acquaintances; some of the latter were men he had known since before I was born. Their talk was principally about sheep, the state of the market, the weather and, for those who had not met since the previous year, kindly enquiries about themselves and their wives and families. Being men almost wholly absorbed in their work, it was not surprising that sheep was their main topic of conversation. They took a pride in the appearance of the lambs they had penned for sale, and were jealous of the reputation of the farm on which they were employed as regards its sheep stock. Obviously they evinced a keen interest in the trend of the sale, and a spirit of competition as to whose lambs would make the most. As a farmer ruefully remarked during a period of low prices, 'A herd disna care hoo little the lambs make, as lang as his pen makes thrippence a heid mair than his neebors!' A certain farmer purchaser was in the habit of decrying the ewe lambs from X, as he moved about the sale, yet he bought them year after year. His motive was, of course, simply to put off other buyers who might be interested. The shepherd at X got to hear of this and he promptly confronted the offender and gave him a good dressing down.

Although most of the shepherds were fond of a dram, not all of them were heavy drinkers. There were some who used the sale days with their company and camaraderie to indulge in deep drinking and get themselves soused. Few would do this until the end of the sale with their sheep disposed of. Father as a teetotaller looked askance at those who took too much drink. 'Jock So-and-so's a'right', he would say of someone like that, 'but I canna dae wi um, when he gits blethery wi drink.' I remember he remarked to me at a sale, while I was still a boy, 'Ye'll no hae mony freends here if ye dinna drink.' A man of independent mind, he was content not to follow the crowd, and he did have some kindred spirits.

Though I was mostly content to listen avidly to the crack, I got bored at times if we were bogged down too long at the same pen. I made for the sale ring to look on and listen to the auctioneer. Being an avid trainspotter I sometimes sneaked away from the mart to go up to the railway station. There at the passenger platform I would watch for the big engines that hauled the long distance trains on the Waverley line between Edinburgh and Carlisle. To see a Pacific or Atlantic type locomotive was a thrill indeed, for most of the engines I saw at Roxburgh were of a smaller type. The locomotives on the Waverley line and its branches were mostly named after the Waverley novels, or characters drawn from them.

The bulk of the lambs left the mart by rail after they were sold, and it was a long drawn out business getting them trucked. Once the waggons on the loading bank were full, there was a delay until they were dawn out by an engine, and a fresh lot of empty waggons substituted. The shepherds had to wait at the pens in charge of their lots, until their turn came to go to the loading bank. Sometimes it was quite late in the evening ere we were free to board a train for home.

At Newtoun the pattern of sheep husbandry was slightly different from that at Burnfoot. A larger proportion of the season's lambs was kept back for fattening on turnips during the autumn and winter. After they had been accustomed to turnips by having them scattered in cartloads over the pasture, the lambs – or hoggs as they were called from the age of six months – were folded on the turnips with wire nets. They were given a portion at a time, which we called a 'brick' or break. In Border parlance, turnips or 'tumshies' were the white or yellow fleshed variety. Swedish turnips of harder calibre we called 'swades' or more often 'baigies'.

From midwinter, the hoggs, now starting to lose their lamb

teeth, were fed on cut turnips, rendered into finger-shaped slices by a turnip cutter, a machine having a hopper set on a revolving barrel with cutting blades, the barrel being rotated by a large hand-operated wheel. The turnip cutting job was usually undertaken by an orraman or a woman worker. It was a hard job turning the wheel, and a messy one in wet weather carrying the cut turnips in a box or creel to the troughs, when the mud could often be ankle deep.

The ewe stock were Halfbreds, the universal low ground Border breed, and they were crossed with Oxford Down and Suffolk Down rams. The replacement ewe lambs were usually bought at St Boswells or Hawick. Mr Bell had strong ties with Hawick, having been a butcher here before he took up farming, and moreover he still had an interest in the farm of Kirkton in that district. He came from there to Newtoun, but left his elder son in the farm there.

On one occasion Mr Bell junior, the second son who was still at home unmarried, went up to Caithness to buy ewe lambs. Up there he found it was still mainly the custom to buy the lambs at the farm; also that the buyer was expected to buy the wedder lambs as well, as opposed to the Border usage of selling the sexes separately, and through the auction marts. The Caithness lambs had to be doubled dipped i.e. dipped twice within a fortnight after they came home, in case of sheep scab infection. Sheep scab had been eradicated in South East Scotland but still lingered on in parts of the Highlands. In consequence all sheep coming into Roxburghshire from north of the Forth, had to be twice dipped in the presence of a policeman.

Caithness ewe lambs, both Halfbred and Cheviot, were making their debut in the Borders in the early '20s. Though they carried a risk of scab, they were free from scrapie, a disease then endemic among Border flocks. Those Caithness sheep were not regarded favourably at first by Border sheep men, who miscalled them as ugly and ill-bred, but as time went on they became greatly improved and more acceptable.

At Newtoun many of the fields were not very well watered,

and in several of them water had to be pumped by hand, from a well into a trough for the livestock. In the summer when cattle were grazed in a field containing a pump, a lot of extra work was entailed for the shepherd to keep them supplied.

At Roxburgh our horizons were widened because of the handiness for trains, and the proximity of Kelso, which we now visited more frequently. As already stated, our parents were incomers to the Borders, therefore our relatives lived outwith the area. From early childhood we had been in the habit of going with one or other of our parents to visit their folk in East Lothian and Midlothian, thus giving us a wider outlook than many of our fellows whose relations lived round about them. At times we experienced a slight feeling of not belonging, since our parents had no ties with the district. For instance when we were very young, we came out with words and phrases in the Lothian dialects, which our playmates were not slow to notice and ridicule. Such words as licht, nicht, fecht and strecht for light, night, fight and 'strite' (Border for straight) fire, byre, chair which the Borderers pronounced with 'i' as in 'life'. We said barn, star, haill, hame whereas our mates said bern, sterr, hyill and hyim; these and many other examples such as witter for water, and the pant for the pump, we had perforce to adopt in order to conform.

Bairns were very cruel in this respect. Anyone coming new to school who spoke 'fine', i.e. with an English accent, was a butt for mocking and teasing. At the same time the bairns from a family who came out of the Glasgow slums to live at the Trows endured a dog's life at school because of their thick Glasgow accents. Although the use of Scots words and phrases was forbidden inside the school, we were not punished for using them in the playground as was the case in some localities. 'Don't speak as your parents speak, speak as you are taught in school', was a widespread dictum among Scots teachers for generations.

Our parents never went on holiday together, for there was the cow, the pig and the dogs to be attended to. There were few fixed holidays on the farms in those days, but father always managed to get a week off once a year, when he went to visit his parents at Dunbar, or his brother and sisters. At times he took his days off during the school holidays in August, and would take some of us with him to our granny's at Dunbar. He went by train all the way from Roxburgh via Kelso and Berwick-on-Tweed, and spent a pleasant time by the sea. Our grandparents stayed in a cottage inside the grounds of Broxmouth Park, not far from the beach. Whilst he was at Dunbar, he would take us on an afternoon trip by rail to East Linton, to visit his brother and family at Phantassie. Afterwards when they had flitted to Seacliff near North Berwick, we went there as well. When father went alone to East Lothian, he journeyed by bicycle, a very long journey indeed. He had a sister at a farm near Humbie, whom he visited by bike as well.

In return our uncles would cycle over from Lothian to visit us for a week-end, maybe once a year. No one thought anything of cycling long distances then. To reach Dunbar father went by Duns and Grantshouse, and to get to Humbie he travelled by Gordon and Soutra Hill. Either journey extending to over 50 miles each way must have been a sore pull on a bicycle – an ordinary roadster at that. In later years when I became owner of a car, I travelled those routes and could not help but marvel at the grit and staying power of those who in the past had made such journeys by bicycle.

Divided as they were by miles of country and seldom meeting, our parents and their respective families kept in touch regularly by writing copious letters, exchanging each other's news. Our uncles, aunts and cousins were regarded by us as special people, and we were scandalized by the offhand way some of our schoolfellows spoke of, and treated their relations. To us, having an auntie and cousins at the next farm or village would seem a luxury indeed.

In wintertime when the cow was not in milk, mother took the opportunity to have a short holiday. She visited her relations in Edinburgh and Midlothian, taking some of us bairns with her. The train journey to Edinburgh was an adventure for us, for we saw a lot of fresh countryside en route. I remember how my young sister and I counted the number of times the train crossed the Gala Water, between Galashiels and Heriot. Little did we know that one day our home would be in that austere valley. We could reel off a list of all the stations between Rutherford and Edinburgh Waverley, though of course the train did not stop at each one.

We became familiar with the capital at an early age, as our aunt and uncle who lived there took us to see the sights both by tramcar and on foot. It was doubly exciting near Christmas, when the shops were all lit up and decorated. I remember we were once staying in the city over the New Year, and when twelve o'clock struck, we could hear the crowds cheering, the shrilling of railway engine whistles, and the hooting of ships' sirens on the Forth, welcoming in the New Year. Our Uncle Jim, mother's brother, was a policeman in the city force. He and Aunt Sarah his wife spent their summer holiday with us most years.

On two consecutive summer holidays I went to stay with mother's sister, our Auntie Meg at Bonnyrigg. She took me and her neighbour's bairns by bus to the Pentland Hills for a picnic trip. It was my first ever journey on a bus, and of course I was travel sick, an affliction which dogged me right into adulthood. Our picnic was near Glencorse, which was mother's calf country, and she often told us stories of her schooldays there. When I got home I was pleased to be able to tell her that I had seen the place, and the scenes of her childhood, made so familiar to us by her reminiscences.

One Saturday, auntie's husband, our Uncle Dave, who drove a horse drawn grocer's van for the local Co-operative Society, took me with him on his round to Newtongrange near Dalkeith. It was a revelation to me to view the rows upon rows of miners' houses and the huge pit bings. He also took me on Sunday walks to Cockpen and the grounds of Dalhousie Castle. It was a great experience for me who had travelled so little. Although I enjoyed my stay at Bonnyrigg, and my aunt and uncle were kindness itself, I felt something alien in the atmosphere of the place, and was relieved to get back home to Roxburgh and the farm.

It was during our stay at Newtoun that the first motor lorries began to appear on the scene, delivering feeding stuff, fertiliser and such like to the farm, and lifting farm produce. Before that, all grain had to be carted from the farms, either direct to the merchants, or to be laid on trucks at the nearest railway station. Farm carts had sometimes to travel several miles to the nearest station with produce, or to fetch cattle cake off waggons, or coal from the depot. The farm folk had their coals carted free as part of their bargain, so we got a cartload – half a ton at a time – delivered when we required it. The coal we had to pay for of course, but I have heard tell of instances where hill shepherds got coal as a perquisite in lieu of peats. By and by when coal lorries began to hawk coal round farm towns, the custom of getting one's coal carted from the depot faded out, but the free cartage of firewood continued right down to the present day.

Roxburgh village was a hive of activity, having a Horti-cultural Society, a quoiting club, a football club, and a rugby club, just to mention a few. At Sunlaws House on the other side of Teviot, owned by Brigadier General Scott-Ker, a fête was held in aid of some charity nearly every summer. It was well patronized by the parish folk; we walked to it from Newtoun, a distance of three miles each way.

Indoor events were held roughly from October to March, and since there was no village hall, these were held in the school. Concerts were always popular though not staged very often. Now and again a travelling concert party visited the village. Those travelling groups, most of whom came from Edinburgh, were common in Scotland then, and put up in country towns during their tour or were the guests of farmers and others. One group I specially remember consisted of a pianist, a male vocalist, three lady artistes who had the role of vocalist, violinist and elocutionist respectively. They gave two performances, one in the afternoon for the schoolchil-dren, and a second to a packed audience in the evening. Their repertoire consisted of Scots and other songs, solos and duets, piano pieces, violin solos and recitations. They drew loud applause from the audience, with much whistling and stamping of feet from the youths, who always occupied the back of the hall at concert. Any concert or entertainment held in the school was invariably followed by a dance, when music was supplied by local fiddlers or melodeon players.

The winter session of continuation classes, or night school as it was called, was very popular with the young folk, particularly the post-school adolescents. These classes formed an integral part of the education scene in Roxburgh county, and were held in all the village schools. I had known of their existence both at Linton and Morebattle. But at Roxburgh, thanks to the enthusiasm and organising ability of the headmaster, the night school was particulary strong. Tuition was given on a variety of subjects by the headmaster and the infant teacher, backed by some of the itinerant teachers. The youth of the parish appeared keen to further their education. Cynics might say of course that the night school offered a chance for lads and lassies to mix together, rather than any thirst for knowledge on their part. Be that as it may, it also showed a genuine effort by our rural youth to improve themselves. Music was one of the subjects taught, and at the end of the session the music class gave an open concert, followed of course by the inevitable dance.

On two successive years a dancing class was run for bairns of school age during the autumn and winter. This was held in Roxburgh school on Saturday forenoons, pupils from both village schools taking part. The teacher was Mrs Brown, the music teacher, and the fee was seven shillings and sixpence for the course. My sister and I and another girl from Newtoun attended both courses. The dances we were taught were the Highland Fling, the Polka, Triumph, Petronella and the Lancers. We staged an exhibition before an audience of parents and others at the end of the session.

I first attended the St James' Fair held annually at Kelso after we came to Newtoun. The fairground was about three miles off, within reasonable walking distance. I shall have more to say on this subject in a later chapter.

For the bairns of the parish there were various events held during the year, but the real highlight was the annual Spittal trip, organised for the schools. Spittal, just across the Tweed from Berwick, is the main seaside resort for the Borders, and even today most village communities have their Spittal trip day.

Pupils from all three school travelled by train for a day at the seaside, mothers and toddlers going as well. Those were the only times I saw the headteachers of the other two schools, Miss Davidson from Heiton, and Miss Eaton from Fairnington, two formidable ladies equal to our own male head at keeping order. The Fairnington Bairns had boarded the train at Rutherford, and were joined at Roxburgh by the hordes from Heiton and Roxburgh. Any High School scholars, which included our sister, came along as well. We had two meals at Spittal, lunch and tea in a local church hall, the rest of the time being spent on the beach, with visits to the ice-cream and entertainment stalls. Our pocket money did not stretch very far, but we enjoyed ourselves. After our hectic day, we left the train in the evening and tramped the two miles home, tired but happy.

We had a sports day at school, just before the summer break up, organised by the headmaster and the drill teacher. We boys were always keenly competitive and spent a lot of time in practice beforehand. I was as keen as any, and though I never really shone in the athletic field, I could do reasonably well in practice, but was assailed by stage fright on the day.

At Christmas time we had both a school treat and a Sunday school treat, events eagerly looked forward to. We had mugs of tea and a bag of cookies each. Once the bag was empty it was customary to fill it with wind and burst it, the popping of bags would resound all round the schoolroom. Grateful as we were for the treat, some of us could be cheeky at times. On one occasion when the tea was a bit stewed, a boy sitting beside me complained that his tea was too strong, when asked by a sympathetic helper if he would like more milk in it, he replied scornfully,'No, it's no milk oo need in't, but mair witter.' After tea the time honoured games were played, such as musical chairs, pass the parcel, the Grand Old Duke of York, etc. but we older ones aged 12 and 13 got keener to have some dancing included as well.

In 1926 the General Strike affected Roxburgh more than many other rural communities, since it was so dependent on the railway, and practically all the railwaymen were out. The daily papers were reduced to four pages only, and feelings ran high in the parish. The farm workers were not affected, but tended to sympathise with the strikers. Our parents took the opposite view, arguing that strikes never settled anything in the long run. One neighbour herd took umbrage at father's attitude saying 'Dive ye no see that the miners are fightin a fight for oo?' which was a dubious argument, for had a rise in farm wages given rise to higher food prices, they would be the first to girn. Townsfolk were quite happy to exist on cheap food dumped from abroad, no matter what effect that had on agriculture and those employed therein. During the pro-longed miners' strike which followed the collapse of the General Strike, coal became very hard to come by. Mr Bell got permission from the laird to have a tree felled, which was cut up and divided among the households gratis. The estate foresters felled the tree, and all the men on the farm staff banded together to cut it up, with axes and crosscut saws, the work being done in the evenings in their own time.

One notable event in 1925 was the start of the rural libraries by Roxburgh County Council. Libraries were estab-lished in every parish usually at the school or village hall. The task of acting as librarian fell in most cases to the teacher The books, both fiction and non-fiction, were changed every quarter, reading lists being supplied with each fresh batch, and distributed to the patrons so that they could choose books for themselves. A lot of the borrowing was done by readers on the outlying farms through the schoolchildren, who were roped in to give out the reading lists, and carry the

A Shepherd Remembers

books to and fro. I had the job of carrying the books for our own parents, for our neighbours the steward and his wife, and for the folk at the farmhouse. The folk at the row were served by the bairns who lived there. With his characteristic skill and enthusiasm Mr Hislop threw himself into the largest readership of any, among the rural parishes of the county. Among the Borders counties Roxburghshire had the best record in education at that time. We did not realise this until we moved into Berwickshire and Northumberland, for both lagged decidedly behind in this respect.

It was at Roxburgh I first came under the influence of the works of Sir Walter Scott. This was not surprising since we lived right in the middle of the Scott country. His historical novels appealed to me, for history was my favourite subject at school, Scots history in particular, which I dipped into much deeper than was touched upon in our school books. I was early aware of the prominent part played by the Borders in Scotland's story. My interest in Scott was first awakened when I read 'The Lay of the Last Minstrel', in which Scott named many places and historical personages in our home district. Curiously enough I first became acquainted with the poem through its being one of my sisters' schoolbooks at the High School. Soon I got hold of a copy for myself, read and re-read it, committing long passages to memory. I did not read any of the Waverley novels before leaving school, but I devoured both Marmion and the Lady of the Lake, as well as Tales of a Grandfather. I was an avid Scott fan right on till manhood, then I cooled off after I realised how biased he was toward the lairds and upper class.

By the time I was twelve years old, I had made up my mind to be a shepherd when I left school. Though I was a good scholar, I declined to sit the bursary examination, which, had I got through, might have taken me to Kelso High School for three or even six years. Both my parents and the headmaster were dismayed and very angry with me on this score. Although father had always encouraged me to take an interest in the sheep, he had cherished the hope that I might make a career in some other direction.

Roxburgh

Apart from my deep interest in shepherding and determination to follow that line, there were factors which made me scared of going to the High School. My elder sister's books and the subjects she had to study over-awed me, plus the piles of homework she was saddled with. Then there was my ingrained dread of the woodwork class and the PT teacher, both of which would have confronted me at Kelso. It seemed an appalling prospect.

Though I am certain on hindsight that I might have done well for myself in the academic world, I never really regretted my choice of career.

For the rest of my life I did not neglect the intellectual pursuits. I remained an avid reader, quite a bookworm in fact, obtaining endless pleasure from books. There is no reason why a person should not work happily with his hands, and at the same time retain an interest in the things of the mind. We have examples of this in the hundreds of manual workers, who never 'rose' in the world, but developed above average intellectual qualities.

3

FOGO

When I left school at the Christmas break in 1926, with the object of being a shepherd, father decided to leave Newtoun at the following May term, and hire us jointly to a man and laddie place. This system of hiring workers on a family basis was prevalent on the inbye farms on both sides of the Border and in the Lothians. There was none of the billeting of single men in lofts and bothies, as in other parts of Scotland. The single farm workers, both male and female, lived in the family home until they were married, and were hired with their fathers in a joint agreement. On the large farms sometimes as many as five members of a family, say the father, two sons and two daughters, might be hired jointly out of the same house. Examples of jobs advertised in the Press would read as follows: Double herd wanted; double hind wanted; double hind wanted with or without woman worker. The bondage systems whereby a householder was obliged to house a woman worker or bondager had died out years before, but it was still an advantage for a man to have a daughter or daughters for farm work. In families without a father, the role of householder was assumed by the deceased's son or daughter; sometimes a boy would hire himself as odd laddie, to provide a house for a widowed mother.

Wages were paid monthly and where a family was concerned, they were paid in a lump sum to the householder. The various members did not have separate pay packets. It usually fell to the mother to handle the money, and dole out to the young ones what cash they required for their own needs. The system which prevailed in most households, I believe, was for the mother to retain a certain sum for board and lodging off each son or daughter's pay, and leave them with the rest.

I have no idea when individual pay packets were introduced on the farms, but in my own case the joint payment continued right up until the time I left home in 1944. I never bothered my head about money when I was young, as long as I had some pocket money for my personal needs. Mother gave me an agreed amount each month for that purpose, and when I required boots or clothing she provided the cash out of the family budget. It all sounds very naive and maternalistic but I was quite happy with the arrangement. How other young folk conducted their financial affairs I neither knew nor inquired; it was not considered the done thing to ask other people about their pay. A man's bargain was sacrosanct and was only known to himself, his employer and the steward. The latter would consider it a breach of trust, to spout about this or that worker's bargain. It was a well known fact, from remarks let slip at odd times, that not all hinds on the same farm had the same rate of pay, but everyone got what they bargained for.

Father need not have left Newtoun to get me a situation, had he been content to stay on there and send me to service under another shepherd elsewhere. Boys and single men were frequently hired under and boarded with a herd shepherd especially in the hill country. Both outbye and inbye the father and son arrangement for double herdings was considered the most satisfactory, but there were plenty of men with no sons of their own at home who occupied head shepherds jobs and boarded single men. On inbye farms when an under shepherd did not live in with the head shepherd, he would occupy a cottage with his parents in the row, or, if married, a house of his own.

Had my parents elected to send me to service, I should probably have ended up as a hill shepherd, for it was outbye where most opportunities were open to boys. Some hill farmers employed what was then known as a summer boy, who assisted the shepherd from the end of lambing till the hay season was past.

A Shepherd Remembers

Mother would have let me go to a small outbye herding, but father was adamant that I should stay at home. My two elder sisters had left home early to follow their careers, and father said, 'Oo canna hae them a' leaving hame sae young.' A humane enough sentiment no doubt but one that was to have its comeback, for it enmeshed us in the family hiring system. I think father felt that since I was to train as a shepherd, there was none could undertake that training better than himself. There was an element of truth in that attitude, for a father was more likely to impart his knowledge to a son, than a head shepherd would do to his hired help.

Father went to Hawick Herds' hiring but could not get a place for a man and boy. Ironically he was offered one or two other places on his own for he was of good character and appearance. Before Kelso hirings he saw an advert in the local newspaper offering a job to a shepherd with boy to assist. He applied by letter and it was agreed that he should meet the farmer at Kelso on hiring day. The place was Fogorig in the Merse district of Berwickshire. Mr Young the farmer and he made a bargain and he was duly hired to go there at the Whitsunday term of 1927.

Between January and the term I had two jobs; first I assisted my father at Newtoun with the lambing in March, then in mid April I was sent to Dodburn near Hawick for three weeks to assist the herd there with the hill lambing. It was through Mr Bruce, the tenant of Priesthaugh, that I got the job. He was married to one of Mr Bell's daughters, and farmed Dodburn along with Priesthaugh. At Dodburn during my brief stay I got my first glimpse of hill shepherding, but it was nearly twenty years later ere I actually tried the life.

Berwickshire was to provide a complete change of scene for us. The landscape was different, with the big rolling arable fields, some of them of 60 acres or more, unlike the smaller fields of the Roxburgh area. Moreover we found that our new house was in a big row of ten houses, a fact with which my mother never came to terms. She had always hankered after having a house by itself, such as many herds had on upland

and outbye farms. This was an ambition she never achieved throughout her married life, poor soul, for father would never go outbye to herd. He always sought situations within easy reach of the kirk and the school. Many hill shepherds' bairns at that time had to walk three miles or more to school.

I am afraid the women folk belonging to farm workers had very little choice then regarding what sort of situation or dwelling house their menfolk would obtain. Unless their move was to a farm which they saw often or knew well, the odds were that farm folk had little idea of what their new abode would be like, until the menfolk went to plant the garden about a month before the term. Farmers at the hirings were notoriously close about housing conditions at their farms; how far their place was from school etc. For example a farmer told a prospective employee, that school was only half a mile or so away, but it turned out that that was by a short cut through fields, a very unsuitable route for young bairns in winter time. The actual distance to school by road was nearly three miles.

It was customary for the outgoing worker to allow the newcomer to see inside the house on the gardening day. Some even offered him a bite of breakfast ere he started to dig, knowing that he had set out early from wherever he had come. At dinner time he got a meal at the farmhouse, and was invited there for a cup of tea after the garden was dug, ere he set out on his homeward journey.

Unless the worker's wife accompanied him to see for herself, which seldom happened, few men could give a satisfactory account to their wives on their return, regarding the dwelling, its surroundings and lay out. Many were not very fussy about the state of the house, as illustrated by the following story: a certain hind went to plant his garden at the new situation, and was invited by the outgoing tenant's wife to have a look inside the house. 'Never mind the hoose let's see the horses an harness', he said. Many herds were no better in this respect, being more concerned with the quality of the sheep stock, the lie of the land, the state of the faulds and shepherding equipment etc. than with the dwelling he and his family were to occupy for the next 12 months.

Yet I know of one shepherd who, not having seen the place until the term, refused to unload his furniture from the lorry when he saw the state the house was in. He went back whence he had come and sought a house off a farmer of his acquaintance.

It must be borne in mind that folk had few options in the period between the wars, when labour was cheap and plentiful. Those who were in secure situations tended to stay put as long as possible, until forced to flit for family or other reasons.

After the slump of 1929–31 which fairly capped the period of decline in farming which had commenced in 1921, many farmers kept fewer horses and laid fields down to grass, putting the emphasis on livestock husbandry rather than grain growing. By and large such a policy operated in favour of stockmen and shepherds, who experienced less difficulty in finding jobs than hinds. Some of the latter applied themselves to shepherding, but never attained the skill and know-how of the professionals.

When we flitted to Fogorig I was sorry to leave Newtoun with its boyhood associations to go to a completely strange district. On the other hand I was looking forward to the fresh scene and the start of my first job. Three long carts, the sort used for carting grain at harvest, were sent from Fogorig to move our furniture and other effects. The number of carts required for flitting was agreed upon by the parties at hiring time.

Everything that folk had went onto the flitting carts, including garden tools, the cuddy for sawing firewood on, the barrels to catch rainwater for washing clothes, and quite often a pig in a wooden crate. Pails, tubs and tin baths were filled with some of the favourite flowers from the flower plot just vacated. The family sat on top of the furniture with the cats in a box or bag beside them. A sofa or couch made a handy seat for the women folk and bairns, being fitted into the load somewhere at the back of the hindmost cart. The cow, when there was one, had to be led separately by a member of the family. If the flit was a long one, say ten miles or more, arrangements were made beforehand to have the cow put up the night before at some farm half way. When we went to Fogorig, father wrote to Mr Greig of Eccles, a place on the way about five miles from Kelso, asking permission to have our cow and pack sheep put up overnight. Mr Greig granted him permission to leave his sheep, but explained that he could not accommodate the cow because he had a pedigree herd of tuberculin tested Shorthorn cattle, but had arranged to have her taken in at the neighbouring Crosshall. Father drove his sheep as far as Eccles on May 27th, leading the cow and wheeling the bike at the same time. He cycled back home, then set off again next morning taking the dogs with him, to move his stock on the next leg of their journey.

The flitting carts arrived at our old home the night before in charge of two of the hinds from Fogorig, the ploughman steward and second hind. As was the custom, most of the furniture was loaded before dark, haps being thrown over it in case of rain. The horses were unyoked and stabled at the farm, then as early as possible next morning they were yoked up, the rest of the things loaded on to the carts and everything was ready for the road.

We youngsters slept on the floor overnight, the adults sitting on chairs blethering or trying to snatch some sleep. Supper and breakfast were supplied by mother, bread and cold ham or salt beef was the fare, with beer for the men.

The distance from Newtown to Fogorig was 16 miles. I can recall it was a cold, dour day, but dry which was just as well. I was fair nithert sitting on the front of the third cart which I had been given to drive. It seemed a long, long journey and I thought we were never coming to the place. The speed of a horse and cart was about five miles per hour, a man's smart walking pace. In that year only the steward and ourselves came new to Fogorig, a remarkable thing for so big a farm. The annual turnover of labour at farm towns varied a lot from farm to farm. Some places had a virtual clean out each year, only one or two families remaining. In our second year at Fogorig (1928) only two households moved out of the ten in the row, neither of the three men and two women involved being replaced, their houses being let to folk not employed on the farm. The following year out of the eight households two moved out, and at our last May term only ourselves moved away.

It was a sight indeed to see all the flitting on the country roads on the 28th May. Carts were a pretty crude mode of conveyance, and had to be loaded carefully to prevent breakages, as they had no springs. Most householders had their crockery, glass and china cabinets well packed and protected. As might be expected not all farm men were dab hands at loading furniture, though it was a matter of pride among them to try to do it expertly. Once off the public road, farm roads were pretty rough and the jolting of the carts sometimes resulted in breakages. One shepherd's wife told mother that when she and her man flitted to Southernknowe, a place well up the College valley, during the First World War, she got all her china broken owing to the roughness of the track.

Accidents were very rare with flitting carts, though I remember clearly when I was a boy at Burnfoot, a little girl was killed by falling off a cart when the horse bolted on Linton Brae. It caused quite a stir at the time, but I never knew what was the upshot.

The May term, too, could be a time of sadness particularly for workers' wives, there were sad partings among friends who had been neighbours for years, and friendships had been forged which lasted for a lifetime. Those farm towns were really little communities, and folk got attached to the place itself after a sojourn of several years. A neighbour of ours used to tell how, when she first came to Fogorig, 'Ah grat for days efter leaving Whinkie' yet 'Whinkie' short for Whinkerstones was a neighbour farm only a mile away. In few cases did flittings incurred through a row with the steward or master provoke rancour up till the actual flitting date, for it was difficult not to be on speaking terms with someone you wrought beside every day. All the same individuals or families who had spent a stormy year at a place were generally glad to shake its dust from their feet.

The lorries were a mixed blessing, for the contractors took on as many removals as they possibly could, often with chaotic results. It was a rule that houses had to be vacated by noon on the term day. This posed no problems in the days of flitting by cart, as everyone was on the road as early in the morning as possible, and all houses were empty long before noon.

But the contractors turned flitting by lorry into a full day's job for the drivers and vehicles; loading of furniture could not start until the lorry arrived in the morning, then having got the first flitting completed, the lorry driver would go on to his next assignment, maybe nearing midday. If he still had a third party to flit, which was not uncommon, it would be getting on in the afternoon ere he got to them.

It frequently happened that a family would have to get all their stuff outside by noon, because the lorry had not arrived, and often had a long wait ere it came to lift them. It was no joke on a wet day as bedding and furnishings got soaked. I knew one shepherd for whom the removal lorry did not come until six in the evening.

To complicate matters still further – and this was a house-holder's nightmare – the lorry with the incoming tenant and his goods, could arrive first on the scene. This gave rise to confusion and friction, as things belonging to the two families got mixed together. A favourite ploy with contractors was to try to obtain contracts to dovetail together, that is, to flit a household from farm A to farm B then lift a family from there, possibly out of the same house, and take them to farm C, which would probably be the nearest to his home base.

Once our flitting carts had arrived at Fogorig they were quickly unloaded with the help of neighbours from the two nearest houses. The men were given a meal by mother, who had got the fire going with the help of some live coals from our next door neighbour but one. She discovered that this wife was known to her, for she and the woman's mother had been neighbours many years before at a farm near Melrose. Our neighbour had then come on visits to her mother with her young family now grown up. Such encounters were quite common on the Border farms; one time neighbours found themselves neighbours again at another place. We moved to Fogorig on a Saturday which was considered slightly inauspicious. There was saying, 'A Setterday flit's a short sit,' and perhaps that had something to do with the fact that we only stayed three years there!

As time wore on down through the late 1920s into the early 1930s, more and more flitting were done by lorry. The owners of the lorries were enterprising men, some being ex-carters who had realised the potential of motor transport. Farmers began at first to hire lorries to move workers from a distance, then gradually it became policy for all removals to be done by contractors. This did not happen overnight for it was well into the mid-30s, ere the horse and cart flitting disappeared from the roads. To engage lorries to do the job was much more convenient for the farmers, and caused less disruption of their everyday work. For instance should three or four families leave a place at the term, it was impossible for the remaining staff to cope with all the removals on the same day. Thus it sometimes happened that by mutual consent between employers, some householder could be shifted on the 26th and 27th May. It actually happened that when we moved to Newtoun, the two men sent to flit us had just come to the place themselves on the 26th.

Fogorig stands on one of the characteristic ridges of high ground in Berwickshire. 'The Rigs o' the Merse' was the title of an old song now forgotten, and indeed there are at least a dozen places in the Merse with 'rig' in their names. The farm commands a magnificent view of the Cheviot Hills some 20 miles away. The English Border is revealed right down to near the coast, and in depth to the Kyloe Hills, Dod Law, Ross Castle etc. To the north lie the Lammermuir Hills, prominent landmarks seen being the Hardens Hill and Cockburn Law. Duns is the nearest town and it was after we came to Fogorig that I first heard the town's motto, 'Duns dings A'. Of Chirnside which comes prominently into view to the eastward, one of the odd laddies quoted to me a rhyme, running:

It stands high an it roars sair,

It hez a heid but nae hair. [Editor's note: this is usually said of a church bell in a steeple]

Of a certainty a body could 'see about them' at Fogorig, and it was not difficult for one to foretell the weather when one left the house to go to work.

The farm was very large, over 900 acres, and carried a numerous staff. During our first year there from 1927–28, there were 28 regular workers on the pay-roll, forbye five Irishmen who worked there from June till November. The total permanent population was about 60. (Now the row of cottages has been demolished without trace; the only one left standing is that which used to house the steward).

The steward's house stood by itself, as was the trend on the Berwickshire farms, but the herds were housed in the row beside the other workers.

I think it is worth mentioning here a list of the various workers on the farm at that period, and their duties. There was the steward, who had oversight of the workforce – the shepherd excepted of course – and who also saw to the engine and the barn machinery; then came the first hind or plough-man steward, who drove the first pair and who could deputise if the steward was off ill. After him came the nine hinds or ploughmen with pairs who were more or less of equal status; at the tail of the horsemen came the odd laddies, two of whom drove a single horse each, and were mostly engaged in carting work. There were four men who did not have horses, called spademen or orramen, who did odd jobs about the farm and mended drains and fences. The term 'spademen' originated during the days of high farming in the nineteenth-century, when men with spades dug the ground at the roots of the hedges to discourage weeds, and utilize the parts that the ploughs could not reach. There were seven women workers, still often referred to as bondagers, all single women. Those were led by one of their number styled the forewoman, and were employed on a permanent basis for a variety of jobs, such as turnip singling, haymaking, stooking and forking at harvest, gathering potatoes and turnip shawing. There were the byreman and byrewoman, who tended the large number of cattle fed in the courts in winter time, and also the milk cows. The byrewoman milked the farmhouse cows. Another boy was employed who helped Mr Young junior with the Clydesdale breeding and young stock, and the pigs. There was a tractorman who drove one of the two tractors, the other being driven by the young farmer when required. Then last but not least came the shepherd and the herd laddie who were in charge of the sheep and the grazing cattle. I found myself in much closer contact with the folk of the farm than hitherto. Instead of being a casual observer, I was one of the staff and dweller in the row.

The year following (1928) saw the staff reduced by six and in subsequent years there were further reductions as the farming depression began to bite. Wages also fell gradually, until they were below the thirty shillings mark.

The farm policy at Fogorig was that of mixed arable farming, with the emphasis on grain, potatoes and sugar beet. A large acreage of turnips and swedes was grown for the winter fattening of cattle and sheep. Most of the grassland was of leys in rotation with the other crops, part of the first year's ley being hained for hay. Only a small portion of the whole farm was under permanent grass. A large number of grazing cattle were kept, both Irish and English bred beasts, of which Shorthorns and Shorthorn crosses predominated. In addition to the grazing bullocks, there was a small herd of suckling cows and a bull, which were also of Shorthorn type. There were cattle in every field, a thing I had never seen before, and two large fields of permanent grass on the outside of the farm, bordering on the River Blackadder, were reserved mainly for cattle; a handful of sheep was allowed to graze amongst them. Mr Young was very much addicted to cattle, and used to stand for hours in the cattle courts watching them. This prompted Dan the steward to remark sarcastically, 'Ah think his faither must hae been a bullick'.

The Youngs also bred Clydesdale horses, so that there were often brood mares with foals, and young unbroken horses running in the fields. Mr Young junior bred and fattened pigs off his own bat, an activity the master thought little of. We were amused one day when he was beside us among sheep in the faulds, when a couple of wandering pigs appeared on the scene. He made some cutting remarks about pigs and pig keeping in general, indicating his dislike.

Our employer was something of a dealer in livestock; he was forever buying and selling, and rented grass all over the countryside, so that stock was always being shifted hither and thither.

The sheep stock in our care consisted of Half Bred and Suffolk Cross ewes, with lambs by Oxford, Suffolk and Hampshire rams. This was the first time I had met with the Hampshire breed, and thought well of their progeny out of our ewes. They were thick-set, with good backs and easily fattened. The numbers of our ewe stock varied, somewhere between twenty five and thirty score, and all the lambs were sold fat, being mostly sent to Edinburgh by lorry. Sheep and lambs were sold all the year round, commencing in May with the early spring lambs, and carrying on till the following spring when the last of the turnip fed hoggs and fat ewes were disposed of. In addition to the home bred lambs, large numbers of lambs were bought in late summer and autumn at St Boswells, Hawick, Reston and Edinburgh, to be finished on foggage, sugar beet tops, turnips and swedes. One year at the Lammas Fair sale at St Boswells, Mr Young bought two hundred lambs. They came by train to Marchmont Station, landing there after midnight, and had to be driven home in the dark. Ewes unfit for breeding, both Half Breds and Blackfaces, were bought in for winter fattening as well, and those were mostly disposed of at Glasgow mart in the spring.

A Shepherd Remembers

Lambing time was a long drawn out process at Fogorig, starting with the older ewes on February 1st to get early fat lambs, going on through March till mid-April, when, after all the ewes had lambed, we started to lamb the ewe hoggs. Those latter would not be all lambed till well into May. Not many flockmasters took lambs off the ewe hoggs, but Fogorig was one place where it was done. Out of the three lambing seasons we had there, two were carried out in fields a mile away from the farmstead, which entailed a lot of extra travelling. We did the lambing our two selves, except for the night work when the farmer's son took a turn at sitting up. Once or twice when the ewes were lambing fast, and we had not time to get the lambed ewes off our hands quickly enough, a couple of women workers were sent to drive some of them to the more distant fields. Driving ewes with young lambs is a tedious time-consuming job, but the women enjoyed it as a break from more arduous work.

Certainly there was no lack of food for the ewes, in the shape of turnips, hay, corn and oil cake, and straw galore to build the lambing field. 1928 and 1930 were both middling springs and we got some dirty weather for the lambing season, but in 1929, the middle year, we experienced the best March weather I have ever seen before or since. The sun shone for the whole of the month, there never was as much as a shower, and with mild, balmy nights the grass grew apace.

Clipping was done in an implement shed, cleared out for the purpose. The sheep were all shorn with hand shears by a band consisting of father, a shearer hired by the day and one or two of the other men who were able to clip. One of the women workers rolled up the fleeces, and wheeled them away in a sort of barrow to a loft in another part of the steading where they were stored. At the dinner hour some of the young hinds used to look in at the shed, borrow a pair of shears and have a go, much mirth being caused by their amateur efforts. I remember one chap who tackled the shearing of an Oxford Down ewe, one of the three or four we kept for ram breeding. Now Oxford Downs have wool on the face, crown and legs down to the hoofs. This lad was so exasperated by the amount of odd corners he was having to cover with shears, that he remarked to the ewe, 'It must be awfa cauld doon about Oxford, hen, when ye need a' that oo on ye!' I was only a learner myself that first year of course, and it took me about three clipping seasons till I obtained proficiency. That involved having the strength to handle the sheep and the knack of holding it in the right positions, as well as plying the shears. In 1929 the two Dodds brothers from Duns took the clipping by contract, so we did not have to clip many. They clipped the sheep by piece-work, at so much a score, a person being provided to roll up the fleeces behind them. Not many herds or farmers were keen on having the job done by contract in this way, for piece clippers, in their haste to get through as many sheep as possible in the shortest time, often made a rough job. Most shepherds liked to see the sheep well and evenly clipped, and this was better achieved by men on days' wages. Machine clipping was then in its infancy on Border farms, and did not became universal till some years after the Second World War.

Sometimes when I was exposed to the elements during the bad weather, I felt a bit disillusioned with my chosen calling, but my deep interest in sheep carried me through. The winter time was the worst to bear, as far as those early years of shepherding were concerned. Many hundreds of hoggs were folded on the turnips, so that a great deal of our time was taken up erecting, taking down and shifting wire nets. Being heavy sticky soil, the turnip land soon got churned up into a sea of mud by the wheels of the carts taking off the shawed turnips to be stored or made into clamps in the field. When the sheep were folded on it afterwards their numerous hooves added to the effect. The hoggs were fed cut turnips by a cutter cart drawn by a horse. The body of the cart was in the form of a hopper, after the same principle as the hand cutter, the turnips falling on the barrel of blades as the cartwheel moved. The cut turnips fell into a large box on the underside of the cart, and from there they were shovelled out into the troughs, which were strung out in two rows across the break. The cutter cart could be put on and off gear by working a lever. It was an improvement on the hand cutter, but was very heavy on the horse in muddy conditions. As time went on, both the hand cutter and cutter cart were replaced by a cutting machine driven by a petrol engine, but that still lay well into the future.

The cutter cart was operated on alternate weeks by the two odd laddies, each having a week 'on the cutter'. It was a middling job in wet weather when muddy conditions prevailed, or in hard frosty weather when everything one touched bit the fingers. Then the turnips would be frozen, even when happed with straw in the clamp, and were hard to fill by graip into the cart.

Both the odd laddies and myself suffered a lot from chilblains in winter time. On most mornings it was agony getting into our boots, and we hirpled along until our feet got warmed up, whereon the pain subsided a bit. Everyone wore leather boots then, it was some years later ere the wearing of rubber wellington boots became general. Shepherds wore the traditional herds' boots, tacketed and with sprung last giving them an upturned toe effect. The boots were generally made to measure and were expected to last for a year at least. Those shepherds' boots were ideal for walking though they tended to be somewhat heavy. The rest of our workaday apparel was a heavy tweed jacket, worn over a dungaree jacket, with tweed trousers. During my early working years, dungaree overalls were only used for clipping, but gradually they came to be worn over our trousers all the year round, and in hot summer weather as a substitute for tweed trousers. Cloth caps and cloth leggings were worn, but many shepherds wore tweed hats. Knee breeches and leather leggings were worn by some workers, but the hinds tended to favour corduroy trousers and leggings of cloth or corduroy. The women workers wore drugget petticoats with an apron of sackcloth or some waterproof material; their headgear was the traditional straw hat worn over a kerchief. All workers had oilskin coats, leggings and sou'westers. Many of the oilskins were homemade in cotton, and waterproofed by dressing with linseed oil.

But to return to the odd laddies, who did all the carting for the sheep, and with whom I had daily contact during winter and spring. A laddie started driving an odd horse at fourteen on leaving school, and after two or three years he graduated to a pair of horses at sixteen or seventeen. Since he came in at the bottom of the male pecking order on the farm (the women workers had their own pecking order), he had to endure a good deal of teasing from the hinds. As an apprentice, too, he was continually under the surveillance of the farm steward who was always keeping him right. For a large part of the year the odd laddies were at the beck and call of the shepherds, laying down turnips in the pastures, carrying out feedstuff to the field bins from the steading, shifting bins and troughs, or wire nets and stakes from field to field. The herds were often pretty hard on the laddies, finding fault with them if they made mistakes in carrying out orders. One extreme case I heard tell of, was a shepherd who ordered a laddie to lift turnips and lay them down again in a grass field, simply because he had not put them in the right place.

A story is told about a farm steward at Sisterpath in Fogo parish, whose own son was one of the odd laddies on this farm, and whose dimness or awkwardness was a thorn in his father's flesh. Exasperated one day by some extra stupid action on the part of the boy, he shouted, 'Man, ye're an awfu donnert laddie ti hae sic a clever faither!'

One phenomenon new to us when we moved to the Merse was to witness the large flocks of wild geese that haunted the large stubble fields in autumn and winter. Late September saw the first gaggles passing over; then in October hordes of them settled on the fields by day to feed, resting by night on Greenlaw moor. Most of these geese moved on elsewhere after a week or two, but there were always a few gaggles which stayed on to winter with us. Their yelping cries never failed to thrill me. I dubbed them 'Grey winged pirates from the misty north', and in my fancy pictured them as the spirits of long dead Vikings from Asgard or Valhalla. To this day when I hear the cry of the wild geese it brings back memories of my early working days in the Merse.

In common with other Merseland farms, Fogorig was not too well watered. The only water for the fields came from the ditches that traversed the farm. To the steading and cottages the water had to be pumped. For the farmhouse and farm buildings the supply had to be pumped from a well over fifty yards away to a large storage tank in the waterhouse, a building by the roadside. The faulds and sheep dipper were situated just across the road from this waterhouse, and all the water for sheep dipping had to be carried in buckets across the road, a most laborious business.

Pumping was done by a windmill which stood by the well, augmented by an engine in spells of calm weather. Windmills were a familiar feature of the Berwickshire landscape and the screeching of their sails in windy weather could be heard day and night. By the time we lived in the district they were being superseded by engine driven pumps, such as that at Fogorig.

The water for the row was pumped by hand from a well just a few yards from the end house. The carrying of water for the cottages was mostly done by the girls and housewives, though sometimes a young man would go for water for his mother, when a chance arose to chat up a girl he fancied. A good deal of laughing and daffing took place at the pump at dinner times or in the evenings. For easier carrying a hoop and harness was used to suspend the buckets, a method used from time immemorial.

Another feature of the landscape worth mentioning was the tall chimneys in the steadings at the larger farms, which were relics of steam power in bygone days.

To touch again on the subject of the workers' cows; there were half a dozen at Fogorig which were summer-grazed in a large field just in front of the row. As the field usually contained a score of thirty bullocks in addition to the milk

Fogo

cows, the women had often difficulty in getting them milked –
milking was done outside in summer – free from interference
from the other beasts. I have seen mother sore trauchled and
delayed at milking, having to go to the far end of the field to
see the cow. In small pasture fields the cows usually came to
the milkers when called, but in a big field among a lot of other
beasts, they were reluctant to leave the herd. Again, once the
milker had sat down to milk, other cattle would come sniffing
around, or the whole herd would just move off. The cow
growing restless would finally follow them, leaving the poor
milker to carry the milk pails after it, trying to coax it to stop
and stand to get the milking finished. No wonder the women
often returned from milking cross and exhausted. The hinds'
cows were mostly milked by the daughters, who were also
field workers. They had to milk before yoking at six in the
morning, during the hour and after lowsing time in the
evening. The farmer's three cows and those of the workers
were housed in separate byres; housing was from autumn till
early summer, and they were fed, bedded and turned out into
and from pasture by the byreman. In summer from mid-May
they lay outside all the time.

The row of cottages at Fogorig was built in the shape of a
fender, the six middle houses faced the road, and the two
houses at each side faced into the centre. There were no back
doors, access to the backs was by two vennels, which went
through at each end of the main middle row. Privies and coal
houses were built on to the backs. Our house was at the end
nearest the steading.

Being such a big place and bordering as it did on a public
road, the row attracted a large number of vans. The days of
the horse drawn vans or 'cadgers' cairts', were over, motor
vans having replaced them. Those were both of the open and
closed variety. A host of vendors called selling different
wares, and it was seldom that a van of some sort was not
to be found on the doors. Coal lorries hawking bags of coal
were plentiful, so that the carting of coals from the station
became a thing of the past. The coal came from Northumber-

land, from Scremerston and places further south such as Broomhill, Shilbottle and Choppington.

The vans included grocers, butchers, bakers, and drapers from the surrounding towns and villages, some of them coming fair distances to follow up regular customers. Mother's own grocer called on her from Kelso. This was James MacLean, the firm she had dealt with since the Burnfoot days. It was about this time that MacLean's business was acquired by Miss Helen Johnston.

In addition to the traders mentioned above, there were hardware merchants, fruiterers, bootmakers and even a chemist's van which came from Coldstream. Basket wives from Swinton called occasionally, selling crockery, pirns, pins and other small household articles. Swinton, like Yetholm, was the abode of muggers or basket folk. They were not the same as the tinkers who frequented other parts of Scotland, in that they had permanent homes in villages like Yetholm and Swinton. They drove around the farms in horse-drawn traps accompanied by lurcher dogs, which trotted along under the vehicle. I could not say what exactly the menfolk did for a living, perhaps a bit of horse couping or collecting scrap metal, but the womenfolk did quite well with their packs. The mugger class were not short of money, in spite of being shabbily dressed, and 'putting on a puir mooth'. They mowed the loanings and roadside verges for hay for their ponies, and some had a bit field adjacent to the village where they lived. As time went on they used carts to hawk around in, and some branched out as contractors, car dealers and garage owners after World War II.

There was life, laughter and bustle on the farms of the Merse in those days, for the whole countryside teemed with people. In Fogo parish, besides Fogorig, there were Bogend and Sisterpath, both large farms with big staffs. Sisterpath was also a full doubled herding, with a first class ewe flock. There were also two shepherds on Eccles Tofts, another large farm bordering the parish, whose numerous staff together with that of Printonan made a big contribution to the population.

Fogo

For a generation farm folk had owned bicycles, which gave them more mobility, and by the time I had started work a fair sprinkling of young farm workers had managed to get motorbikes. As regards rail travel, the nearest railway actually ran through part of Fogo parish. This was the Berwickshire line which ran from St Boswells to Reston, connecting the Waverley line with the East Coast route. Marchmont, our nearest station, was two miles away. In the late 1920s buses made their appearance on the Border roads, which helped further to make the folk more mobile.

The buses were mostly owned by small local operators, though in a few years the big companies such as the Scottish Motor Tractor Company were to step in and run them off the roads. Such companies had the backing of the Traffic Commissioners who regulated the issue of licences, and gradually they built up a monopoly of road passenger transport. It came to pass that if a private individual applied for a licence to run a public bus on a route covered by the SMT they immediately lodged an objection, and the Traffic Commissioners would block the application in their favour. Thus did the big fellows gain a monopoly in public transport on the more important routes.

Since we were equidistant from Duns and Greenlaw, on the road between these two towns, the buses that plied between them passed our doors.

The two chief summer gatherings were the annual games at Swinton and Greenlaw, which attracted large crowds of farm folk. The Berwick May Fair was another popular event, drawing crowds from both sides of the Border. The bus could be taken from Duns to Berwick and back, with a good connection either way on our local route.

Quoiting had been a popular sport with farm women for generations, and was still carried on with enthusiasm in Fogo parish. The men practised on the wide road verges or on waste ground during the summer evenings, for it was essentially a summer sport. Most parishes had a quoiting club, which held contests among its own numbers and tournaments

93

in which parish was matched against parish. At the two village games previously mentioned, quoiting contests figured prominently.

On Sunday evenings when there was nothing better to do, the young folk from the farms went for long walks in groups, youths and girls separately of course. The young men gathered in numbers at certain crossroads, Fogomuir being one of these venues, where they compared notes about their various places of employment, how the farm work was progressing, how they were treated by steward or farmer, and other items of gossip and local interest. Banter was rife and arguments arose now and again, and facetious remarks would be shouted at passing girls and courting couples.

Amongst the farm chaps were to be found fiddlers and melodeon players, these instruments were the favourites then, just as the accordion and guitar are today.

Dances were held in Fogo school from time to time during the winter, mostly following a concert or some other gathering. Kirns were given sporadically at neighbouring farms, but never at Fogorig in our time. It is said that a kirn had been given a few years previously but Mr Young, an abstemious man, had been so disgusted by the drunken behaviour of some of the men that he had vowed never to give another. Although the majority of the workers were not heavy drinkers there was a minority who had themselves a skinful on a Saturday night.

Concerts of a homespun variety were held in the school now and then. The Girl Guides staged one annually, but by far the most popular concerts were given by a troupe led by Mr Malcolm Dickson, a butcher in Duns, which toured the surrounding villages. I forget now exactly how many members there were in the party, but one of the artistes, a lady whose name I have forgotten, was a beautiful singer. Her rendering of that rousing song 'The Scottish Bluebells' was superb. This stirring song, once so popular, I have never heard sung since. It appears to have sunk without trace in the intervening years. Apart from the soloists, the party acted out a humorous sketch, with Malcolm himself dressed up as a lady. He also did one or two solo turns in drag; he had a portly figure and the sight of him cavorting in female guise drew hilarious applause from us rustics. The only other artistes whose names I can recall were Miss Horsburgh, another singer who also did recitations, and Tommy Cunningham a ventriloquist, whose repartee with his puppet Joey was a star turn, especially since Joey's remarks were often spiced with references to individuals in the audience. They of course took it in the right spirit – a bit of harmless fun.

Good old Malcolm! He and his party brought a lot of cheer into our lives, even if his repertoire and that of his fellows was somewhat hackneyed. He never failed to draw a good crowd wherever he went. Looking back and comparing him with the present day television and radio stars, he did not do so badly. They too tend to have a limited repertoire of songs and patter, and when they descend on one of our Border towns to give a performance, they do so with the sole aim of publicising themselves, and to sell their records.

It is not to be denied that life was pretty hard for landworkers in the period between the wars but we managed to have fun as well. There was a warmth, a neighbourliness and community spirit abroad, which is totally absent from the deserted rural scene of the present day.

At Fogo, as at other places where we had been, the kirk played a prominent part in the life of our family. Except during the lambing time, father and mother attended kirk regularly, scarcely missing a Sunday. We young ones were expected to follow suit and never questioned it. We enjoyed going to the kirk and meeting folk at the kirk gate. At that time the women and girls walked straight into the kirk whilst the men and boys remained outside chatting in groups until the final bell rang. I don't know how long this habit had been in vogue, but it certainly persisted for some in the Borders.

After the service folk lingered in groups for a few minutes, greeting friends, before setting off for home. The folk from each farm, the farmers' folks excepted, walked in company to and from the kirk.

In winter time when there were large numbers of sheep on turnips to be attended to, father and I attended the kirk on alternate Sundays. The byremen and odd laddies did Sunday work too during the winter, the former in the cattle courts and the latter at the cutter cart. It was accepted that folk in charge of livestock must need to work on Sundays, but other farm work, even at hay and harvest, was never undertaken on Sunday. It was not until the Second World War that Sunday work became general on the Border farms, and then only at harvest. Since then Sunday work on the farm has been extended all the year round. The ministers never frowned upon stockmen and shepherds undertaking Sunday tasks; theirs was considered to be work of necessity and mercy, but they did not take kindly to the idea of Sunday work in general. Some farmers who were staunch kirk men held out against the practice of Sunday working even during the war and after.

We had perforce to attend the Auld Kirk at Fogo, because the nearest UF kirk was at Leitholm three miles away. In any case, we had compromised at Roxburgh, and the two kirks were now on the verge of uniting, which event took place in 1929. I joined the kirk that year as a full communicant member. Before that I was classed as an adherent, so that I and a married lady from Bogend were the first new members at Fogo Kirk after the union.

I also joined the choir and attended the week night practices held on Tuesday evenings for most of the year, barring seed time, hay and harvest. One other youth and three young women from Fogorig were choir members as well.

Like my native parish of Linton, Fogo was a parish without a village. The only remnants of what must have been a village were the kirk and manse, the school and schoolhouse. The nearby farm of Fogo Mains was still called Fogo East End locally, which denoted that Fogo must have extended in that direction at one time. The original village or hamlet had probably been swept away in the agricultural improvements of the late eighteenth and early nineteenth century. There was a smithy and joiner's shop at Fogo Muir about a mile away but those may have been the remnants of a separate hamlet. There was also the ruins of a school at Pilmuir, between Fogorig and Bogend where another hamlet had probably existed.

The minister at Fogo was the Reverend John Hunter, a young man recently ordained and still single, who had one of his sisters as housekeeper.

From childhood upward I had been familiar with our Church Hymnary, though it was mostly the children's hymns that I knew and loved, but now as a member of the choir at Fogo I began to appreciate and enjoy the adult hymns and psalms. From then I can date my love for the Scottish metrical psalms and paraphrases, especially their tunes, a regard that has stuck with me all my life. Those tunes and many of the words are, one could almost say, graven on my heart. What solace and sustenance I have derived from them throughout life and my career as a shepherd.

Many times when sitting at night in the lambing hut after a day of ceaseless rain, I would hear it still lashing down throughout the night. I would be filled with fears regarding the welfare of the young lambs outside, being battered by the elements. With the approach of dawn the rain would cease, and when I was out looking over the ewes in the shed, I would notice a line of light on the horizon where the clouds were lifting. Then I would call to mind two lines of a hymn, commonly sung to the psalm tune 'Irish':

And lo! already on the hills,

The flags of dawn appear

I would hum it to myself, thanking God that the storm was over at last.

My other favourites among the psalm tunes were Ballerma, Martyrdom, Kilmarnock, and Stracathro, just to name a few. It is a great pity that in this secular age those tunes are being consigned to oblivion. The Kirk itself is not above criticism for the way many ministers neglect in services the use of psalms and paraphrases with the fine, sweet, dignified tunes. What gave joy and solace to generations of our forebears will soon be merely a memory.

The various allusions to sheep and shepherding in the scriptures, I have found to have parallels in my own experience. The parable of the lost sheep; what shepherd has not felt the anxiety of the search and the subsequent joy and satisfaction of finding the stray? The story of the good shepherd laying down his life for his sheep has its equal in the many cases of shepherds perishing on snowstorms on the hills, when going to succour their flock. The scriptures speak of sheep knowing their shepherd's voice, and sheep being led by the shepherd rather than being driven. How often have I myself led sheep from one field to another through mud or deep snow, when to have tried to drive them with dogs would have been useless.

A Bible class was held in Fogo Kirk on Sunday evenings during the winter. This was common practice in all parishes then, the idea being to provide post-Sunday school religious tuition and Bible study for young adolescents. Ours was well attended by young folk of both sexes from school leavers to those in their early twenties. No doubt many came just for the company and the lack of something to do on a dark Sunday evening. After the meeting was over the girls usually took the short cut home to Fogorig, via a farm track, but the youths went all the way round by Fogo Muir, and joined the others at the crossroads. To mark the end of the session a social and dance was held. I remember the minister remarking jocularly at one such function that the Bible class was an agent of matrimony! Maybe he wasn't far wrong for many a lad and lass found romance after the Bible class on Sunday evenings. A rhyme we used to chant when we were bairns to the courting couples who strolled sedately past Burnfoot ran thus:

Lad an' lass, kiss the cass'
Mary in the Bible class.

That was before people started to use the anglified terms 'boy friend' and 'girl friend', for when I was young, a young fellow had his lass and a lassie had her lad.

The beadle at the kirk was Tom Paterson, a forester on the Charterhall estate, who lived in a cottage called Rashie, a few hundred yards from the kirk. The cottage stood in a field of the same name, and possibly there might have been a croft there in former times. Tom had been the precentor, and although the kirk had an organ, he still led the praise from his stance below the pulpit. He was a jovial kindly man with a very fine singing voice. Tom was our choirmaster as well. At the annual kirk soirée, he was one of the leading artistes, giving some fine renderings of Scots songs. The soirée was held after the turn of the year and consisted of a tea, followed by a programme of songs, readings, recitations and choral items, interspersed with a succession of witty stories told by our own ministers and those from neighbouring parishes who had been invited along to take part. The audience both young and old was always a large one, and filled the kirk in which the soirée was held.

The short cut from Fogorig to Fogo already referred to was a field track. It was not very clean at times, and when the field was in grass folk tended to leave the track and keep to the grass for cleaner going. In misty weather this could lead them to wander off the direct route completely. One chap who was returning from a function at Fogo on a very foggy night got temporarily lost. Next day when relating his experience to his companions he said, 'If Ah jumpt that ditch yince, Ah jumped it a dizzen times', referring to a ditch which lay across this path through one of the fields. His tale caused much hilarity among his listeners, for it was obvious that he had been wandering in circles. What struck them as most funny was the number of times he had crossed the ditch. Once he had jumped over the ditch the first time why had he not the sense to avoid crossing it again, and him stone sober too!

When we were at Fogorig my young sister was still at school, and just left it at the Christmas term before we flitted from there. She did not like Fogo school very much. She found it inferior to what she had been used to at Roxburgh, scholars of her own age lagging far behind her in many subjects. Indeed all Berwickshire was backward compared with Roxburghshire as far as education was concerned.

Fogo was a two-teacher school, with a schoolmaster and an assistant lady teacher. The schoolmaster was very harsh on the pupils and ruled by the tawse. My sister was sickened by the daily thrashings meted out to some scholars for the most trivial offences and for their failure to grasp the lessons.

We had no circulating rural library or evening classes. In our first autumn I made enquiries about a night school and the schoolmaster said he would try to get one going. In the event only another youth and myself turned up so it never got off the ground.

Right up till after the Second World War lighting in farmhouse, farm cottage and steading was by paraffin lamps and lanterns. A very small minority of farms had their own generators for producing electric light in the farmhouse and steading. At some farms, for example Bogend, the lighting was extended to the cottages, each householder being charged a shilling a week. Hanging lamps or table lamps were used in the kitchen-cum-living room, hand lamps or candles in back kitchen, pantry and the bedrooms. Paraffin oil was purchased by the gallon or more from a grocer or the hardware van. I remember our own grocer's van had a distinct odour of paraffin. Mother kept her oil in an empty whisky jar called a 'greybeard'. The daily trimming, cleaning and filling of lamps was part and parcel of the household chores in the dark season of the year. Though those lamps and candles may have presented a fire hazard folk were very careful and fires were very rare, certainly not as many as those arising from the present day chip pans. One thing I can remember, though, is being flyted at for spilling candle grease on the stair or in the bedroom.

The steading was lighted by hurricane lamps, which were called stable or byre lamps. The hinds and byremen were provided with lanterns, which they carried to and from the steading during the dark season, hanging them up behind the stall in the stable, or at some strategic point when feeding the cattle. It could be difficult in a high wind to keep the lanterns from being extinguished when out of doors.

When tending their horses in the early morning, the men would venture out in the black darkness to get straw from the barn or hay from the hayshed; it was quite easy for them to make their way when they knew where to go. On one occasion a young chap went to the barn to get an armful of straw for bedding, but as he stooped down to scoop up the straw there was a terrific roar, and he found himself flat on his back. He got the fright of his life, and wondered what had happened, till he realised he had been bowled over by the farm boar, as it started up from where it had been sleeping amongst the straw.

In spite of the universal use of paraffin lanterns about the buildings, and by the shepherds in the straw-built lambing sheds, there were remarkably few farm fires. When fires did break out they were usually devastating, destroying steadings or stackyards ere the fire brigades got them under control. Lack of water was a crucial factor, unless the farm had a pond or was near a stream or river.

When the alarm was raised that fire had broken out all the workers rushed to the scene, and folk from neighbouring farms rallied round to help. The first object, should the steading be full of animals, was to get them to safety. Many were the deeds of heroism performed by hinds in rescuing their terrified horses from a burning stable.

Farmers lived in dread of farm fires, especially after harvest when the stackyard was full, for there was little that could be done once a fire really got a hold. When we were at Fogorig, in 1928 it was, a fire occurred at the nearby farm of Whinkerstones. The buildings were gutted but the farmhouse was unscathed, and since it was summer there were no animals involved.

Tramps were frequently blamed for farm fires, as they would be careless with matches when sheltering overnight in farm buildings. Most farmers absolutely refused to allow roadsters into their steadings, and who could blame them. Those who did harbour tramps usually insisted that they surrendered all matches, pipes or cigarettes they had about their persons.

Fogorig was one farm that did not harbour tramps, but the cottages were pestered by plenty of them when passing through. At such a big row they were assured of getting pieces and tea at one or other of the houses. Mother never turned a tramp away empty, and used to feel heartsore for the bairns which some women tramps dragged around with them. A cute move by those women was to send the bairns to beg for them as they knew it would tend to soften hearts. Mother would sometimes flyte at men of the able-bodied sort, though she never refused them tea. One chirpy character when asked his occupation said, 'Ah'm an inspecturr, an inspecturr of milestanes'.

Occasionally singing tramps would appear on the scene, or one with a melodeon or some other instrument.

Many of the tamps were regulars who covered a fair bit of country in their wanderings. Notable among those was Yorkie, of English extraction and reputed to be a broken down son of the gentry. He could be very noisy and aggressive and bairns and some housewives were terrified of him. He would knock on the door and demand food in a threatening manner, but if he was treated firmly, he was easily cowed. Nervous housewives at lonely hill cottages however, could be terrorized into providing him with a substantial meal, which he insisted on eating at the table. The story goes that one such young wife had just complied with his demands when her husband returned from the hill unexpectedly. Sizing up the situation, he promptly threw Yorkie out of the house, and gave him a right good hiding. His roars of pain and rage awoke the echoes as he retreated down the valley. 'Stickie' was the nickname given to another tramp, who always carried a bundle and a stick under his oxter; Bet the Boar and Nellie the Sweep were two well known female tramps, and Puzzle Bobbie, another familiar vagrant, used to make puzzles out of pieces of wire, which he sold to the bairns.

A curious fact about the tramps was that those from the English side of the Border frequented the Scots side and vice versa. I imagine this had some connection with the differing poor laws of the two countries.

The big house where the laird resided was Charterhall, fully a mile up the road from us towards Greenlaw. The then laird was Colonel Trotter, an ex-army man, and very gruff and testy. I remember meeting in with him and the head gamekeeper during our first summer at Fogo. He gave me instructions about what to do should I chance upon a pheasant's or partridge's nest. 'Be sure and tell Smith' (the under keeper on the Fogorig beat, who lived at Hunthall). 'Do you understand?' he ordered, in a very fierce voice.

The Trotter tribe had held Charterhall estate for a considerable time and still do. The same clan had estates in Midlothian, and I believe they had originally been Edinburgh merchants or lawyers or such like.

Most of the lairds in Berwickshire were ex-army types who were not at all popular with the farm folk. Like all lairds they were aloof and arrogant, being doubly so because of their military background.

A notable exception was Mr Guthrie-Smith of Caldra House close to Fogo, who was a retired sheep farmer from New Zealand. He once gave a lantern lecture in the school, on his experiences in New Zealand, which was much enjoyed by a packed audience.

He impressed father and me when we met him on the road one day in June 1928. There had been a severe storm of rain and hail earlier in the month, just after the ewes had been clipped. He had noticed the sheep rowed up against the hedgebacks, sheltering from the storm, and asked us if we had had any perished. He indicated that in New Zealand they often suffered heavy losses among their flocks when hailstorms struck just after shearing time. This concern for our sheep from an interested onlooker, coupled with his approachable and unpatronising manner, awoke a response in us. Farm workers were used to being talked down to by the upper and middle classes.

Father, in common with many other shepherds and farm stewards, was ambitious to rent a small farm for himself. Small farms were scarce in the Borders, and competition was keen. During our sojourn at Fogorig, he made offers for two small farms, Orange Lane near Eccles in 1928, and Harcus near Eddleston, Peeblesshire in 1929. In both cases he went and walked over the farm, after perusing the Conditions of Lease. Conditions of Lease under which farms were rented were formidable documents drawn up in legal jargon and heavily weighted in favour of the landlords. Many clauses were never fully enforced I suppose, judging by the state of some farms when they became vacant, but they were binding nevertheless. Well, all the money father had was his savings, with the backing of his bank to advance an equal sum. Many working men seeking farms obtained financial backing, over and above what they could raise themselves, from big farmers to get themselves set up. In father's view this put one too much in the hands of the big man, however benevolent he might be, so he would have none of it. In the event he offered what he considered to be a reasonable rent for each of the farms, but neither offer was accepted. Had he got a farm then it would have had a far-reaching effect on the fortunes of our family.

In the back end of 1929 father decided he had had enough of Fogorig. It was not exactly a very good herding, as the sheep stock was irregular and too often much of the breeding stock was being grazed elsewhere. One thing he particularly disliked was Mr Young's practice of taking turnips at other farms, to be eaten on the ground by the grit ewes in the weeks prior to lambing. 'Ye send the yowes away tae other folks' places at the very time Ah should be lookin efter them', he grumbled to the master. We had had a lot of trouble among the ewes at lambing time in both '28 and '29, as a result of them being badly looked after by other men while agisted on turnips.

Fogo

He and Mr Young had a row at lambing time 1929, during which the master flew into a rage about something or other, making some cutting remark concerning father's work. Mr Young was one of those of whom it is said, 'His bark's worse than his bite'. He would say things in a temper then forget all about it, coming up as nice as ninepence in a few days afterwards. But father, like many of his calling, was a proud man and felt he had been slighted. The insulting remarks rankled, and though he would not leave at May 1929, cutting off his nose to spite his face, he resolved not to make another bargain for the following year. Besides I would be ready to partner him in a full double herding by May 1930. Thus he intimated to the Youngs in December 1929 that he would be leaving at the following term. They were surprised and dismayed, never dreaming that he had a grievance, and sorry to lose a good man, for they realised his worth. With my feeble help he had accomplished a lot.

Mother was relieved to be making a move for she had never really liked the place; my sister was not bothered either, and as for myself I looked forward to the prospect of a better job.

4

GLENDALE

Having intimated his intention to leave Fogorig at May 1930, father set about looking for another double herding to start at that date. For nearly a month prior to post-New Year hirings for shepherds and stewards at Hawick, Kelso and Berwick, vacant situations for these key men appeared in the local papers. More and more then newspapers were being used as a medium for hiring workers, and in the run up to the traditional hiring fairs, column after column of situations were advertised.

We scanned the 'situations vacant' notices in search of something suitable without having any luck. Father went to the Kelso Hirings to see what he could find. I did not go since it was usual for the father to do the bargaining, while the son stayed at home to look after the sheep. There were other shepherds at Kelso that day seeking double herdings, who had left sons at home.

When father returned home in the evening he informed us that he had hired us to a situation near Wooler in Northumberland, and reckoned that he had made a good bargain. We were all relieved that we had got a situation, as we had grown not a little anxious during the past weeks, lest we could not get a place to go to at the term. At that time when men were all hired by the year, the hiring season was restricted to certain periods. This custom arose from the fact that the hiring fairs were the only dates set for hiring workers, and once they were past everyone was assumed to be settled for the ensuing year commencing in May. The seasonal rush of 'situations vacant' in the newspapers coincided with the 'speaking time', and reflected that state of affairs. Anyone unlucky enough to be still unhired after the traditional hiring period, had perforce to try to rent a house from a farmer, and get seasonal farm work wherever possible or even work outside agriculture.

The place we were hired to was North Doddington in the district of Northumberland called Glendale. The farm was owned by Alderman Rea, a typical gentleman farmer. His old shepherd, Alec Rutherford, was due to retire after forty seven years of service, first at Middleton and then at North Doddington, to which place Mr Rea had moved in 1915. Farmers often asked long served trusted employees to accompany them to a new farm rather than part with them. The under shepherd, a young single man who boarded with Alec, was also leaving for another job.

Alec Rutherford held the job with an antiquated bargain little modified since the 1880s. His wage was all in kind; he had a full pack of thirty or forty sheep, a quantity of corn to be ground into meal for household use, and for pigs' food, the keep of a cow, potatoes as lifted and a house and garden.

This system was considerably modified to suit father, who ended up with a part cash wage and certain perquisites. Those perquisites consisted of a small sheep pack (ten ewes and three ewe hoggs), a cow's keep, sixty stones of oatmeal per annum, two tons of undressed potatoes, house and garden, plus some cash. My wage was to be thirty two shillings per week, paid monthly in cash. In addition mother was to get fifteen shillings per week for boarding and lodging the lambing man for four weeks. The farmer was to provide a sheep's carcase to feed the clippers at shearing time.

It may seem strange that Mr Rea, a Northumbrian farmer, should come to Kelso Hirings to engage a man. But we found out later that he had hired Scots herds and stewards in the past, when he farmed more extensively on the Middleton estate, an enterprise covering six hirsels.

Father went to plant the garden at Doddington near the end of April, and one of our neighbours from Fogorig volunteered to accompany him to lend a hand. It was as well he did, for they found that no one at Doddington turned out to help as was customary on the Scots side of the Border. He was a bit put out by this and it gave him a rather poor impression of the English, even though the retiring herd's household gave them dinner and tea. We were told afterwards that the English term being much earlier, i.e. May 13th, it was not considered necessary to get the garden set beforehand. Men came in April just the same to see the place and view the house, but they only did the very minimum of work in the garden.

To reach Doddington, father and his companion cycled the six miles to Coldstream, took the bus from there to Wooler, and completed the three mile journey from Wooler to Doddington by taxi. They carried some tools with them and a few cabbage plants. The seed potatoes had been sent beforehand to Wooler station, where they collected them.

The English term was on May 13th and the Scots term on May 28th which raised some problems. However, it was agreed between Alderman Rea and father that, since the outgoing head shepherd was retiring, he might be willing to stay on until May 28th, if I were to go down there to take the place of the single assistant shepherd, who was leaving on May 13th for another situation. Alec Rutherford agreed to this and to put me up until my parents came at the Scots term. Mr Young of Fogorig was quite agreeable to let me go, and meantime my place would be taken as father's assistant by a boy who had just left school.

Thus I went to our new abode a fortnight before the rest of the family. Mr Rea sent his chauffeur and car to fetch me, dog, baggage and all. I remember that on that particular occasion it was a terribly wet day, and the flitting carts we met and passed on our way after crossing the Border presented a forlorn appearance.

The other members of our family duly arrived on May 28th by lorry. The lorry, which belonged to Redpath Bros., a Wooler firm of contractors, had deposited our successors at

Glendale

Fogorig from Crosbie near Earlston. Their goods and chattels were unload at the house, ere ours could be picked up. As I have already explained that was a method frequently used by contractors, to link flittings to and from the one farm. It was not altogether a satisfactory arrangement from the workers' point of view.

My two sisters (one of whom had come home for the occasion) cycled to Doddington, a distance of at least twenty miles, and they were pretty tired when they landed. Mother and father came with the furniture lorry; mother rode in the front in the cab beside the driver, and father perched on the roof of the cab with his two dogs. He always wore a tweed hat, and they had not gone far ere his hat blew off. His efforts to attract the driver's attention were unavailing, so he was obliged to make the rest of the journey bareheaded, catching a heavy cold as a result.

Our cow and the pack sheep had been sent off by lorry on the previous day. For some reason or other it did not arrive at Doddington until the small hours of the following morning. This caused me some embarrassment for I had perforce to arouse my host from bed to help me to unload and dispose of the animals. I think the owner-driver of the lorry – a one-man business in Swinton – had wasted time in a pub en route, for he smelt strongly of drink.

The Glendale district of Northumberland into which we moved covers roughly that part of the county lying between Wooler and the Tweed at Cornhill. It takes its name from the river Glen which joins the Till at Ewart.

Although it entailed a move of only some twenty miles, this move into Northumberland was a traumatic experience for us. We seemed to have landed in a strange land alien to us in speech and customs. Of course we had met with folk from Northumberland before this, but it was something new to be living in their midst, and to hear everyone speaking with a 'Geordie' accent, which we had some difficulty in understanding at first. I might remark, however, that the folk of North Northumberland in those days, hotly resented being called 'Geordies', that term in their opinion rightly belonging to the pitmen and townies of Tyneside.

It took us some time to get settled in our new environment, and I for one never accepted it. I fretted for Scotland, longing for the day when we would return there. I am afraid I was a very discontented youth, and must have been a pain in the neck to my parents with my grumbling. Since father and I were hired jointly, any move from home by me would have meant either that they would have had to flit as well, or give board and lodging to someone else. For my own part I realised that living at home and herding under father was preferable to living and working with outsiders. So I just tholed England for twelve years, mellowing some in the process, though I never abandoned my Scottishness and tended to maintain a nationalistic stance.

As Scots interlopers we encountered hostility in some small ways, and such snide remarks as, 'The stone lions on the gates of Alnwick wag their tails every time a Scotchman goes back to Scotland', implying that this was a thing that never happened! Once when I had a row with another chap, he shouted at me, 'Git away back tae yer own country, ye bloody foghriner!'

We soon found that there were a lot of Scots in the area, and a great many more who were of Scots descent. Curiously enough some of those who had Scots parents proved to be more English than the English themselves, and more prone to run down Scotland.

Certain Scots folk we met with, went as far as to say that Scotland held no happy memories for them, and that they had been far better off since crossing the Border. Their statements contained a grain of truth, for Agricultural Wages Boards had been in operation in England long before 1930, and were not brought into force in Scotland for several years after that. The result was that with a fixed minimum, wages in Northumberland never fell to the very low levels offered to workers in Roxburgh and Berwick shires, during the depression years. I don't recall that the Northumbrian minimum wage fell below thirty shillings a week, whereas we were told that on the Scots side hinds were only getting twenty-seven or twenty-eight shillings, with some being offered only twenty-five shillings a week. The Wages Boards laid down a floor for wages, but at the same time the minimum wage was regarded by farmers as the standard wage, and few of them paid their men any more than that.

One person who was as bewildered and homesick in his new surroundings as we were was a Mr White who came to farm at Chillingham from West Linton in Peeblesshire, in the same year in which we crossed the Border. Father happened to meet him at the mart at Wooler one day, and hearing father speak he said, 'Ye're a Scotsman man, gies a shake o yer haund!'

Doddington village is situated about three miles from Wooler, on the Wooler to Berwick road. It consisted then of two large farmsteads, North Doddington and South Doddington, with their cottages, a church and vicarage, school and schoolhouse and a post office. There were some other houses, not farm cottages, notably those occupied by quarry workers who worked in the famous freestone quarry situated on the side of the Dod Law. This quarry had provided stone for many notable buildings up and down the country, amongst them I believe the Scottish National War Memorial in Edinburgh. The quarry was still being worked, but owing to the depression and the fall in demand for building stone, the staff was drastically reduced in the early 1930s and work only continued on a limited and selective basis.

The steadings of the two farms were adjacent to each other with only the public road between, that of South Doddington containing the ruins of an old pele tower.

We found that the fashion of building two farms together to form a hamlet was common all over north Northumberland. Not far from Doddington were East and West Horton, and East and West Fenton, better known as Fenton Town. In the case of Doddington it might have been for the convenience of water supply, for the Dod Well was situated in the centre of the village. This well, converted into a stone fountain, gave an abundant supply of pure cold water to the inhabitants. Apart from the examples noted and several others, the farms of North Northumberland were scattered about the countryside, after the same pattern as in Scotland.

Up till the Great War the lands of Doddington had been part of the Chillingham Estates of the Earl of Tankerville, but had been sold to owner-occupiers about that time. The farm of South Doddington contained all the hill pasture tract of the Dod Law, as well as extensive inbye fields. It was farmed by Mr Harvey who bought it and took possession in 1930. The Harveys were a family of working farmers whose forebears hailed originally from Holy Island.

North Doddington on the other hand was owned and farmed by Alderman Rea. He and his family had farmed extensively in the area for three or four generations. I believe his forebears were local millers who had attained the rank of yeomen farmers and married into the local gentry. The Alderman maintained a large staff of workers, nineteen in all. There were twelve men and boys and seven women employed on the farm, and in addition he had a gardener, a gamekeeper, a groom-cum-chauffeur and three maids in the farmhouse.

The ground at North Doddington lay up to the Berwick Edge, the name given to the moorland rim where the Berwick road climbs up from the village, stretching right down from the edge to the river Till and beyond, into that large flat area known as Milfield Plain. The Plain, much of which is little over a hundred feet above sea level, was undoubtedly the bed of a primeval lake. This was borne out by the fact that the soil of the fields bordering the river was of solid alluvial clay, whilst the soil of those nearer the farm on each side of the Doddington to Milfield road was of pure sand, and in dry windy weather in Spring such of those fields as were under cultivation, were liable to dust storms. A good few years before our time the road itself was blocked in parts by sand, blown off the red land fields in a Spring gale.

Glendale

The fields in the middle and top part of the farm were tilled frequently. The rotation of crops was that which prevailed on both sides of the Border: two years ley followed by oats, a little wheat and a small acreage of potatoes in the first year; second year was green crops, that is turnips, swedes and a few acres of mangolds; third year barley under-sown with grass seeds. Hay was usually taken from the first year ley, and in addition a large permanent grass field was also mown. The amount of tillage was not large and some fields were allowed to lie in grass for more than two years. The whole farm embraced an area of eleven hundred acres, but much the greater part of it was in permanent pasture. The fields bordering the river and those beyond it, nine altogether, were all in grass. Access to those fields beyond the river was by a stone one-arch bridge which served both farms and which carried the right-of-way track to Ewart.

Apart from the extensive haughs by the riverside, those fields were protected from flooding by a series of water dykes, which ran for miles on either side of the Rivers Till and Glen. Floods occurred when those two slow winding streams overflowed, the point at the junction of the Glen and Till being particularly vulnerable. There was an elaborate system of ditches with sluices at the waterdykes, which could be shut down when a flood threatened, to prevent back water covering the fields behind the dykes. In spells of good weather, the flat green haughs dotted with cattle and sheep, with the lazy shining river winding between its sandy banks, presented quite an attractive picture. In springtime and summer with redshanks, lapwings and sandpipers making music the river bank took on an idyllic atmosphere. On scorching summer days it provided the cattle with a respite from the tormenting flies, when they stood belly deep in its waters, and the sheep too would lie low on its many shingly beaches or under the overhanging banks.

But the Till was a constant menace in wet weather, especially during winter and spring, when it could be swollen with rain or melting snows on the Cheviots. When a flood was anticipated we had to clear the stock off the haughs into the fields behind the dyke, and shut down the sluices. On the subject of haughs, here is an illustration of one of the many difficulties we met with regarding the Northumbrian speech. On my first day at Doddington I was greatly intrigued, when I heard the old shepherd refer to the riverside fields as the 'Howffs'. I thought to myself 'Howffs' that's a funny name to give to fields, not realising that this was the local pronunciation of the word 'haughs' and had nothing to do with our Scots word 'howff' meaning a drinking house.

The worst flood we experienced was in April 1934, when a heavy sudden snowstorm took place on the 10th. There was a heavy fall on the hills, followed by a thaw and two days and nights of incessant rain. On the morning of the 12th the river was bank full and rising fast. Luckily we had not much stock in the fields lying across the river and I was able to get them behind the dykes. By afternoon our bridge was surrounded, as was the bridge on the Wooler to Berwick road near Turvelaws. So being cut off from the fields beyond the river entirely, we could only hope that the flood would not top the waterdyke or the waterdyke itself give way at some weak spot. By the late afternoon on the 12th the rain had ceased, and by dawn on the morning of the 13th the river had started to fall. We spent a very anxious night indeed, only one of many such suffered on account of the Till, during our stay at Doddington. I used to have recurring nightmares in which I or the livestock would be caught in a flood, nightmares I kept having for years and years after we left Glendale.

That particular flood of April 1934 was the worst that had occurred since a more serious flood in May 1906. In that year the flood had so silted and polluted the riverside pastures that the two farmers involved had had to graze their hained hay fields for much of the summer. One day soon after the flood of 1934, I met with our neighbour herd on the bridge at the march when we discussed the flood and how it had affected us. 'Well', said Geordie, 'they say it's been the worst flood for twenty eight years, an' I'm no carin if there's no another wan again for twenty-eight years.' In actual fact there was another, far worse flood in August 1948, sixteen years later, when the bridge over the Berwick-Wooler road was swept away, and the flood surmounted the waterdykes. At Ewart Park hundreds of sheep were drowned after pars of the waterdyke collapsed. But neither Geordie Dunn nor I were there to see it.

One thing we noticed when we came to Northumberland, was the large numbers of cattle kept on the farms, as compared with the Scots Borders There the sheep were predominant and kept much thicker on the ground, two to two and a half ewes with lambs per acre. In Northumberland cattle were much more in favour and the sheep spread more thinly on the pastures for their benefit, only one to one and a half ewes per acre. Slag was widely used as a top dressing on the pastures, making them more beneficial to cattle.

North Doddington with its large acreage of grass, carried a big cattle herd, which was the responsibility of us shepherds during the summer grazing season, and this also extended to those being outwintered. During winter fifty to sixty lay outside and we were expected to keep an eye on them, though the job of feeding them with hay was done by an odd laddie with a cart, helped by one of the women workers. A large haystack was built each year, in a corner of one of two fields in which the beasts were outwintered, for convenience when haying them. The stack was used in sections as required, each new section being cut with a hay knife. The hay was forked loose on to the cart, then laid out on the ground in forkfuls for the cattle.

We shepherds had to do everything with the cattle, such as shifting them from field to field, driving them to the mart or railway station, and fetching a new batch from the station or from the master's other farm at Barmoor South Moor. We only got help from the byreman when a lame beast had to be thrown to sort its feet, or a sick beast held for the vet. We had not been accustomed to working so much among cattle, but this was just one of the different customs we met with in England. The cattle stock consisted of a number of forward bullocks and heifers of two years old, which were outwintered and fattened on grass in summer. These were sent to market as they got ready, starting in June with the heifers, followed by the bullocks in July, most being disposed of by October. Other grazing cattle were kept, some of those were fattened on turnips and cattle cake in the cattle courts during winter, while others were outwintered; the youngest class of beasts were wintered inside on straw and turned out to graze in spring.

The beasts kept were homebreds and Irish, plus a number of English bred Shorthorns. Mr Rea maintained a herd of breeding cows at the led farm of Barmoor south Moor, their progeny being brought over to Doddington at weaning, to be kept till they were sold fat at two years old. These we called 'homebreds' as opposed to the other English bred cattle which came principally from Teesdale. The Irish and English cattle were bought in from dealers as stirks in the later summer as room became available for them.

With so many cattle to attend to in summer, we had the extra chore of rounding up beasts which had broken out when running from the flies. Those fields where the Till formed the boundary between us and our neighbours were a constant source of bother. Some of us shepherds complained of the extra work entailed with cattle. One man alleged that the farmers got their cattle herded for nothing, as we were only paid for tending the sheep!

When first we went to Doddington, the ewe flock numbered thirty-two score in regular ages from one to four crop. We noticed that the local usage was to describe the ewes in terms of years of age, rather than the number of crops of lambs they had produced as we did in Scotland. Thus they called a four crop ewe a five year old, a three crop ewe a four year old and so on.

The ewes were all Suffolk crosses and bred on the farm. Suffolk cross ewes were kept on a good few farms, and were the progeny of the Suffolk ram and the popular Half-Bred ewe of the Border Country. Our North Doddington ewes were unique, however, in that they were not direct first crosses, but were sired by Suffolk-Border Leicester cross rams, and had been so bred for many years, being, one might say, almost a fixed breed on their own. The rams were homebred and produced from the two small flocks of Border Leicester and pure Suffolk ewes, about half a score of each, kept for that purpose. The only sheep bought on to the farm were the stud rams. One of either breed was bought every two years, a Border Leicester and a Suffolk alternately for use on the pure bred ewe flocks. In this way cross bred rams were produced, and pure bred ewe lambs to perpetuate the Border Leicester and Suffolk flocks.

In addition to the ewes, there were eight score of ewe hoggs for replacements, seven score of grazing hoggs, and about a hundred fat hoggs clipped ready for market, these last being the remnant of the winter fatteners.

The grazing hoggs were clipped and sold fat off the grass throughout the summer as they became ready. Those still left in the autumn were finished off on turnips. A few fat lambs were sold in summer and autumn, but the bulk of the lamb crop was kept to be fattened on turnips. A few score of lambs were wintered on a lighter diet, to be put to pasture in spring and fattened on the grass. The summer grazing and fattening of large numbers of young sheep was an antiquated system of sheep husbandry which was then fast dying out, as more and more flockmasters sold their lambs fat in summer. Indeed it has all but disappeared from the Scottish Border, but in Northumberland the policy of keeping clipped sheep for finishing on grass lingered on for some time. This was possibly because of the large number of cattle kept, young sheep being considered more suitable for mixed grazing with fat cattle, than were ewes with lambs.

At lambing time we had a permanent lambing shed adjoining the steading, the ewes running by day in the same field year after year. There was also additional shelter available for young lambs in bad weather, for then we had easy access to an empty cattlecourt, or other shed of some kind.

A Shepherd Remembers

We got the help of a lambing man who lodged with us for four weeks. These lambing men, all local, proved to be interesting companions to me over the years, at a season when I was isolated from everything else. Under father's lambing time rules one was not allowed away from the place for the whole period. We gave our undivided attention to the sheep, and cut ourselves off from all other activities, and that included attendance at kirk. I never questioned the rules, having been inured to such isolation and dedication from boyhood.

Shearing was done by two machines, but these were only hand driven. The shearer sheared the sheep, whilst a man turned the big wheel that operated the shearing head. The job of turning the wheel all day was a hard and monotonous one, and was delegated to an odd man, as the spademan was called in Northumberland. We clipped the fat hoggs and the grazing hoggs earlier by ourselves, but for the clipping of the breeding stock two or three men with hand shears were hired as well.

Mother had to feed the whole lot, clippers, wheel turners and the woman who wrapped up the fleeces. According to the bargain made, a sheep was killed to provide mutton, but in hot weather or in the event of the clipping being spread over the best part of a week in wet weather, mother found that the meat went stale, and after a couple of seasons a new arrangement was sought. An agreement was made with the master, that mother would buy the meat from the butcher and he would foot the bill, a much better system she thought. Not only did it do away with the risk of meat spoiling, but it also allowed her to vary the clippers' diet, instead of feeding them with mutton all the time. Occasionally one or other of the hired clippers, who lived some distance away and did not have motor bikes opted to lodge with us. They of course paid their lodging themselves.

For a few years, until 1936, we washed the sheep prior to clipping. This was another old custom that was also fast losing favour. Although the washed wool was worth a few pence more per pound that the unwashed stuff, there was a marked loss in weight on the fleeces. The sheep were washed by swimming them twice through the river, and a pen was erected at a favourable spot on the bank, from which to push them into the water. There was a lot of driving to and fro attached to the sheep washing, as well as general disturbance of the flock. Finally the master decided that it was not worth all the trouble for a penny or tuppence on the pound of wool, so the practice was discontinued. It so happened that ours was one of the last places at which sheep washing was done. Many years later after the Second World War, when the Wool Marketing Board had been set up, the price gap between washed and unwashed wool was as much as five or six pence per pound. Washing could have paid at that, but no one was inclined to revive the custom; besides, all the old ponds and washing places at streams had disappeared. Ancient sheep washing sites are commemorated in some English place names, such as Alrewas, sheep-wash by the alders.

As I have already stated, most of our lambs were kept for fattening on turnips. The turnip cutting cart was in use as at Fogorig, but there was one difference; instead of the cutter season finishing in April when the turnip land was cleared for ploughing and spring sowing of barley, the remnant of the hoggs were folded on a piece of pasture and fed with cut mangolds right on till mid May.

The winter fed sheep were sold at Newcastle mart, a batch going there by lorry every Monday from New Year onward. The lorry mostly called between 2 and 3 am to lift them, the idea being that the same lorry should accomplish two journeys to Newcastle with livestock. The drivers of stock waggons had a hard life then, for that was before the fixing of maximum driving hours. Most of those men, however, were glad to have a job at all in the 1930s.

Loading sheep on to a lorry in the dark with only the aid of a hurricane lamp was a tricky business. Yet we always managed to get them away somehow. On Sunday evenings we put the hoggs in a little field that was handy for the faulds. The lorry stopped on the road outside our house and the driver gave a small toot. It was handy for me to pop out of bed in the upstairs bedroom, open the skylight and shout 'Right'. The lorry then proceeded to the faulds, whilst father and I got dressed and sallied forth with lantern and dog to round up the sheep and pen them. One dog we had which lay in the house became really keen on the job; the minute the door was opened he was off like a shot to the field, and had the sheep gathered and at the gate waiting for us. He was always restless on the night before if there were sheep due to go, and whenever he heard the lorry stop was on the alert. Yet if no sheep were being sent he never paid any heed should a lorry pass by. So ingrained did this habit of being awakened in the small hours become that I never slept soundly on Sunday nights, and the mere sound of the lorry stopping would wake me. After the sheep were gone we went back to bed for another three or four hours.

Disturbing though those nocturnal goings-on were, they fitted in quite well with our routine. Once the waggon had been dealt with in the early morning, we were free to go about our business from seven o'clock, unhampered by waiting for a lorry to appear. At least we were spared the ordeal of the Lowick Hall shepherd who had to accompany the lorry driver to Newcastle with the sheep, on his boss's orders.

One of the usages in connection with our work which we found different in Northumberland was at the sheep dipping. In contrast to the Scots side where ample help was always given to the herds in the operation, we found that where there was a double herding the two shepherds were expected to keep the sheep themselves. Even on farms having a single handed shepherd, no more than one man was sent to help with the dipping. In our case I put the sheep into the bath and father dipped them. I found it a hard job handling over a thousand sheep into the dipping bath. The dipping could not be accomplished in one day, but covered several days, for we had all the separate lots of sheep to drive to and from the dipper. Our method was to go out on our rounds in the early morning just after dawn had broken and fetch in a batch of sheep each. After a quick breakfast we commenced dipping and carried on till both lots were dipped; then if we had time before dinner we would go out and fetch in another lot of sheep apiece, whilst the first two lots were drying. We always deemed it advisable to have all the sheep we hoped to dip in the one day gathered in before noon to allow them to cool off and empty themselves before dipping. After dinner the dipped sheep, now well dried, were returned to their fields, and dipping resumed as soon as possible. The afternoon quota were usually through the dipper by 4 pm then we would go home, change our clothes and have some tea while the sheep were drying.

At first we resented the lack of help with the dipping, and having to return to the dipper for days on end, but over the years we found this more leisurely method more beneficial to the sheep than the hurry and scurry of getting them all done in one day with additional help. We shepherds knew the right way to handle sheep at dipping, whereas the other men were often rough and noisy. There is nothing that frightens and bewilders sheep more than for strangers to pen them and work among them.

At Christmas time we sensed a different atmosphere south of the Border. In Scotland at that time Christmas was still largely ignored, the New Year being held as the traditional holiday. In our home circle we had always recognised Christmas, gave and received presents, but work went on for us menfolk just like any ordinary day.

In Glendale the farm folk had a holiday, church services were held by all denominations and there was a distinct air of festivity all around.

On Alderman Rea's orders a sheep was slaughtered a day or two before, and each householder presented with a piece of mutton for Christmas dinner. Father had the job of killing and dressing the carcase, cutting it up and distributing the gifts of mutton. This was done every year (until the outbreak of war and subsequent rationing of meat), and to ensure fairness of distribution father instituted a rota system for the different cuts of meat, so that each household had a chance each Christmas to get the best or plainest cuts in turn.

Mr Rea also entertained his three key men, the steward, head shepherd and byreman to Christmas dinner. This appeared to be the old custom as practised by the yeoman farmers, which he still kept alive. I never knew of any other farmers in the district who kept it up.

After our first two Christmases at Doddington the custom was discontinued, for the Alderman died early in the New Year of 1932 after suffering from a stroke. His death spread gloom over the village and the whole district, for he was a man devoted to public service, much respected and a just master. His widow continued to occupy the farmhouse until her death some years later. Their only son, Major Rea of Berrington near Ancroft, a few miles south of Berwick, took over the farm and ran it as a led farm from his own place. As a result the steward and father had more responsibility thrust on them since there was now no resident master on the farm. Harry the steward was a Scotsman as well, who had come over the Border as a young single man many years before. Unfortunately he died suddenly a couple of years after the Major took over, and the ploughman steward being next in the pecking order was promoted to the post. This poor chap was stricken by ill health just a year or two later, and died after a lingering illness. His place was taken by the ploughman steward who had stepped into his shoes, when he had been promoted to steward.

Major Rea did not make many changes, apart from the fact that he had to reduce the ewe stock and let a couple of grass fields for four years, to help meet the death duties on his father's estates. The late Alderman's life style had not been equal to the farming depression which now set in with a vengeance. Yet he had employed a lot of folk and left his farm in good heart, and in impeccable condition as regards fences, gates, drains and farming buildings, which could not be said of many farms in Glendale.

The fields which were let for grazing were rented by Mr

Glendale

Robinson of Tughall, Chathill, who also farmed Langleeford
in the Cheviot Hills above Wooler. This man grazed cattle on
the fields and sent sheep down from the hills at different times
of the year. We tended the stock for him as part of our duties.

Changes which took place under the new regime that
concerned us, included the switch over to a Half Bred ewe
stock, and the reduction of the number of young sheep on
grass. These latter were phased out entirely after a year or
two, for it did not pay, even allowing for the value of their
wool, to keep them over a year at the prices then going. With
regard to the ewe stock, the Major had Half Breds on his own
farm, and preferred them to the cross Suffolks. Though the
Suffolk-Leicester ewes were big and most prolific, they were
less hardy than Half Breds, and took more upkeep. It was
decided to phase them out gradually by buying in Half Bred
ewe lambs from Caithness. Those were obtained through Mr
Waite, a dealer in Berwick. The first Half Bred lambs were
bought in 1933 and by the back end of 1936 the whole flock
were of this breed. The small flock of pure Suffolk ewes were
retained to breed Suffolk rams for home use, but the Border
Leicester sheep were disposed of. They were the last remnant
of what had been the ram breeding flock of Leicester sheep,
owned by the Reas for at least a couple of generations. A
shepherd who had served the Reas as a young man told us
that about 1900, the Half Bred ewe stocks on the Reas' many
farms were maintained by the use of Half Bred rams, produced by using a Cheviot ram on the Border Leicester ewes, a
reversal of the usual practice.

The various duties of the farm staff were much the same as
in Scotland. The four hinds had each a pair of horses in charge,
but in Northumberland one hind was designated as carter, and
it was he who undertook most of the carting work to and from
the farm when two carts were required. A few differences of
methods in Glendale, in contrast to Scotland, might be mentioned here. When carting with a pair of carts, the second or
led horse had a collar round its neck with a chain attached, by
which it was fastened to a ring on the tailboard of the leading

cart. In Scotland the horseman managed the second horse by a lead rein which he held in his hand as he sat on the front of the first cart. Again in contrast to Scotland, the horses were out at grass from May till November, doing all the harvest work off the grass with a feed or two of oats per day, instead of being stabled at the start of harvest and being fed on oats and hay. We found that the Wages Board fixed a sum as value of the perks such as a house and garden, potatoes, milk (where provided), all deductible from the weekly wage as laid down in the Schedule, though it was not every employer who deducted house rent. Overtime rates were in force for extra hours worked. Shepherds were entitled to a certain sum per dog per week, to buy food up to a maximum of two dogs. Most herds fed their dogs on maize meal or flaked maize, but we fed ours on oatmeal, as father still had the oatmeal in his bargain in the Scots fashion. Major Rea never queried my father's oatmeal bargain but continued to provide it right on till 1940, when, under wartime regulations, it became illegal to feed oatmeal to animals. A species of pig meal was substituted, much to father's disgust, for we had used the oatmeal for household purposes as well. At harvest time the hinds never went on shift work as they did in Scotland, but cut the corn within their customary hours only. At leading-in time they worked late but got overtime.

We got confused at first with the linguistic differences. We found that cattle courts were not 'closes' but 'hemmels' or 'coortins'; cart shafts 'limmers' instead of 'trams', corn bin and sheep troughs we called 'kist an boxes', the English called them 'tun an trowes'; to set up the wire nets we used a 'piercer' to make the holes for the 'stabs', and a 'mell' to drive them into the ground, but our Northumbrian mates spoke of the 'pinch', the 'stakes' and the 'mill'. What we called 'wrack' the Scots for couch grass, they called 'whickens'; the 'coo gang' was the 'cow pasture'; the sheep 'faulds' were the 'pens' and so on. Before long we had mastered their lingo, but never copied it as many of the other Scots settlers did.

The farm workers of Glendale had a half day on Saturday

all the year round, an advance on the Scots system of having half days in summer only when the horses were at grass, between the completion of turnip sowing in June till harvest in August. In addition the English had several fixed holidays: Good Friday, Whit Monday, August Bank Holiday and Christmas Day. New Year's Day was recognised as a holiday on most farms too, the wily Northumbrians getting the best of both worlds because of their proximity to Scotland.

Any workers who had to turn out to feed livestock on the prescribed holidays were entitled to be paid. Of course shepherds obviously could not enjoy all those holidays, but instead of being paid, we preferred to have days off in lieu at a more convenient time.

In Glendale the horse fork was then in general use for stacking the hay, which was built in oblong mows, rather than the round stacks favoured on the Scots side.

The horse fork was a two-pronged steel contraption, suspended from a pulley attached to a high pole erected alongside the site of the haystack. The pulley was worked by leading a horse backwards and forwards. The fork's prongs were stuck into a hayrick i.e. a haycock, which had been brought in from the field intact on a hay bogie, and set down beside the stack. When the horse was led forward the forkful of hay was raised till it was posed above the haystack, then it was lowered onto it and released by backing the horse a certain distance. The empty fork was then raised and brought down again ready for the next plunge by manoeuvring the horse.

As at Fogorig, the odd laddies or, as they were called in Northumberland, the 'turnip dicks', were the workers with whom I had most work-a-day dealings, as they and their horses were at the beck and call of the herds when required. There were two boys on the job; in winter and spring one was on the cutter cart and one carted hay to the outwintered cattle. The latter was a morning job only, but the former was an all day job, and was really too heavy for a young boy; indeed on some farms it was delegated to a full man who was

125

hired to do the cutter in winter, and as orraman for the rest of year.

During the first three years we were at Doddington the laddies were big hefty chaps, but from 1933 when those two left for promotion elsewhere, there was a succession of beginners who had just left school at fourteen, and they were a bit too light for the cutter work. Father and I helped them as much as we could, on whichever of our beats the cutter cart happened to be in operation. We would clean out the turnip troughs for them in the morning, and help them to yoke the heavy loaded cart, filled up in readiness on the previous day. In the afternoon I went out with them and helped to fill the hay hecks, to yoke and load up the cart, then go the first round with them, shovelling the turnips into the troughs.

The women workers at Doddington performed the same tasks as we had been accustomed to see the women doing. They were all single, living with their parents and hired for permanent work. In summer they thinned turnips, forked hay, cut thistles; at harvest they bound the corn into sheaves behind the men with the scythes at the 'opening up', when roads were cut for the binders round the perimeters of the cornfields. They stooked the sheaves behind the binders and forked the sheaves on to the carts when the corn was led in; some stood beside the stackers upon the stacks, handing them the sheaves as they came up. This task was called 'striddling' or 'stack heading'. The women helped with the thatching of the stacks; with threshing, potato lifting, and shawin the mangolds, turnips and swedes. In spring one would be sent to the field where sowing was in progress, to serve out the seed grain from sacks to the 'ribbers' (corn drills). It was the women too who gathered stones off the fields which were to be hained for hay to prevent damage to the reaper blades at mowing. The stones were deposited in neat little heaps to be lifted by a cart. Another spring job they performed was scraping whickens into heaps for carting off or burning, in the fields designated for the root crops, or picking whickens off the drills after the turnips were sown. The whickens were picked into a sack apron called a 'daidlie' or a 'brat'. A job the women did for the sheep in winter was 'picking shells'. When the turnips were eaten on the field, once they were eaten down to ground level, the remains or 'shells' were picked out with a tool called a turnip pick. This tool had a blade about five to six inches long, wedge shaped, with a sharpish point about two inches broad, and it was fitted with a wooden shank like that of a hoe. The picker was used to enable the sheep to clean up the turnips with the least waste.

Another usage we found different south of the Border was the treatment of the workers' cows. The byreman tended the farmer's three cows, but the cottage folk had to feed, muck and bed their own cows, the byreman only being responsible for turning them in and out from pasture. Few of the workers beside ourselves kept cows; only one at a time as far as I can recall. Throughout the Border country the keeping of cows by any farm workers except shepherds had virtually ceased by the mid 1930s.

After Alderman Rea's death the farm cows were dispensed with, and mother sold milk to some of our neighbours. About this time the Glendale Co-operative started a milk round in the country places from Wooler.

With the passing of the years we got used to the North-umbrians, their speech and ways. Though we had found them reticent at first, they gradually thawed out as we came to know them better. My youngest sister and I joined in the activities of the young folk in the area. She had left school just before we crossed the Border, but mother kept her at home to help out, since we had now two cows. She worked occasion-ally on the farm at peak periods, and also got work as an extra maid at Fenton House, when Lord Durham and his retinue were in residence there.

This state of affairs was not fair to my sister, who ought to have been able to choose a career of her own, the same as our two elder sisters had done.

All too often it was the case that a daughter was expected to stay at home to help the mother, or to keep house if the mother was invalided or had died. The family living next door to us were an example; they had lost their mother a year or two before we came to stay beside them in the row, and as there were seven of them in the house including the father, one of the girls had to be housekeeper. When she got married another daughter left her job on the farm and took her place.

There was plenty of amusement for young folk on both Doddington and Wooler. We had a Reading Room for the young men, which also had a billiard club. Billiards was a popular pastime in Glendale, with clubs in nearly every village. Competitions were arranged between the various clubs, the teams travelling to assignments by taxi.

The Women's Institute had a flourishing branch in the village, membership being drawn from the village itself and the farms in the neighbourhood. The leading lights were the schoolmaster's wife and the postmistress.

The Reading Room building was also used as a hall for dances, concerts and other functions. A fine new village hall was built and opened in the summer of 1933. It abutted the old reading room which was used as an annexe. In order to raise funds to pay off the new hall, a series of dances were held. Soon our hall, which had a very fine dancing floor, became a centre for dancers, who flocked to it from the surrounding countryside. The dances commenced at 8 pm on Friday evenings and carried on till 2 am on the Saturday morning. The Saturday night dances finished at 11.30 pm. The large crowds which flocked to our hall were always well behaved, until one night a party of men and girls from the Hunt Kennels appeared, the worse for drink, and caused a fracas. From then on the hall committee ruled that no one the worse for drink, or with drink on their persons, would be allowed into the hall. Thus trouble was nipped in the bud, which saved our hall from becoming a haunt of rowdies, a fate which overtook Ewart ballroom nearby, where fights were frequent. Drinking among girls was virtually unknown in rural areas in those days, and none but the most disreputable females would darken the door of a public house.

Glendale

The Women's Institute had a hut of their own, where they held their monthly meetings and occasional whist drives. Whist drives were popular as a pastime, and for raising funds for various causes. WI used the village hall for their annual party, and for the big whist drive and dance which they organised each year in aid of the Royal Victoria Infirmary at Newcastle. Before the new hall was built this annual event was held in the granary of South Doddington Farm, kindly lent by Mr Harvey. 'Infirmary' whists and dances were held in many of the villages and hamlets, and I can remember cycling along with some others to one at North Middleton, three miles beyond Wooler on a night of wind and rain. The dance was held in a building with a stone floor and, by gosh, my legs and feet were sore the next day.

In the early 1930s music for the dances was supplied by local farm chaps with their violins. We had three such players in Doddington, and when they stopped at the interval for supper someone would improvise with a melodeon. Buffet supper and lemonade for refreshment were supplied to the dancers at each event. As the years passed and folk became slightly more sophisticated, bands were hired from neighbouring towns to provide music, some calling themselves by such high-falutin' names as the Regal, the Rialto etc.

All our night journeys to Wooler and elsewhere were done by bicycle, lighted with acetylene lamps. On Saturday and Sunday evenings in the winter gloaming, one would hear the rattling of tins 'on the doors', as the young folk riddled the carbide out of their lamps, in a can with holes in the base, prior to refilling them with fresh carbide. We were always having to fork out cash on tins of raw carbide and burner nipples. Acetylene lamps gave a good light, but were liable to be blown out in a high wind. Gradually we swopped them for electric battery lamps and dynamos. Reflectors fixed to the mudguards of rear wheels of cycles were obligatory for a time, then tail lights came into force. The latter were a nuisance, for one never knew if they were working properly.

The parish church at Doddington was Church of England

of course. For some years after we came the vicar, who was unmarried, stayed in Wooler, and the vicarage was let to Major Taylor, a retired military man. Eventually the vicar married and came to live there himself.

A large part of the population of Northumberland were dissenters and not members of the established church. Presbyterianism had a strong following all over the county, due partly to the number of folk of Scots descent that it contained, but there was also a strong native Presbyterian tradition which stretched back for centuries. In Wooler there were two Presbyterian churches, known locally as meeting houses, or just plain 'meetin', the word church being bestowed only on the Church of England. 'He disna gawn tae the meetin he's strang church', would be an apt description of a zealous Church of England adherent.

Besides the parish church in Wooler, there was a Methodist chapel, a Roman Catholic chapel, and a Plymouth brethren Hall. The latter sect were very numerous in the district.

We joined Cheviot Street Presbyterian Church; the other Presbyterian church was called the West Church. Both were well attended and held morning and evening services. We travelled the three miles to church by bicycle or bus. The Berwick to Wooler bus service ran to suit the morning church of 11 am till 12.30 pm. Except in bad weather most of the young folk who attended from Doddington cycled to and fro.

There was a preaching station at Fenton Town in the parish which was linked with the Presbyterian Church at Etal, and Mr Dunlop, the minister there, conducted services in it.

Cheviot Street Church had two separate ministers during the twelve years in which we were members, and both were called Mitchell. The Rev Thomas Mitchell who retired in 1936 was a native of Newmilns in Ayrshire. He had been a minister of the United Free Kirk in Scotland, before crossing the Border to Blackhill Presbyterian Church, Newcastle, from whence he came to Wooler sometime in the 1920s. His successor the Rev James Mitchell, inducted in 1937, was a native Northumbrian, who hailed from the Alnwick district.

Glendale

He came to Wooler from a church at Reading. Mr James Mitchell was one of the finest preachers I ever heard; his sermons never failed to impress. Moreover he had a phenomenal memory, and before starting his sermon he took off his glasses and then held forth with out a single note.

Cheviot Street Church was the focal point for a whole range of activities. I became involved with two of those, namely the choir and the Literary Society. A workmate of mine who was already a member of the choir, persuaded me to join, so I enrolled as a bass singer. We attended choir practice once a week, and church services twice on most Sundays throughout the year.

The monthly meetings of the Literary Society of which I became a member extended from October to February. The syllabuses were varied and interesting, papers were read by individual members and discussed at length. I myself contributed papers on the Gaelic language, and on surnames, two subjects in which I was keenly interested. From time to time speakers were brought in to give talks. Subjects of papers which I can recall were the Battlefields of Glendale, Sir Walter Scott, and the First Earl of Durham (of Reform Bill fame), to name but a few. One controversial subject which evoked much heated discussion was a talk on the New Church Hymnary by the Presbyterian minister of Belford. Our members were not slow to express their disapproval of many of the new hymn tunes that it contained. At the end of the session two social evenings were held, a Ladies' Night and a Gentlemen's Night, at which the respective sexes entertained each other with songs, recitations and a humorous sketch.

In the first year of my membership the Literary Society had a summer outing to the Border Abbeys, so I went with the trip, for a day back home as it were.

Our choir was about twenty strong and our role was to lead the praise each Sunday, and to sing anthems on special occasions such as Christmas, Eastertide and Harvest Thanksgiving. We played a leading part in the annual church soirée, held in the Archbold Hall, when we sang choral items and some individuals contributed solos. There was usually a guest speaker as well, and on two occasions the Rev James Barr, an eminent United Free churchman and politician, gave lectures on Robert Burns and on the Minor Scots Poets. At some soirées the choir would be given a rest and outside entertainers engaged for the evening. One of these was Charlie Hipp's Company from Newcastle.

Our organist and choirmaster was John Green who lived in Alnwick and travelled to Wooler every Sunday. After his untimely death a lady organist also from Alnwick got the post. I have forgotten the lady's name, but she played the organ till she was called up to the forces in war time.

The Harvest Festival was an event celebrated on different days at the various churches in the town. There was some rivalry between the two Presbyterian churches, as to who would have the best decorations and choral features. Sometimes our choir was invited to give a performance at one of the rural Presbyterian churches. I recall going to both Chatton church and Lilburn Glebe meeting house.

On one particular year I joined a concert party organised by Miss Baker, the organist at the Methodist chapel, consisting of singers drawn from the choirs of the two Presbyterian churches and the Methodists. In addition to giving recitals in the Methodist chapel itself, we went to Crookham and Beaumont Presbyterian churches to perform.

Cheviot Street church choir had an annual summer trip on the Wooler Trades' Holiday at the end of June. Funds were provided partly from a grant from the church, and partly from a whist drive and dance early in the New Year, promoted by ourselves. Some of the elders were not too keen on having a whist drive in connection with the church, but neither were they keen to provide cash to give the choir an outing. Our trips were mostly by a bus hired for the occasion, which took us to some seaside resort or place of note. My enjoyment of those trips was invariably marred by travel sickness, though it only affected me on the outward journey. As often as not, too, we got a pouring wet day.

Glendale

In 1931 we went to Roker, near Sunderland, but I was not impressed by the rain-soaked view of the Tyneside conurbation through which we passed. Of Roker itself I remember little, except that we went to a show after lunch at a seaside theatre, which was very funny indeed.

On two occasions we joined with the rest of the townsfolk and the Tweedside Co-op from Berwick, in a special rail excursion from Wooler and Tweedmouth stations, to Loch Lomond and Loch Long in 1932, and to the Trossachs in 1935. Those were my first glimpses of the Highlands and I was greatly thrilled. It was wet at first on both days, but the sight of the torrents of water cascading down the mountainsides was one I never forgot. How fitting, thought I, the words of Burns:

> Farewell to the forests and wild hanging woods,
> Farewell to the torrents and loud pouring floods.

And of Sir Walter Scott:

> Land of brown heath and shaggy wood,
> Land of mountain and flood.

The 1934 trip took us to Edinburgh and for once it was a fair summer day. This trip was memorable because of our experience on the return journey. Our homeward journey had been planned by the bus company to take us via Gifford and across the Lammermuir Hills to Duns, which would have been a glorious run in daylight. Unfortunately we were a bit late in leaving Edinburgh, as most of the party had gone to the cinema, and it was black dark ere we reached the Redstane Rig, a notoriously steep ascent just beyond Gifford. The bus driver got into difficulties on the steep gradient, and asked us to leave the bus and walk behind it, till he surmounted the hill. Once we got back on the bus, the driver was a bit confused as to whether he would go by Cranshaws or by Longformacus. Panic set in among the passengers when the bus was stopped again to ascertain which road was which, as they thought they were lost in the middle of nowhere. However, confidence was restored when things were sorted out, and the bus driver proceeded to take the Cranshaws road. Little did we know that this road led us over another fearsome gradient called the Hungry Snoot. It was just as well for our peace of mind that it was dark.

In 1936 the trip took us to Keswick and Derwentwater. It was an enjoyable day, marred by rain in the morning, and louring cloud over the Lakeland Fells. Our outward route was by Hexham, Alston and Penrith and we had a stop in Carlisle on the return journey in the evening. 1937 saw us at Barnard Castle, up Teesdale to Alston, then home by Hexham and Rothbury. We visited the noted Bowes Castle Museum at Barnard Castle. I remember passing through Staindrop on the outward journey, which I thought was the bonniest village I had ever seen. I re-visited it along with my wife and family thirty years on, after I had acquired a car.

Going up Teesdale on that choir trip I was impressed by the many thriving small farms in the valley, which a friend told me later was the rearing ground of the Shorthorn steers that were bought in for grazing at Doddington. On my 1966 visit I was saddened to see that many of the homesteads had been abandoned and the farms amalgamated.

The 1937 choir outing was the last of its kind, support for it having fallen away as many of the Wooler choristers preferred to take their summer holidays around Trades' Week and go off for a fortnight to the Isle of Man, Blackpool and other resorts. The choir trip was one of the few holidays that we two country members had. I used to envy my choir companions from Wooler, who had a full fortnight's holiday every summer, but, let me hasten to add, that was the only respect in which I envied townsfolk. I would not have swopped jobs with them for anything.

Although Wooler was little more than an overgrown village, its inhabitants had quite a bit of civic pride, and some of them even tended to look down their noses at us farm folk. It was amusing to hear talk now and then of 'going out into the country'. But I confess I was not much better myself with my rural pride. Some Wooler girls tried to coax me to join their Tennis club, but I would have none of it, deeming tennis to be much too cissy a game for a country chap to play!

Before leaving the subject of Wooler, I might add that it was then a favoured resort for holiday-makers from Tyneside. They came for the angling, rambling and so on. Its holiday reputation had links with the past, when folk of delicate constitution or invalids on convalescence repaired to the hillside town to drink goats' milk, one of their number being Sir Walter Scott.

'Cheviot' was one of the key names in Wooler, derived from the hill range which sloped down to the town, the chief peak Muckle Cheviot being only about six miles away. There was a Cheviot Street, a Cheviot this and Cheviot that. The local newspaper, the *Wooler Advertiser*, which was circulated gratis throughout Glendale from the 'capital' had as its motto:

> When they talk o' their high hills,
> An' brag o them scornin;
> I'll think o the Cheviots
> An scorn them again!

A beautiful sentiment, which I, a Scots Borderer, could feel proud to echo. This motto was a stanza from a poem by a Northumbrian poet called Storey. I have never been able to trace anything about him or his works.

I used to explore the countryside on my bicycle in the summer evenings after church, sometimes faring as far as Coldstream. The road north seemed to draw me like a magnet. On occasions such as Kelso Show, St James's Fair and Kelso Ram Sale, I cycled to Kelso twenty odd miles away. I also cycled the thirteen miles to Berwick when necessary. I much preferred cycling where possible for I was a poor traveller on buses, though train journeys did not affect me.

A Shepherd Remembers

I enjoyed most cycling to Longformacus once a year to stay for a week-end with father's sister, our Aunt Mary, and Uncle Bill her husband. Uncle Bill was a partner with his two brothers at Caldra Farm, Longformacus, and I found my brief stay there, right in the heart of the Lammermuir Hills, a fine change. Our aunt's house was a place frequented by many callers; I met some fine folk there, and greatly enjoyed their crack. I would go with aunt and uncle to the kirk on Sunday. What a pleasant place it was, that wee kirk among the hills, so friendly and informal.

On one visit to 'Lockerie', to give the village its pet name, I went to a concert in the village hall. The place was packed with folk, and guess who the artistes were? None other than Malcolm Dickson and his party from Duns!

The journey to Longformacus from Doddington was a long one, well over thirty miles, and it was a hard pull over the Hardens Hill from Duns in both directions. Whilst at Lockerie I went once or twice on a bike run, up to the top of the Redstane Rig, and down by Mayshiel and the Whitadder Valley to Ellemford, and from there over by Whitchester to Caldra. How I revelled in the Scottish scene!

Father's mother died in April 1933, and father took me with him to her funeral in Dunbar. We went by bus to Berwick and took the train from there to Dunbar. It was the first funeral I ever had attended. On the subject of funerals, I might add that when we crossed the Border to live, my parents were amazed to see women turning out at funerals on the English side. At that time no women were ever seen at funerals in Scotland.

After Granny's death our links with East Lothian became less strong, and I never was back at Dunbar for many, many years. Uncle Will, father's eldest brother, came to visit us once a year from his home at Seacliffe, near North Berwick.

Shepherding in the 1930s was pretty hard work, and only persons with a dedication to the job, and they were many, could stick it out. I have often thought since of how inefficient and cumbersome our working facilities were, how meagre the

136

veterinary aids that we had at our disposal compared with the present day.

Yet we managed to have some very successful years at North Doddington; if the financial returns from the livestock were meagre at the time, it was no fault of ours but that of low market prices.

Father had full charge of the sheep stock and the grazing cattle, having virtually a free hand in their management apart from buying and selling. That was common practice on the bigger and better class of Border farms, where the sheep were concerned, the shepherd being left to use his skill and initiative. The results of such delegation of responsibility were invariably good, and made for job satisfaction where the shepherds were concerned. Few experienced shepherds could tolerate busybody farmers who interfered too much, and tried to dictate the day to day details of the sheep work.

We were still at North Doddington when the Second World War broke out. That event caused so many changes on the farms, and in the countryside, that it must be the subject of another chapter.

5

WARTIME

The outbreak of World War Two brought about a change in the whole system of Border farming, the aim now being to get maximum production of food, as soon as possible. Plans were already in hand to increase the home production of food, following the Munich crisis of 1939, encouragement being given in the shape of a subsidy for ploughing up old grassland.

The plough up policy was intensified in the autumn of 1939, and a War Agricultural Committee (the 'War Rag' in common parlance), was formed in every county with compulsory powers to oversee farms and enforce Government directives.

A gradual change took place in the countryside as fields were ploughed up for the first time since 1918 or even further back. This change was most marked in North Northumberland and caused not a few headaches. Although farmers in some parts, notably Glendale, had kept the plough going on a limited scale, a great deal of land had long been under grass. A number of farms had not the staff, horses and implements to cope with grain and other crops, for their whole farming policy had been for years geared to cattle, sheep and haymaking only.

On one large farm in 1940 there were six hundred acres of grain to harvest and only one binder to cut it; on others in 1939 not even a plough or arable implement was available, and for the first time cultivation and harvesting had to be undertaken by men who set themselves up as contractors, thus laying the foundations of the farm contracting business, which is so widespread at the present day.

Wartime

More and more tractors appeared on the scene and for these, horse-drawn implements had to be adapted, either by local blacksmiths or at implement works.

An early casualty of the newly awakened urgency for increased food production was the traditional rotation of crops. This ancient rule, built into farm leases, forbade the taking of two white crops in succession from the same field. It was now abandoned and crops could be grown in any order other than the traditional five course rotation. The hitherto common practice of fetching the whole grain crop into a stackyard was discouraged, and farmers were advised to dispense with the cornstacks to lessen the risk of fire from possible enemy action. Thus cornstacks were to be seen standing in groups or rows all over the farm, instead of in a cluster close to the homestead.

Overnight the nation realised that its long neglected agricultural industry was vital to its very existence. Farm workers suddenly became important persons, so much so that we were exempt from military service. It had dawned on the powers that be that the despised peasant, yokel or country bumpkin or by whatever other name he was known to the city slickers, was a national asset. Under the food rationing system, which was quickly introduced after the war started, we were allowed a special extra ration of cheese.

We were still living at Doddington when the war broke out, and I can well remember the scene. The prevailing atmosphere was one of gloom, hand in hand with a resolution to see it through. No one was under the illusion that it would be a short war, some prophesying that it might even last ten years. We had the issue of gas masks and the enforcement of blackout regulations. The latter were a real headache at first as folk wrestled nightly with improvised materials such as blankets or tablecloths fixed with drawing pins. After a while we got black outer frames made to fit the windows. These factors coupled with the bad news from Poland made their contribution to a far from cheerful outlook. We knew what we were in for, since the horrors of the 1914–1918 war were still fresh in folks' memories. We also knew that nothing would ever be the same again.

There was a general feeling of frustration and anger that no move was being made to help the Poles in their agony. Why must the Allied armies sit immobile behind the Maginot Line? Why can't they advance on to German soil? Why not drop a few bombs on Germany instead of skittering about dropping leaflets? These were the questions on the lips of ordinary folk.

No pacifist views were expressed that I was aware of, but one elderly man in the village, for reasons unknown, was pro-German. His neighbours in the village treated him more as a nutter than an enemy. Another man, an avowed communist, was all against the war as a capitalist caper, but when Russia was attacked by Hitler in 1941 he changed his tune, and grumbled that the Allies were not doing enough to help the Russians.

The early autumn weather of 1939 was glorious, perfect for the prosecution of the harvest, which was early that year. The corn was all cut and stooked without a hitch and the leading in was in full swing, an unusual feature for the early days of September when war was declared. On the shepherding side, things were going well too. The sheep were in good shape and, as a result of the early harvest, we got the use of the corn stubbles to augment the grazing much sooner than usual.

The first indication that war was gong to have an impact on country life, was the arrival of the evacuees, children and their mothers from Tyneside. They were billeted with families in the village and on the surrounding farms. This first attempt at the evacuation of mothers along with the children did not work out very well. These mothers with toddlers and babies found rural life boring; they missed their menfolk and their neighbours. As the weeks passed and the expected bombing of cities did not materialise, those women with their very young bairns drifted back home, only the bairns of school age being left.

It took a while for those city bairns to fit into their new surroundings, the way of life they had been used to was so much different from that of us country folk. It must be said that the rural households made a good effort to make them welcome, and to overcome any snags that arose.

Early in the war the local Territorials, the 7th Battalion Northumberland Fusiliers, were mobilized and departed for the south. I remember the night on which the Wooler contingent left. It was a rather sombre occasion with little of the ballyhoo and wild cheering that had heralded the departure of troops in 1914. A sprinkling of farm lads who were in the Territorials were called up, including one or two farmers who were officers. One or two local chaps had already been called up with the Militia draft during the summer, these were the twenty year olds, the first age group to be conscripted.

In the first half of September the first Land Girls appeared on the scene. North Doddington got its quota early on, for the master's wife, Mrs Rea, held the post of local commandant of the Land Army or some such post.

To begin with the Land Girls were billeted with householders on the farms on which they were employed, but later in the war, hostels were arranged for them at local centres, from which they travelled to their places of work. This latter arrangement worked well enough, the girls being provided with bicycles. It gave rise however to some abuses on the employers' part. Certain farmers used the girls as casual day labour, and would even, on occasion, send them back to the hostel after only half a day's work. This was tough on the girls who had to make a contribution to their keep at the hostel out of their earnings. A rule was made therefore that should a farmer engage any girls from the hostel, he had to guarantee them a full week's work at a time.

The Land Girls who came to Glendale were chiefly town-bred girls drawn from Tyneside conurbation, and comprised girls from all walks of life. They were cheerful and willing, and did a good job of work after some training, but seldom matched in efficiency the native born outworkers. Quite a few of them stayed on in agriculture after the war, and some of them got married to farm workers and young farmers.

A Shepherd Remembers

As the war progressed and the call up of both sexes got under way, the local girls who were not in farm work, as well as the men, disappeared in the Services. Not many of the girls when called up opted to join the Land Army, being eager to seek adventure elsewhere. One girl from Doddington who worked in a shop in Wooler asked to join the Land Army when called up. Though she was a girl with a rural background who had some inkling of what farm work was like, her request was refused, and she found herself packed off to Gloucester to train in the Women's Air Force. On the other hand one local girl I knew told me after the war that she had volunteered for the ATS (the Women's Army), to see the world, but spent all the years of her war service at Catterick Camp in Yorkshire!

In September 1939 it happened that the farmhouse at North Doddington, a miniature mansion, was empty. Major Rea's sister-in-law had lived in it for some years, but had died in the early part of 1939. So along came the Army and requisitioned it for soldiers. At the same time they took over the village hall, the Women's Institute hut and a loft at Nesbit Farm about a mile out of the village. At the end of September the first batch of troops was brought in, a company of the 5th battalion the Border Regiment, a Territorial unit. The men were billeted in the various requisitioned buildings, and the officers were billeted in the vicarage, much to the disgust of the vicar and his wife.

Their conditions were on an active service basis and very realistic, the cooking being done on an open air field kitchen. The troops complained of shortage of rations and badly cooked food, which roused the indignation of us local folk. We held that nothing but the best and plenty of it was good enough for the men who were being sent to fight for us. We went out of our way to show them kindness and hospitality.

The men of this Border Regiment company were mostly miners from Whitehaven and Workington, who had been in the Territorials for years. There was a fair sprinkling amongst them from other trades, but very few country lads.

Troops were billeted in other places around Glendale, at

Wooler, Ewart and Milfield, the army strategy being to disperse the units all over the countryside in case of bombing and strafing from the air. The battalion HQ was at Wooler, and there the higher ranking officers were billeted in a hotel.

This was Glendale's first taste of 'army occupation' which was to continue throughout the war. Various regiments followed each other into the billets as they were moved around. The King's Own Royal Lancasters followed the Border Regiment, and they in turn were followed by the Lancashire Fusiliers. All these units were part of the same division, which was scattered over a large part of North Northumberland.

In January 1940 the Fusiliers moved out and our village was clear of soldiers until the first days of April when a large group of new conscripts arrived. They were attached to a battalion of the Essex Regiment, and had not even been issued with uniforms on the day they came in. Those men were all conscripts except for the NCOs; they numbered about three hundred and remained at Doddington for many weeks till they had completed their basic training. The air around the village was filled by day with raucous bellowing of NCOs and the tramp of men as the rookies were being knocked into shape. The drill sergeants seemed to take a special delight in parading their various sections on the roadway in front of the rows of cottages, and haranguing them there. The youth of the village, myself included, lost some of their hankering after Army service when they saw with their own eyes what men were subjected to after call up in the way of invective and abuse. It appeared to me that men were shorn of their dignity and manhood, and treated like children or dogs. I suppose it was all necessary in the disciplining and brutalizing of men for the savage business of war.

By this time hutments and tents had been erected to house the soldiers, and proper indoor kitchens and other facilities had been installed. The place took on the appearance of an army camp and the military greatly outnumbered the inhabitants.

We got on well with the soldiers on their off duty hours,

A Shepherd Remembers

and invited one or two from whatever unit happened to be in residence up to the house of an evening for a bite of supper and a chat. Many other folk in the village did the same, and the men appreciated the home atmosphere.

Two chaps in the Lancashire Fusiliers, one from Kearsley near Manchester, and one from Bacup, became special friends of mine, as did a lad from Norwich in the Essex Regiment. I corresponded with them regularly for several years and am glad to say that all three survived the war.

The soldiers used to hang around the steading or walk the roads on their off duty hours. They were mostly city blokes and amused us sometimes with their ignorance of country life. One chap was amazed when I told him that some very young lambs, which I was driving along the road with their dams, were only two days old. He could not believe they would be able to walk at that age. Some thought the country must be a terrible place in which to live. One asked me how long I had been living at Doddington; when I told him, ten years, he said he would have been dead long since, if he had had to live in such a place. My reply was, 'Well lad, I bet you'll be in worse places yet before this is finished'.

In addition to the Army, the Air Force was brought into Glendale too. In 1940 work was begun on the aerodrome at Milfield plain, and a few years later the district got a large influx of Air Force personnel. I am not sure when the aerodrome became fully operational; it may have been before we left the district in May 1942. A ring of searchlight emplacements was built around Glendale in 1940, to protect the airfield under construction.

In July of that year a bomb was dropped close to Milfield by a stray raider, an event which caused quite a stir at the time.

During the first three winters of the war we experienced some of the severest weather for many years. In 1939–40 there was a spell of hard weather which lasted from Boxing Day till mid-February. There was a heavy fall of snow in January, with severe drifting which blocked roads, accompanied by a

Wartime

very hard frost. Both the soldiers and local men, the latter out
of work because of the severe weather, worked hard to keep
the roads open. There were none of the modern type of snow
ploughs then in use; snow ploughs were towed behind trucks,
and deep drifts had to be tackled by men with shovels.
Weather reports on the wireless were forbidden for security
reasons, and it was years after the war that we learned just
how widespread and disruptive the snowstorms had been at
that time. A train had actually got lost in a blizzard in the
West of Scotland. After it had lain for several weeks the snow
finally disappeared in the third week of February, after which
we enjoyed lovely spring-like weather. March was a fine
month and both seed-time and lambing time were successfully completed. The lovely weather of spring 1940 was
continued right into May. It was a month of glorious sunny
days and mild nights, indeed it was one of the best May
months that I can remember. Yet the beauty of the scene
appeared to go unnoticed, so preoccupied were we all by
events on the Continent.

The summer of 1940 was very hot and dry, Glendale with
its light soil suffered severely from drought, and the pastures
got really brown until the weather broke temporarily with
heavy thunderstorms in July. The heavy rain caused flooding
on the river, and the haughs had to be cleared of stock for a
day or two, not a common occurrence in summer. After the
rain there followed a period when the sheep suffered a lot
from attacks of maggot flies, and we were forced to do an
extra dipping.

The months of August and September were exceptionally
good with capital harvest weather. The sheep did equally
well, the lambs coming forward to market in fine fettle.

We again had a hard winter in 1940–41. The frost was
particularly vicious in early January, the hardest I had ever
yet experienced, but there were one or two short breaks of
mild weather later. In mid-February following one mild spell
we had a very heavy fall of snow which lay for two weeks.
There was no drifting but a level fall of two feet, which was

A Shepherd Remembers

very deep for our area for we were only 150 to 300 feet above sea level. The snow lay so deep that no vans could get through, and horses and carts had to be sent to Wooler for provisions.

The ewes suffered a good deal from this storm, as it came a bit too near lambing time. That season for the first time we had an outbreak of twin disease (pregnancy toxaemia), a malady affecting in-lamb ewes, when their plane of nutrition is lowered by a check in their food supply too near lambing time.

The lambing season of 1941 was far from being good, there was hard frost and snow toward the end of March, and April was a bitterly cold month. I shall always remember how the Home Guard went in snow to church parade in Doddington church on St George's Day.

Our lambing man was with us for only three weeks that year; he had been reluctant to take an inbye lambing at all, for the severe winter had prevented him from completing his rabbit trapping contract.

It was during the full moon in March that the first big blitz was delivered by the Luftwaffe on Clydebank. When we were on night shift in the lambing shed we heard the German bombers flying over like a swarm of bees.

The winter of 1941–42 was also severe after another good summer and harvest. A black frost struck in November, which did a bit of harm to the mangold crop as it was being lifted. Fortunately the worst of the wintry weather had passed before March, so that we had reasonably good weather for lambing. We did not have a lambing man that year, the ewe stock having been so reduced in number that we could manage to lamb them ourselves. Hard frost in April and May blighted hopes of a good spring. The pastures were terribly bare at the English term when normally one could expect to have plenty of grass, and hand feeding of ewes could be slackened off.

The work of the farm had to go on as usual war or no war, our farm duties being discharged in much the same way as they had been for generations. As far as the state of the crops and livestock went, things could not have been better. Far more potatoes and sugar beet were being grown on Border farms than hitherto. In the autumn of 1941 a couple of tractors were introduced at North Doddington, of the grey Ferguson type, and the horses were reduced to three pairs. The farm staff was as large as ever, augmented by four land girls.

The life of the village was somewhat disrupted with the presence of the military. It was a blow to have our village hall and the Women's Institute hut commandeered. In course of time however the troops organised dances, concerts and whist drives in the hall, for the benefit of both soldiers and civilians alike, to make up to us for the loss of our premises, and as a mark of appreciation of the kindness shown to the soldiers by the village folk.

After Dunkirk the call to form the Local Defence Volunteers brought a quick response from the local men, both 1914–18 veterans and the younger sort. Soon we were drilling and manoeuvring just like the soldiers in our midst, and since we were not far from the east coast, our local company was delegated to man road blocks in conjunction with the regular troops. The Home Guard, as we eventually became, was labelled 'Britain's Last Hope', and was the butt of much derision on the part of the populace at large. Our leaders were always lecturing us on what would have to be done, should the 'balloon go up', referring to the event of an invasion. The 'balloon', however, never went up and there was no invasion, so our prowess under fire was never put to the test.

Our local company, the Doddington and Fenton Company of the Northumberland Home Guard, was under the command of the Earl of Durham, a most benign gentleman, who had served as an officer in the Great War. Mr Logan, farmer of East Fenton, another war veteran, was second-in-command. I enjoyed my duties with the Home Guard during the rest of our stay at Doddington. From time to time we got a spot of drill from army NCOs to smarten us up a bit. The exercises we engaged in often gave rise to humorous incidents, about which we often had a good laugh afterwards.

The Home Guard almost invariably met on Sundays, which interfered with my attendance at church, though I was able to get to an evening service occasionally.

From time to time some of our number, gardeners, road-men and artisans, who were not in reserved occupations, would be called up with their age group to the regular forces. Conscription was carried out in an orderly manner, all men had to register with their age group on a certain date, but several weeks might elapse ere those eligible would be summoned for a medical examination, and a further pause ere they got their call up papers. Volunteering for service was not encouraged, though two pals of mine, both shepherds, were dead keen to join up, and presented themselves at various army depots to do so, but were told to remain where they were – in farm work.

In June 1940 the local community received a blow when the 7th (Berwick) Battalion of the Northumberland Fusiliers, was among the regiments captured by the Germans at St Valery. A fair number of my acquaintances were among those taken prisoner, and it was a good while before their folks received any word about them.

A similar fate befell the second line Territorial Battalion the 9th (Berwick) in February 1942 at the fall of Singapore, just shortly after it had arrived there. Again many local families were involved, and it was not until the end of the war in the Far East that those prisoners of the Japs who had managed to survive were heard of again.

Food rationing was brought in gradually during the first few months of the war, and worked tolerably well and fairly throughout.

The abolition of auction sales for fatstock destined for slaughter took place almost immediately after the outbreak of war, and a grading system of marketing was introduced, and was soon working smoothly. All cattle, sheep and pigs destined for slaughter had to be presented at a grading centre,

Wartime

which was usually the nearest auction mart. There they were assessed and graded on the hoof, at an estimated dead weight, by a couple of men appointed by the Government. Grades were Super, A, B and C according to quality. The auctioneers and their staff did the supervising, handling and paperwork. The producer was paid a price fixed beforehand for every week of the year with seasonal fluctuations. The grading system gave farmers a stabilised market, which hitherto they had never enjoyed. Moreover they could forecast for a year ahead exactly what price their fat stock was likely to fetch in any given month. Sales by auction of store stock went on as usual of course.

Entry of livestock to the grading centres was regulated, that is to say that a producer having notified his intention of presenting X number of animals on a certain day was required to stick to that number and not exceed or fall short of it. To avoid gluts and shortages, producers might be asked to decrease or increase their entries. This compulsory grading system was not finally abolished till 1954 with the ending of meat rationing, when freedom of marketing was again allowed and the auction sales of fat stock resumed.

The bulk of the livestock from the grading centres went to the thickly populated areas, and butchers in country towns and rural areas were only allocated a small quota. It was particularly galling to see hundreds of cattle, sheep and pigs being entrained at Wooler station for distant centres, and only a mere handful retained for our local needs. We realised of course that we had to be rationed like everyone else, and that this was the fairest way of doing things.

The embargo on killing of sheep on the farm for home consumption was rigorously enforced. In normal times any carcases of sheep that had to be butchered at home owing to sickness had been disposed of to the farm workers. Now such carcases or 'fallen mutton', had to be delivered to the local slaughterhouse along with the sheep's heads, skins and offal. A heavy penalty was incurred by anyone who breached the regulations by home killing and consumption. In remote

149

areas it was certainly done, but on inbye farms with so many folk around, no one considered it worth the risk in case someone should spill the beans.

At the same time farmers and farm workers had to have a special permit to kill pigs for home cured bacon; only one pig per year per household could be killed. Officialdom was very pernickety too that the killing should be carried out on the date stipulated on the form, and thereon hangs a tale:

It was a well known fact among country folk that it was inadvisable to slaughter a she-pig, when it was 'a-breemin', i.e. in season, as the meat would not cure properly. Our neighbour's wife got her permit from the local food office to have her pig slaughtered on a certain date, but as the appointed day approached she noticed that her sow was in season, and would continue so over the killing date. She, therefore, went off to the food office to get her permit extended or altered, but met with a refusal. It was only after a furious argument that she obtained her wish. 'By gosh! Ah gien thon weemen in the office a reid face, when Ah telled thum why Ah needit ma permit changed. Ah sayed "Sows are no like you, ye knaw, in season a' the time" she crowed afterwards.

Many townspeople thought that country folk lived the life of Riley with plenty of home grown meat, butter, eggs and bacon, but this was not strictly true. Those who owned cows, pigs and hens certainly had the use of some of their own produce, but surplus eggs and butter had to be delivered up as well. Folk without animals, who formed the majority, were no better off for rations than anyone else.

By 1941 the ploughing up programme had begun to bite deeply into the grazing grounds on the mixed arable farms. As a result sheep stocks dwindled in number, and the shepherds, for so long the most important men among farm workers, had to take a back seat. Flockmasters were obliged to cut their sheep numbers drastically, and the autumn ewe sales saw the disposal of more than just the ordinary annual drafts of breeding ewes. Ewes were only fetching prices of fat stock for killing, as there was little demand for breeding stock. The

North Doddington draft ewes only realised forty-two shillings each, about a pound below their value to breeders. One of our neighbour farmers, a keen sheep man, complained bitterly in conversation with father, about having to cut down the numbers of his ewe stock, 'My sheep never were better, an here's me hivvin tae putt away maist o' them', he said. The situation was slightly better on the upland stock rearing farms, which were not being required to plough so much.

Our ewe stock at Doddington was now well below the number that would provide work for two full men. We decided therefore to leave at the May term of 1942, and gave in our notice early in December 1941.

I was keen to return to Scotland, and with this object in mind, we placed an advert in a Scots Border newspaper seeking a situation as a double herd. We were sure we would get a job in some upland area where sheep still held sway. We had only one reply to our advert. It came from Mr Cranston of Morridgehall Farm near Maxton, who was vacating that farm at 28th May, in order to take over the tenancy of Cortleferry, in the Gala Water district of Midlothian, for which he would require two shepherds. We contacted him by telephone and he came down to see us, and we hired to go with him to his new place in May. We agreed to the Wages Board rates of pay, as Scotland also had a Wages Board by this time, with the perquisites of potatoes and oatmeal, but no cow or pack sheep. Although Cortleferry was unknown to us except by name, we deduced from the description given by Mr Cranston that it would be alright, and that included the house.

At the English term our employment at North Doddington ended and we were left virtually homeless for a fortnight. We had arranged to stay in the interval between the terms with relations in Lothian, father and I near Gorebridge with mother's brother and mother at Musselburgh with her sister. My sister was invited to spend the time with friends near Wooler. A lorry from a Galashiels firm was sent to fetch our belongings to Cortleferry on May 13th, where they were stored in an empty house, but not the one we were to occupy. Unknown to us this house had been used to lodge Irishmen, and as a result our furniture and bedding became infested with fleas, which proved very distressing and embarrassing for us for a considerable time ere we finally got rid of them. Father and I accompanied and unloaded the furniture, then went on to Middleton to my uncle's place. Father left to stay elsewhere after a few days, but I stayed on dividing my time between helping my uncle and cousins on their farm, and cycling down to Cortleferry to plant the garden.

6

GALA WATER

Cortleferry, our new home, was a typical upland marginal farm situated in the Gala Water district of Midlothian, near the village and railway station of Fountainhall. It was in the parish of Stow, that village being about four miles further down the valley.

The valley of the Gala Water, called Wedale of old, divides the Moorfoot Hills from the Lammermuirs. It is bleak, steep and windswept, especially on the eastern side, where the farmlands stretch back in strip-like fashion from the banks of the Gala to the Lauderdale watershed. On the western side the slip is more gradual and the fields less steep. The district has long been noted as sheep rearing country, and has always enjoyed a high reputation for the soundness of its stock.

In 1942 most, if not all, the ewe stocks were Half Breds and Cheviots, Blackfaces being only met with on the higher hills.

At Fountainhall there was a two teacher school, a post office, a shop and of course the railway station. The place itself was mainly a railway village, many of the men being railway employees. It had grown up around the railway junction where the Waverley line was met by the short branch line to Lauder with its two stations at Oxton and Lauder. The Lauder railway then had ceased to have a passenger service, but goods trains still ran on it. The Waverley line traversing the Gala Water valley was at that war-time period very busy with numerous trains both of passengers and goods.

Another source of employment at Fountainhall was the large Hazelbank quarry which provided road metal.

Cortleferry was about half a mile from Fountainhall, which was very handy but it stood at the top of a very steep brae

beside the road leading to Middletown, which was a drawback in winter should the road be ice- or snowbound.

We all forgathered at our new place on May 28th from our
various havens; father and I had attended the farm sale two
days before when the stock and implements of Mr Brodie, the
outgoing tenant, were disposed of. When we came to Cortleferry we received a shock, for it was obvious we had not
made a very good move. The farm was in a much run down
and neglected condition. The drystane dykes which formed
the majority of the field boundaries were in a dilapidated
state, what wire fences did exist were not in good shape
either. This was indeed a slap in the face for us, used as we
were to first class fences, gates etc. There were no faulds
worthy of the name near our house, the main faulds and the
dipper being situated about a mile up the burn, fairly central
for most of the farm but a long way from houses and
steading. The latter too was in pretty bad repair, though
that did not affect us in any way.

There were six cottages in the row at Cortleferry, which
was built in the form of a T, three facing west and three facing
south. We occupied the house at the end of the south facing
row, which had been vacated by the steward of the outgoing
tenant, since father had expressed a wish when we were hired
to have an end house. The gardens at the back of the houses
were a bit steep and stony, but we managed to grow some
fairish crops of potatoes and vegetables. Only three houses
had front and back doors, of which ours was one.

There was a kennel of sorts for the dogs, but it was not big
enough for all our dogs, and I bought a second-hand sectional
kennel to house them better.

Formerly the shepherd had stayed at Hoppringle, where
there was a house and outbuildings. This house was now
empty, having been abandoned a few years previously, at the
time when the cottages were being modernised and an inside
water supply and sanitation installed. It had not been considered feasible to upgrade that house, because of problems
with its water supply. No doubt Hoppringle was ideally

situated as a base from which to herd the farm, as it stood beside the road leading to the Clints, overlooking the deep glen of the Toddle Burn, which split Cortleferry ground in two. How our mother would have enjoyed staying there, with her hens, her cow and no neighbours to bother about.

Father did not take any animals with him to Cortleferry save the dogs. We had to dispose of our cows and the pack sheep before we left Doddington. He now had an all cash wage plus potatoes and meal for the dogs. He was enraged to find at the end of his first month when we got our pay, that a sum for house rent had been deducted from his pay, a thing that had never happened to him before. He had taken it for granted when he was hired that the house would be free. Our employer was quite within his rights to deduct house rent from wages under the terms of the Wages Schedule, though only a minority of farmers exercised that right.

Another bone of contention betwixt us and Mr Cranston was the house itself. We had been told when he hired us that it was a good house just recently reconditioned, but all that had been done was the installation of cold water with tap and sinks in the back kitchen, and water closet. Apart from that there had been no other improvements wrought on the house; the stair was very steep, just a sort of ladder, and the upstairs rooms had skylights and no plaster on the ceiling. However mother was quite pleased to have a house with inside water supply and lavatory at last, after forty years of marriage. In no time she and my sister had it trig and comfortable, for our farm womenfolk were nothing if not adaptable.

Our neighbours in the row were three horsemen and an odd man. There were two empty houses at first but in the following year, a byreman was engaged who lived by himself. There were two tractors on the place, a caterpillar driven by the master's brother-in-law who lived in the farmhouse with the Cranstons, and a Fordson which the farmer sometimes drove himself, and which was also used to drive the threshing mill. This barn mill was of a lesser size than those we had met with, and of a type more common on small or upland farms where the grain crop was less.

Mr Cranston brought all his livestock with him from Morridgehall. These came by train to Fountainhall station, and included his Half Bred ewe flock, and a full complement of Half Bred and Cheviot ewe hoggs to suit his new farm. He brought a large part of the Cortleferry ewe stock at the sale two days before, to bring the numbers up to strength. Those last had been left on the farm and proved to be a perfect nuisance to us, as they had been used to jumping the dykes and going more or less where they pleased. To make matters worse we found that the ewe hoggs he had brought with him had been at spring grazing at another farm, and had acquired equally bad dyke jumping habits there.

We had a difficult task that summer keeping the sheep in the fields where they ought to be, and also out of the corn fields. We did our best to break them off their jumping habits by building gaps and confining the ringleaders to the few fields enclosed by wire fences. It was a dour battle and we felt very sick at times, more especially since our employer unfortunately refused to back up our efforts. He said he had leased the farm on the understanding that the estate would put all the dykes and fences in order. In truth his stance was logical enough, but it was painfully evident that it was going to take a long time to get things put right. However, with a bit of prodding the estate folk started to do some fencing and repairing and wiring of the dykes. We fell between two stools as it were, and had to battle on grimly to try and cure the sheep of their jumping habits, which we were determined to do. We developed a 'thing' about jumping sheep, and whenever we found a single sheep or two or three out of place, we would transfer to a field behind a wire fence, even though it meant turning back on our round. But sometimes the breakout would be on a big scale, as happened on the morning after we had spained the ewes, when I found six hundred of them in a cornfield adjoining the grazing. On another occasion two hundred of them broke into a cornfield on Middletown overnight. it was not long after that Mr Elliot erected a wire fence against his side of the dyke to protect his crops, which helped matters greatly.

We cast envious eyes on the domains of our neighbour herds, whose dykes and fences were kept in reasonable repair. The farms adjacent to us, notably Middletoun, Pirnataton, Burnhouse Mains and Haltree, were very well run and farmed at that time, with good crops of corn and turnips, and first class sheep stocks. Nowadays some of them have sadly deteriorated and are little more than glorified ranches.

By the time we had been two years at Cortleferry, we had managed to bring the sheep under satisfactory control.

Apart from the drawbacks already mentioned Cortleferry was a good herding. The ground was steep in parts and very much exposed to the elements, but the sheep were hardy and good doers, the death rate being low indeed. We were fortunate in that the winters were open whilst we were there.

The ewe stock numbered thirty five score with two hundred ewe hoggs over and above that. It consisted of equal parts to Half Breds and Cheviots, the Cheviots being of the North Country type, which was then approaching its peak of popularity on marginal Border farms. The Half Bred ewes had Oxford Cross lambs, the Oxford tups being then predominant for crossing in the Borders, having made a comeback over the Suffolks, owing to the wartime demand for size of carcase in the lambs. The Cheviot ewes had Half Bred lambs to maintain the Half Bred stock. Cheviot lambs were produced from the Cheviot stock, but a number of Cheviot ewe lambs had to be bought in to augment the number of home bred ones.

There was ample scope and interest for a keen shepherd, and we were able to lay the foundation of a reasonably good sheep stock. To be fair to Mr Cranston, in spite of the differences we had with him, he allowed father a free hand in the management of the sheep.

There were a few cattle kept in the Gala Water district then, and we had only a dozen or so suckling cows with their calves and a few stirks to look after. Few of the fields were well enough watered for cattle.

We found ourselves right in the middle of sheep country, most of the neighbouring farms having been for long well known by name and reputation at the sheep sales. There was a healthy sense of competition among both flockmasters and shepherds at the sales, and we critically scanned each others lots in the pens. Everybody 'ran off' their lambs, that is, fed them separately from the ewes during the summer. The artificial feeding helped the growth and quality of the lambs, and at the same time helped to fertilise and improve the rather poor soil of the farms. A fashion which had died out in Northumberland, but which we found to be still rampant in Scotland, was the colouring or 'blooming' of sheep and lambs for sale. This practice only died out slowly after the war, when tinted wool was penalized by the Wool Marketing Board.

For clipping and dipping we 'neighboured' with the Clints' shepherd; he came down to help us to clip our sheep and we went up to the Clints to help him. The custom of joining neighbours to get the sheep clipped had largely died out on inbye farms, but Mr Rodger of Muircleugh near Lauder, who farmed the Clints then, was one farmer who kept up the custom. He organised a band of local helpers for the clipping of his Blackface hirsel. In addition to his own staff from Muircleugh, a shepherd and three other men, he brought his brother from Langshaw and the shepherd there, the shepherd from his other brother's farm of Wooplaw, and the shepherds from Crookston and Torsone Mains; the latter had been shepherd at Cortleferry for many years previously. To complete the band were father and I and the farmer of Justicehall, Oxton.

Some folk criticized Mr Rodger for his action, alleging that he was getting his sheep clipped on the cheap, but I don't think that ever entered his head. He was pleased to maintain what had once been the widespread custom of neighbouring. The Clints clipping had come to be regarded as a sort of social occasion, an annual institution one might say. Certainly all of us who took part, and there was usually a dozen all told, got a good deal of enjoyment out of the event.

All the clippers used the hand shears, with an element of rivalry among us younger set. The Rodger brothers caught and fetched the sheep for the clippers, and wrapped up the fleeces. They were hard put to it at times to keep their feet clear, for the work of clipping went fast and furious, and so did the crack and banter amongst the men. The badinage reached hilarious heights at times, with quip and counter-quip bandied from one to the other. The crack went on at meal times too, and some of us young ones were so reduced to helpless laughter by the jokes of our elders that we had difficulty in eating our food.

Mrs Coltherd the shepherd's wife, and the farmer's daughter Miss Rodger had the job of feeding the multitude. They did us proud too, providing us with three good meals, breakfast, dinner and tea.

After the clipping was done we all mucked in at the packing of the wool before taking our several ways homeward.

The sheep sales played a very important part in our lives, for the lambs were all sold as stores from July to October at the Newtown St Boswells auction mart. The draft ewes and gimmers were sold there too in September. Sheep and lambs from the area were sent by rail from Fountainhall station, which was indeed a busy place on sale mornings. All stock had to be loaded by 7 am. There could be as many as ten waggons of lambs from the surrounding farms. In addition to the local waggons, the special train would be swollen by waggons from Heriot and Tynehead stations, and a few waggons that had come down the branch line from Oxton and Lauder.

At Cortleferry I continued my membership of the Home Guard. Membership of the force had now been made compulsory for those eligible, and laggards could be fined for non-attendance at parades. I found myself attached to the Fountainhall platoon of Stow company of the Midlothian

A Shepherd Remembers

Home Guard. The platoon commander was Mr Elliot of Middletoun and his second in command, whose name I have forgotten, was a man who lived in Fountainhall and commuted to Edinburgh to work. The company commander at Stow was Mr Ramsay of Bowland. We did most of our parades and exercises as a platoon on our home ground, joining hands with the Stow lot only occasionally. By means of the Home Guard I got to know the local chaps much sooner than I might have otherwise done, though I never enjoyed the exercises as much as I did at Doddington. This was partly due to the fact that the urgency had gone out of the situation, and we tended to get bored. Once we went by truck to the rifle range at Dreghorn in the Pentlands, for shooting practice, which was quite an experience. In my experience the Home Guard did very little shooting practice with live ammunition, and we were told ammunition was scarce, and had to be saved in case the balloon went up.

My attendance at the kirk suffered severely because of Home Guard duties. We all joined the parish kirk of St Mary of Wedale at Stow, after having tried both it and the other kirk which had once been the UF. Mr Waugh was minister at St Mary's and Mr Elliot was the name of the other kirk's minister. We could get a bus to Stow to the kirk, but there was a time lag between the skailin of the kirk and the departure of the bus. Father took the bus but my sister and I preferred to cycle. The minister came and held services in the village hall at Fountainhall about once a month.

There was quite a lot of social activity in the winter at the villages of Stow, Fountainhall and Heriot. Those usually took the form of whist drives and dances, promoted to raise funds for projects connected with the war, such as Comforts for the Forces, Wings for Victory etc. It was common too for the farming communities to organise dances in someone's granary in aid of the Red Cross. One such event was held in the granary at Cortleferry, and on another night I went to a Red Cross dance at Lugate near Stow. I did not hesitate to take part in what social life was on offer. I cycled along to the functions that were held outside the Fountainhall – Stow – Heriot orbit, as the local fellows were reluctant to go where the 'gang' was not congregating. I did not mind at all going to strange places on my own, cycling on one occasion to a whist and dance at Blackshiels about six miles away. It was an eerie experience travelling up the Armet Water and over by Soutra Aisle in the blackout, on a road which I had never traversed before, with nary a light to be seen. Another time I got an invitation to a kirn at Tynehead, seven or eight miles away. I felt a bit guilty about that, for the kirn, held on a Saturday night, did not break up until after 1 am on the Sunday morning. I could not leave before it finished because I was with a partner, but I was ashamed at having violated my religious principles.

Though most of the local girls were away in the Services there were still a few left to partner us, and the Land Army had a hostel at Crookston House, from which the girls worked on local farms. Those Land Girls were recruited from the Edinburgh area.

After we had been at Cortleferry for more than a year father felt that herding was getting to be too much for him, so he decided to retire whenever he could get a suitable house. In those days getting a house was a problem as there were no council houses to rent for farm workers. A retired man's best chance of obaining a house, apart from buying one, was to rent a house on a farm. There were always farmers who had a house available, but the trouble with a rented house was that there were always some strings attached; one was expectd to do some casual work or perform some service or other in exchange for the house. Or again the farmer might decide that he required the house for a worker, so that one had no alternative but to get out. I knew of several retired men who were, as it were, chased from one farm to another in this respect.

As an alternative I could have taken a herding to provide a house for my parents, as was often done by unmarried sons, but father was not keen on this. He said he would not want to look on at someone else after herding all those years. For my part I did not favour such a move either, and felt that if I were to herd on my own, I would be better to be clear of family ties.

Having saved a little money, father's plan was to purchase a small house in or near some Border village, where he would have security for the rest of his life, with no more flitting for him and mother. We spent most of 1944 in house hunting, making offers here and there for the few suitable properties that came on the market, but without much success. When at last father obtained a house at Morebattle in September 1944, we gave notice to our employer that we were quitting.

Since the Essential Works Order, nicknamed the Standstill Order, had come into force in 1940, the yearly engagements of farms were in abeyance. A month's notice on either side was sufficient to terminate an engagement, but a permit had to be got from the Ministry of Labour for a worker to change jobs or a farmer to dismiss a worker.

This heinous order, which caused much bad feeling between employer and employed, and which effectively tied a farm worker to a particular farm, was imposed only in Scotland during the war years. In England so long as a worker remained in agriculture, which incidentally he was obliged to do, he was free to move from one farm to another. The excuse given for the tighter application of the rules in Scoland was the excessive movement from place to place of farm workers, as compared with the more static conditions of workers in England, particularly southern England. No notice was taken of the fact that in the English Border counties the same flitting around took place as in Scotland, yet the Standstill Order did not apply. In actual fact the whole aim of the Order was to prevent bad employers from being left short of labour, during the vital war years. The Order was heavily weighted in favour of the farmers, for it was significant that should a farmer want rid of a worker, he had no problem getting a permit to do so. I blamed the Farm Servants' Union for giving their assent to make this order valid, for they must have known that it had a different face in England.

It was when we applied for permits to leave Cortleferry, that I got caught up in this nefarious Order. Father was over seventy years of age and due to retire so he was granted a permit right away, but my application was refused, Mr Cranston opposing it. Both he and I had to appear before tribunal at Galashiels, to argue our respective cases. Although I pointed out that I was hired jointly with father, and that I'd be left stranded in an empty house, when my parents flitted, the tribunal brushed aside my argument. They said I would be able to obtain lodgings of some sort. When I persisted in my refusal to consider staying on and working at Cortleferry, the chairman of the tribunal made some very nasty snide remarks, about how lucky I was not to be overseas like many other lads, fighting for their country. When I retorted that there were many men in the Forces who had cushy jobs, and had never been outside the country, I think that put the tin hat on it, and hardened the tribunal's resolve to reject my application. I was eventually browbeaten into a compromise position, in which I was obliged to stay on at Cortleferry, until such time as Mr Cranston got two other shepherds, and would try to obtain lodgings of some sort. I asked my friend and neighbour Sandy the herd at the Clints, if he could help me out and he agreed to do so.

Little more than a week after my tribunal appearance, our employer came to us and said we could shift whenever we pleased, as he had been able to hire a father and son for shepherds, from a place in Northumberland where no restriction was placed on their movement. Thus was I freed from my obligation to stay on alone, which was a mighty relief.

We flitted to Morebattle on October 25th 1944, back to the dear calf country I loved so well. Of course I was soon faced with the prospect of getting another job off my own bat, after a partnership of seventeen years with my father but that is another story.

PART II

Border Farm Life Between the Wars

7

SHEPHERDING

For some generations before and up till the Second World War the pattern of Border shepherding and sheep husbandry changed very little. The chief changes which took place were in the breeds of sheep employed. Whitefaced sheep dominated the scene, with Half Bred and Three Parts Bred ewes inbye and Cheviots outbye.

The Border Leicester-Cheviot cross or Half Bred was the favourite choice of ewe in the field herdings. The term Half Bred, with the emphasis on the word 'bred', is derived from the old nickname for the Border Leicesters, which were commonly called 'Bred' sheep by Border flockmasters and shepherds away back in the nineteenth century.

Until the introduction of rams of the Down breeds from England for crossing with Half Bred ewes, Border Leicester rams were used, the resultant progeny being called 'Three Parts Bred'. I can faintly remember seeing both lambs and ewes of this cross in my boyhood.

Another widespread policy in sheep husbandry was the use of Half Bred rams on the Half Bred ewes; the progeny were called 'Half Bred and Half Breds', and in Northumberland, 'Second Crosses'. Whole flocks of Half Bred sheep were maintained in this way, only the rams being bought into the flock. These rams were of course, first cross Border Leicester-Cheviots. Just prior to the First World War father herded a large flock of this type at Harelaw, Lammermuir.

Gradually the Down breeds, in particular Oxfords and Suffolk, gained ascendancy for putting to Half Bred ewes on such farms as kept them, and Three Parts Bred and Half Bred lambs of the second cross type disappeared from the scene.

A Shepherd Remembers

The true Border-Leicester Cheviot type of Half Bred now held sway, bred on upland marginal farms from flocks of Cheviot ewes, and sold as replacements to the inbye flockmasters. Up till the mid 1920s such Cheviot ewes were all of the Border or South Country type, some being produced on field or park farms as 'top' lambs. 'Top lambs' are the first 'draw' or selection of the season's crop of lambs of either sex. The majority of the Cheviot ewe lambs, however, were 'mid' ewe lambs from the hill hirsels. 'Mids' was the term used for the next draw of hill ewe lambs after the best had been retained for breeding. Though they were not extra big sheep, those Half Breds out of hill Cheviot ewes were hardy and good milkers.

When I was a boy and youth most of the lambs off the inbye farms were Oxford crosses, and on the Scots side of the Border especially they greatly outnumbered the Suffolks. The latter played a minor role, most farmers preferring to mate them with the gimmers only, as their progeny were easier to lamb. When we crossed into Northumberland in 1930 we found the Suffolk crosses to be most numerous. Oxford crosses lost ground there until the advent of the war, and the call for size among mutton producers helped them to stage a comeback.

In the 1920s the North Country Cheviot sheep from Caithness and Sutherland became more numerous in South East Scotland. This breed was descended from the Cheviot sheep taken up north by Border Grazers early in the nineteenth century there they had become a fixed type vastly different from their cousins in the south, larger and much more prolific.

The reason for their introduction into southern Scotland in the first place, was the prevalence of 'scrapie' in south country flocks. This wasting disease, which is held to be both hereditary and contagious, caused havoc among sheep stocks from about the turn of the century. Both Border Leicester and Cheviot sheep were susceptible to the disease, and consequently their Half Bred offspring.

Shepherding

Research into the causes of scrapie by the veterinary world was greatly hampered by the hush-hush attitude regarding it adopted by sheep men. One could hardly blame them for this, for although everyone knew that it occurred in all flocks to a greater or less degree, it was policy to deny its presence, and the faintest whisper that a breeding flock was not 'clean' led to a slump in demand at the sales for its female breeding stock or rams.

When it was discovered that Half Bred sheep bred in Caithness and other northern counties were less prone to take scrapie, flockmasters in the south started to go north to purchase their ewe lambs. Southern breeders of Half Bred ewe lambs followed suit and imported North Country female stock.

During the 1930s the north country type of Cheviots practically took over, and the demand for South Country Cheviot females dwindled considerably.

One outcome of the North Country invasion and their gain in popularity was a loss of hardiness in the Half Bred ewe. Many places which had hitherto carried Half Bred stocks switched over to Cheviot ewes producing Half Bred or pure Cheviot lambs, thus severing the closer connection with the hills which had been a feature of the old South Country type and had made them easier to maintain.

Inbye breeding between the wars was a much harder job than it is today, and basically methods had changed little for many years.

Equipment was antiquated by today's standards, and varied a great deal from farm to farm, depending upon the size of the flock or the affluence of the flockmaster. The big double herdings were usually the best equipped, but many single herds could be just as good. A lot depended on how much interest the individual farmer took in his sheep. The poorest equipped places were often those farms tenanted by working farmers, who were not well endowed with capital. I soon learned that where shepherding was concerned, the next best thing to working for one's self was to work for someone with plenty of money.

The standard inbye hirsel contained from twenty to twenty-five score of ewes, plus ewe hoggs, and double herdings ranged between thirty and forty score. We found that double herdings were definitely smaller in Northumberland than in Scotland. Single herdings of below seventeen or eighteen score were, on both sides of the Border, regarded as less than full herdings and were mostly made available to older men.

The shepherd's work varies with the seasons, which rules out the element of monotony. The lambing season is the most important event in his calendar, and one might say it corresponds to the harvest on the arable side of farming.

On Border farms the lambing was organised on the following lines: the ewes were brought into a field chosen for the purpose in weekly batches as they were due to lamb, and were housed at night in a permanent or temporary shed, so that the shepherd and his assistant could sit up with them and tend them through the night.

Where there was a permanent shed, it could either be a part of the farm buildings occupied by cattle during the winter months, then thoroughly mucked out and disinfected for the lambing season, or it could be a stone built enclosure at or near the farm steading, partly covered over and kept for the sheep alone. This latter type was a relic of the days early last century, when the New Leicester sheep, forerunners of the Border Leicesters, were kept on inbye farms. A stone built shed in which to house them at lambing was regarded as a piece of standard equipment on the farm.

Again, a permanent lambing shed might be situated in a field near the steading or the shepherd's house, and consisted of an enclosure made with posts and rails with rows of parricks ranged round the perimeter, to house individual ewes with their lambs. The parricks were roofed with straw or corrugated iron, the straw roof being renewed every year.

It was essential that a permanent lambing shed should be

well cleaned out, and treated with lime or disinfectant as soon as the lambing was past. This was a precaution not always taken on some farms, elementary though it may seem in the fight against such diseases as inflammation in ewes and navel ill in young lambs, both dreaded in those days.

For instance a shepherd colleague once told me that on the approach of lambing time, the farmer came to him and said, 'Is't no aboot time that ye got the lambin shed ready?' To which my friend replied, 'Is't no aboot time that it was mucked oot?' – an example of what some shepherds were up against, as regards their employers' indifference to the welfare of the sheep.

On some farms the permanent site had had to be abandoned because of an outbreak of 'inflammation', a sort of fever that affected newly lambed ewes, which was highly contagious, and in former times usually fatal. According to some opinions the inflammation germ could lie in the ground from one year to another, and nothing save ploughing and renewing the pasture could eradicate it. Some folk considered it good policy to erect the lambing shed in a fresh field every year. I never subscribed to this theory, but as I never encountered a bad outbreak of the trouble I had no way of proving it right or wrong. I was taught by father that whenever a ewe was suspected of having inflammation, she must be promptly isolated from the rest of the flock. Thanks to modern antibiotics the trouble has now lost its terrors for sheep men.

Those temporary lambing sheds were made with posts and paling rails, or posts and wire net, to which were laced bunches of wheat or barley straw. The roof of the parricks consisted of batons on which were laid bunches of straw three or four deep. It was very important to have a good thick straw roof, for prolonged rain or melting snow would seep through, and literally drown the young lambs in the parricks. I remember a neighbour shepherd confessed to me that he had lost a score of lambs, 'at yin crack o' the whip', on one particularly stormy twenty-four hour spell, because his parricks were not adequately covered. He said the farmer only allowed him enough straw to make his shed roof one bunch thick. The straw roof of a lambing shed had to be securely tied down every five feet or so to prevent a high wind from lifting it off. This was done with esparto ropes over stock props or wire netting.

Another lambing time requisite provided on the better run farms was a lambing hut or bothy, complete with coal stove and bunk bed. In this hut the herd and his assistant would spend alternate nights, sallying forth at intervals to inspect the ewes with a hurricane lamp. Also in the hut were kept all medicines and appliances required for the job. The hut could also be a haven of warmth for a weakly or half perished lamb, though many such were carried to the hearth in the shepherd's own house to be revived.

Some farms did not possess a lambing hut, and the shepherd and lambing man had to pass the time between lambing shed inspections, sitting by the fireside in the shepherd's house. This was not very satisfactory, since the kitchen, as the living room was then called, would also be the sleeping quarters for the herd's wife and some of the bairns. On one farm at which my father was shepherd before I was born there was no lambing bothy. When, on the approach of his first lambing time there, he broached the subject with the farmer the latter said, 'Oh, they (that is the previous shepherds) just sat up in the house'. Father's reply was, 'Hoo wad ye like somebody champin oot an in your bedroom through the nicht'? His point was not lost on the farmer, and he gave permission for a bothy of sorts to be rigged up in the steading close to the lambing shed. Mobile lambing huts were equipped with wheels or skids, so that they could be moved by horse power from place to place.

The practice, just mentioned, of housing inbye ewes overnight during lambing had been handed down for many generations and is still prevalent at the present day. Most shepherds approved of the system, for it meant much less risk of loss, and less work in the morning, than if the ewes were left outside in the field overnight. I never grudged sitting up at nights, and on a fine night it was good to walk around the shed, lantern in hand, among the recumbent ewes calmly chewing their cud, and listening for the soft muttering of a newly lambed ewe as she licked her offspring, or the faint cry of the new born. Having got the new arrivals and their dams safely penned, one noted what else was going on, calculated how long it would be ere they required attention, then slipped quietly out of the shed and back to the bothy, to have a seat or a bit dover till the next turn. The lambing shed was a snug place in cold or stormy weather, and what a relief it was on a bad day to get the newly born lambs 'into the shelter of the fold'.

The faulds, pens or buchts, as they are variously called, for sheep handling, were very often quite rudimentary, usually of very poor lay-out and practically bottomless. Any floor they had consisted of rubble and earth, interspersed with large stones over which one was prone to trip and fall when catching a sheep. In clatchy weather after rain they would be in a terrible mess; indeed, following one right wet day, they could be impassable for sheep work for the best part of a week. The woodwork too was often in bad repair, and one had to have a hammer and nails handy each time one went to work in the faulds. Certainly some of the larger hirsels boasted a good set of pens, but I had been herding twenty years before I arrived to work on a farm where the faulds were really good. Long after the advent of tractors, combine harvesters etc. and the erection of buildings to house them, the sheep faulds on some farms were still a shambles.

The first major job among the sheep after lambing was the lamb 'cutting' i.e. the tailing and castration of the lambs. We cut the lambs' tails for reasons of hygiene and the male lambs were castrated to provide better meat. The castrated lambs were known as wedders or wethers.

Cutting was done when the lambs were about a month old, in a temporary pen moved from field to field. A cart loaded with flakes, wire nets and stakes accompanied the shepherd and those sent to assist, round the farm, about four or five lots being dealt with each day. Once the pen had been erected in a field, the ewes and lambs were gathered and driven into it, accompanied by much shouting and bleating. Once the job was done in that field, the pen was moved to the next field and so on.

The lambs were caught and held up for the operation by a couple of men or often by women workers. The shepherd castrated the lambs by cutting the tip off the scrotum, exposing the testicles. These he would pull out with his teeth or a pair of special pincers, some sort of disinfectant being applied to the wound. The lamb's tail would then be cut off before it was released, by the farmer himself or by the farm steward, should the master not be present. The female lambs of course had only their tails docked, but I have read in old sheep books about ewe lambs being spayed.

I have heard tell of shepherds in the past, who dropped the lamb stones into a pail of water, and took them home for frying, but neither I nor father ever tried that one on. When I was a boy, one farmer's wife asked to have the tails kept and skinned to make lamb's tail soup. When father asked the farmer later what the soup was like, he replied, 'Decidedly hairy!'

I never liked the lamb cutting by the old method; I reckoned it was a hashy barbarous job, and welcomed the advent of the rubber rings in use today. An improvement on the time-honoured testicle pulling act was castrating with clamps which crushed the cords leading from the stones without breaking the skin, the stones thereafter disintegrating. This, the Burdizzo method, did not catch on universally, as it was alleged to be less than 100% effective.

Though the cutting was such a drastic operation, there were astonishingly few casualties, and after a day or two the lambs were little the worse. Small number of deaths, much less than 1%, occurred from blood poisoning or from excessive internal or external bleeding. The vast majority of the tails would have dried up before the shepherds' evening round, yet one had to look very closely to see that every lamb had stopped bleeding at the tail. Any that had not done so had to be caught and a string or a ligament tied on. This ligament had to be removed within a couple of days.

I have already described the washing of sheep about a week before shearing, which used to be normal practice but which did not survive the mid 1930s.

With the steep fall in farm prices in 1921, after the post war boom, wool prices suffered a drop in common with other farm produce. Some farmers, rather than sell at the lower price, decided to hold on to their wool clip, in the hope that prices might improve. Many of them had two or even three years' wool clip stored in lofts or sheds. In some cases rats got in among the fleeces, and caused havoc, making part of the wool unsaleable. In the end those men had to sell at a much lower price than that which was offered originally, for the market remained depressed for many years. Half red wool was fetching as little as five pence (2½p) a pound by 1932. In that year I paid five guineas (£5.12½p) for a made-to-measure suit of clothes, which I reckoned contained only two and eleven pence (17½p) worth of raw wool.

Prior to the introduction of DDT and the sheep dips based on dieldrin, maggots or 'mauks' as they were called, were the plague of the shepherd's life in summer time. The 'mauk' season started in late May before shearing; if the weather was hot, then the maggot flies struck the unshorn sheep, and from then until October we never were clear of them.

The eggs laid by the maggot fly in the sheep's fleece hatched out, and the larvae burrowed into the sheep's flesh causing great discomfort and pain. It behoved one to detect their presence as soon as possible, or else they could make a right mess of the sheep, even causing death from shock in extreme cases. Fly strike was most common on dirty-tailed scouring sheep, which could be prevented by clipping off the dirty wool, but when the fly struck on the clean wool over the sheep's back and shoulders it was more serious. It was not uncommon in bad 'maukin' weather, that is humid, sultry

weather with hot blinks of sunshine, to encounter thirty or
forty mauked sheep in a single morning. Sheep struck on the
clean wool were hard to detect in the early stages, and one
had to gather them into a bunch, and walk them past, looking
carefully for any sign of maggots. A wriggling of the body or
jerking back of the head, with a slight tell-tale streak of
moisture on shoulder or rib, were what the shepherd looked
for. A dark streak on the fleece indicated a heavy or advanced
infestation, so that it was essential to pick up the earliest
signs.

There were numerous proprietary preparations on the
market for the treatment of mauked sheep, but Cuff's Fly
Oil, diluted in water, was by far the best application for
turning the mauks out of the fleece. Methinks I can feel the
smell of it in my nostrils as I write, for it had a distinct sharp
tang, which adhered to one's hands and clothing. No shepherd went on his rounds all summer without his 'mauky
bottle' and shears. The bottle, containing an anti-maggot
solution, was of a handy size and usually carried in one's hip
or jacket pocket, though lots of shepherd carried their sheep
stuffs in a cloth bag, like a school satchel, which was certainly
less hard on one's clothes.

Even after the mauks had been doused with Cuff's solution,
and shaken out of the fleece, one had to make sure and get the
last one, for as long as any were left the fly would strike again
and again. We used to dust the affected parts on a sheep that
had been struck with sulphur to repel the fly, but the stale
mauky smell was hard to smother. Terebene balsam or other
healing oils were applied to any sores caused by the burrow-
ing maggots.

Dipping was, of course, our sole protection from the
maggot fly, but the summer dips then in use were only
effective for a short time, up to a month at most. They were
based mostly on sulphur, and arsenic with a dash of methy-
lated spirit. Shepherds dipped the lambs separately just after
clipping time, and a second time in late July at weaning time.
The ewes were not dipped until then, for they had only now

Shepherding

grown enough wool to hold the dip. This gave some protection during August, which could be a bad month for mauks given the right weather conditions. But sometimes one could experience an outbreak of fly strike on the ewes previous to spaining time, or again in the interval between late August and the back dipping in September. More frequent dipping might have helped, but was seldom undertaken, owing to the toxic nature of the dips then in use.

I have dwelt on the subject of the maggots at length for they were such a scourge in those days. They made the summer months an absolute hell for the herding fraternity, and we welcomed a spell of cool windy weather now and again, to hold them at bay and give us a respite. What a relief it was to get the autumn dipping done, and to know that there would be no more maggots to bother us until summer came again. To parody some lines from one of Burns' songs:

> The dark dreary winter an the wild drivin snaw,
> Alane can delight me, the mauks are awa!

After World War II when DDT and dieldrin were introduced into the manufacture of sheep dips, they proved to be extremely effective in the prevention of fly strike. To the shepherd it was like coming out of hell into heaven, for during the twenty odd years that those substances were in use I never saw a maggot. The fly population was drastically reduced as well and sore heads and fly sores among sheep became a thing of the past. But since the above ingredients were banned from sheep dips, there has been a large increase in the number of flies, and mauks have appeared on the scene once more. Any shepherd over 50 will agree that, whatever its demerits and drawbacks vis-à-vis wildlife, the fact remains that dieldrin was the greatest thing ever to benefit the sheep industry.

Autumn dipping was carried out to waterproof the fleece against the elements and prevent infestation by lice and keds. Originally sheep dipping had been adopted for the prevention and cure of sheep scab, a disease which had been non-existent in the Borders for many years; neither I nor father before me had ever encountered sheep scab. The autumn dips we used were based on carbolic and phenol, and came in the form of a thick paste which had to be sliced and melted with boiling water. A fire had to be kept going all day beside the dipper for that purpose.

The dipper or sheep dipping bath was part of the fixed equipment of every farm where sheep were kept. The types and quality of dippers varied greatly from farm to farm, some had good spacious dippers, some even had swim baths, but many dippers were small affairs, stuck away in some clarty hole beside a burn, for convenient access to a water supply.

Dippers could be of concrete or of an old fashioned wooden type; the latter would be prone to leak, and had to be plastered with daubs of clay, to prevent the dip seeping into the burn, whereby the farmer would get into the black books for poisoning the fish.

Except for the rare swim baths into which the sheep were pushed head first, and as they swam through were pushed under water by a man with a stick, dippers were mostly all built on the principle of putting the sheep in hindside first at one end, and emerging after a short swim into a dripping pen at the other end. The shepherd stood at the side of the bath, up to his waist in a manhole; he gripped the sheep as it was lowered by the person catching and laid it on its back to ensure complete immersion. That was the ideal method, but as often as not the catchers would put the sheep into the bath, in any old way and far too fast, with the result that the shepherd had a struggle to get them properly dipped, and got drenched with splashes in the process. His only protection would be an old raincoat and waterproof apron, or an oilskin coat worn back to front. Father always wore an old shirt and jacket, with a sheepskin for an apron.

A further use for the dipper was the blooming of lambs for the sales. This fashion was rampant right up till after the Second World War, when the Wool Marketing Board came into being. It discouraged colouring by penalising dip tinted wool.

For blooming the dipper would be filled with clean water, to which would be added melted soft soap, soda crystals, and colouring matter of various shades of yellow according to the taste of the flockmaster. The sheep were scrubbed in the bath and when they emerged they had taken on a striking new appearance. In the absence of rain to rinse the sheep's wool before the sale day and fluff it out, the sheep were made to swim through a bathful of plain water. The sheep and lambs had a gay enough look after their shampoo, tint and rinse, but I doubt if ever this fashion deluded a discerning buyer. It certainly made for a lot of extra work on the shepherd's part.

Turnips always played a vital part on the inbye sheep farms of the Borders. Apart from their use for the fattening of hoggs, they were also the main winter diet of the ewes and ewe hoggs. The ewe hoggs ate turnips on the ground with an allowance of hay, right up till February, after which they were fed cut turnips. The reason for this was that they were losing their teeth by then and could not deal with the whole turnips.

The ewes were put on the turnip break for most of the day from New Year till lambing time in March, being run off into a grass field to spend the night and there they were fed hay. During my early years of shepherding the ewes never got fed with concentrates until they came into the lambing field.

Large quantities of turnips were stored in December in clamps, which were called 'hots' or 'pits', for spring use. The big square-built turnip pits made at strategic points up and down the farm, for convenient loading into carts and laying out in the fields in spring, were a feature in the Borders countryside. In most years turnips would be available for putting out to the ewes, right up till nearly the May term. A late spring held no terrors for shepherds in those days, for there was always an ample supply of food in the shape of turnips, to nourish the ewes and keep the milk on them.

Hots of turnips were also made on the shawed or cleared ground in the turnip fields, for the cutter, care being taken to space them over the field so that the troughs would cover all the ground, as they were shifted from block to block. This was done to prevent the following barley crop from lodging or going down, should the sheep be allowed to lie too long in one part of the field, thus concentrating their droppings on certain spots.

The folding of sheep on turnips, or 'on the break' as we called it, had been done with rope nets for generations until the introduction of wire nets. I never had much to do with them myself, for wire nets had come into general use by the time I became a full man, but I can remember watching father setting up when I was a boy. The hares were bad for chewing them, and they could be torn if a sheep got its head caught in a mesh. Mending rope nets with twine was for long one of the shepherd's tasks. Some shepherds preferred rope nets, and carried on using them long after wire nets were in general use. The rope nets were certainly easier to carry when one was shifting a break. An expert could set one up in a surprisingly short time.

The wire nets and the stobs for holding them up were usually carried on our backs when shifting the break. It was an arduous job, made even worse in wind, rain, snow or mud, and whenever we got the chance we could have the odd laddie come and shift them with his horse and cart. In hard frost the stakes had to be slackened out of the ground with a pick, and in the same conditions making holes for them on fresh ground with the piercer could make one sweat hard.

It was between the wars that the routine dosing of lambs during the summer months, to kill or prevent stomach worms, came into general practice. Before that, should a field of lambs be scouring badly, shepherds would administer a couple of worm tablets to each lamb. The lambs had to be fasted for twelve hours prior to dosing, so they were separated from their dams and shut in overnight and were treated first thing in the morning. This treatment usually dried up their scour in a few days.

In the summer and early autumn of 1932 our lambs at

Shepherding

Doddington throve very badly, they lost condition and shrank instead of growing, and some even just pined away and died. We were puzzled, not knowing just what was wrong, as the lambs were not scouring much. Major Rea decided to call in Dr Lyle Stewart of King's College, Newcastle, a celebrated veterinary researcher. When he came he diagnosed that our lambs were heavily infested with worms. He made us kill a lamb and open it up, and then he showed us the shoals of roundworms in the fourth stomach, battening on the blood cells of the stomach walls and causing anaemia.

Dr Stewart told us to drench all the lambs with a copper sulphate solution which he prescribed, to help to kill the worms. He also advised us to take time by the forelock, and prevent heavy infestation from building up, by embarking on a dosing routine with the new crop of lambs next spring. This we did, using the copper sulphate solution, and dosed the lambs once a month from May to September. The results were good and never again were we to have such wormy lambs.

Drenching against worms became a part of our summer work from then on, and as the years passed new drugs came into use. We changed from copper sulphate to nicotine, a by-product of tobacco, which proved just as efficient, and easier to prepare. But when phenothiazine came along about 1940, it tuned out to be the best yet and produced striking results. It was a by-product of the dye industry, and came in both tablet form to be administered with a balling gun, and a powder for dilution as a drench. The main drawback with phenothiazine was, that when used in liquid form any drips or drops that got onto the lambs' fleece left a heavy stain.

Shepherds' hours of work were very elastic and varied from season to season. We did not yoke and lowse at set times as the hinds and other workers did. Our general routine would be as follows: get out in the early morning after a cup and bite, come in for breakfast around eight o'clock, then go out again for a forenoon's work, then back in for dinner about midday. Except in winter when we finished at dusk, we would come in for a tea break in mid afternoon, then out again on the evening round finishing about 7 pm. Our meal times would vary according to what job we were at, often finishing a job before knocking off for meals. At lambing time hours were from daylight to dark and after dark; at seasons like clipping and dipping we would start at dawn to gather, and it would be late in the evening when we got sheep returned to their fields and the rest of the fields looked. Herding was also a seven day week job, though on Sundays we only did the morning and afternoon rounds for most of the year. Few shepherds undertook big jobs among the sheep on Sundays.

For the most part masters did not bother the herd regarding what hours he worked, as long as they knew that the sheep were getting proper attention. In places where the herd stayed in the row, the hinds' wives sometimes jealously marked the shepherd's movement, and commented on the fact that he might be in the house or at his garden, whilst their men were out at work in the fields. They never stopped to think that come five o'clock their men would down tools and be finished, but the herd could not leave the sheep at that hour until next morning, for it was considered sound policy to give them a look as late at night as possible.

Some of the harder employers were inclined to challenge the shepherd's right to flexible hours. One such found fault with his shepherd for having afternoon tea and indicated that it should stop. The herd complied but watched his chance for a comeback, and he got his chance when the farmer landed at his door about 8 pm one evening, to tell him that a waggon-load of cattle had arrived at the railway station, and he would have to go and fetch them home. 'Nae fear' said the herd, 'Ah'm no gaun, seein there's tae be nae efternune tea, Ah'm lowsed at five o'clock noo'. So the farmer had to climb down and let things return to the status quo.

Farmers whose flocks were not big enough to constitute a full time herding expected the shepherd to help out on the farm as well. 'Working Shepherd Wanted' was a favourite advert in the 'situations vacant' columns of the newspapers, inserted by farmers of this class. Such notices drew some mirth and caustic remarks from us herds. 'Are herds no supposed tae be working? What dis folk think herds dae if the dinna work?' was our rejoinder. A 'working shepherd' was a man who went to look his sheep in the morning, joined the other men in the fields till five o'clock in the evening, then went to look his sheep again after that.

One great ploy indulged in by shepherds was to meet one another at the march fence to have a crack, when they were on their rounds. As a boy accompanying father, I used to enjoy the occasions when he met with a neighbour herd, and listened avidly to their crack. When shepherds met, the main topic of their conversation was of course sheep and their work among them, but they would also converse on dogs, general topics and their employers. The latter often came in for some adverse criticism. Sometimes the crack lasted for half an hour or more, and they would part company refreshed and stimulated by having compared notes and aired problems.

Quite often neighbouring herds and their wives would strike up a friendship and visit each others' homes now and then. There is no doubt that we shepherds were a race slightly apart from the other workers and like drew like.

Shepherds have always been notorious for talking shop when they forgather, and there is a story about a shepherd's daughter, who got so fed up with the sheep talk between her father and a visiting herd, that she burst out, 'Did ony o you twae men ever happen tae see a *horse* in yer traivels?'

At one time shepherding tended to run in families, sons having followed their sires for generations back. This trend has now entirely died out, but throughout my time there existed some noted herding families on both sides of the Border.

On the Scots side there were the Laidlaws; two separate families of Scotts; three unrelated families called Young and the Brockies, just to mention a few. One shepherd called Young had nine sons who were all shepherds too, and they

183

and their descendants cropped up all over the place. In Glendale there were the Currys, the Newlandses, the Lumsdens and different families of Scotts.

Hill shepherds were a slightly different breed of men, and although there was a good deal of interchange of shepherds between hill and inbye places, there remained a hard core, one might say, of herds of either kind who stuck to their own type of herding in which they had been bred up. It was during our stay at Doddington that I really first came in contact with the hill shepherds. Through talking to them I got an insight into what their work was like and how it differed from my own. I never dreamt then that I would one day go herding outbye myself.

A class of men closely attached to sheep farming and with whom shepherds were seasonally involved, were those who acted as lambing men and shearers during the respective seasons. They hired themselves for two four-week periods of lambing, inbye in March to April, and outbye April-May. After the lambing was done they engaged in clipping from late May till July, moving from one farm to another. Their clipping season usually started with the hoggs on the low ground, then on to the ewes, finishing up among the hill hirsels.

From July onward they took part in haymaking, and on the arable farms some spent the autumn at the harvest. Their mainstays for winter and early spring work were rabbit-catching and hill draining. The cutting and clearing out of hill drains was all done by hand.

The rabbit catchers either rented the rabbits on one or more farms, or caught them on a share basis arranged between them and the farmers.

This class of men were footloose and in a manner of speaking self-employed, their mode of life was called 'workin louse' or 'workin tae yer ain hand'. Many of them were shepherds' sons and had started life as shepherds. They were mostly single men living at home with their parents, or in lodgings when the work took them some distance from home. Those who were married would have a house in a country town or village, or maybe a cottage rented from a farm or estate. In some cases they occupied a farm cottage on the understanding that they assisted with the lambing, the clipping, hay and harvest work on that particular place. Theirs was, however, a way of life mainly followed by single men, who, when they married, settled down as shepherds, game-keepers or foresters.

Many of those chaps returned year after year to the same farm to do the lambing and the clipping. At times two or three of them would club together to form a clipping gang, pre-ferably doing the job by piecework at so much per score of sheep. Clipping on day's wages was mostly done by men working on their own.

Those seasonal workers were amusing characters and had a fund of stories about the places they had been and the sights they had seen. As a youth I listened with interest to their tales, secretly envying their footloose existence. Still, in later years, when I tried to sample their lifestyle for myself, I found that it did not appeal to me. I had by then become too long accustomed to having a secure regular job.

Lambing men and clippers were full of wisecracks, and one which came from a clipper has stuck in my mind. We had been hanging about a good part of the day waiting for a batch of wet sheep to dry, groping them from time to time to see if they had become dry enough to clip. 'Aye', says Wat, 'they're drier than they were, but they're no as dry as if they were right dry!'

One of the lambing men we had at Doddington was noted for his zeal in twinning ewes that had borne single lambs. It was usual when spare lambs were plentiful to make singles into twins, by adding to the ewe's family if you caught her in the act of lambing. Dick made it a point of honour almost, not to let a ewe away with a single lamb if he could help it. One day he came to father with a very red face, and confessed that a ewe he had twinned, had had a second lamb of her own. Her first lamb had been very big, and he had jumped to the conclusion that it was a single, forgetting in his zeal to give her twins, to grope her and see if she had another lamb inside her.

Another man who was with us had a very headstrong dog which was not always very biddable. Jim seldom beat his dog, but addressed it often with the threat, 'Now watch it, or you an me will come tae blows!'

When I was young I used to miss the lambing men when they left, and was apt to feel flat after the bustle of the clipping. These were breaks in what was on the whole a rather lonely existence for a youth.

A feature of the inbye farms were the shedders in the fields during summer for nearly everyone 'ran off' the lambs to boost them for the early sales. In order to feed the lambs, and not their dams, throughout the summer, shedders were put up in the fields. A shedder consisted of two pens, a holding pen into which the sheep and lambs were driven, and another pen for the ewes, the lambs and ewes being shed or parted by manipulating a small swinging gate between the pens. The lambs were let out to the feed troughs and the ewes went into the other pen where they were held until the lambs had eaten the feed. Once the lambs had cleaned the troughs the ewes were let out. The shedders were mainly brought into operation after the ewes were clipped, since there was less chance then of a coupit ewe waiting to be lifted in some other field on the herds' round. 'Couping' or 'lying awalt' were the Borders terms for the habit some sheep had of lying on their backs. The sheep do this because their backs are itchy with no harm to themselves when newly clipped, for they can easily rise again, but after the wool has grown the heavy fleece make it impossible for them to right themselves, and if left to lie they eventually die of suffocation caused by gases from their swollen bellies. For most of the year the shepherd has to be on the alert to detect sheep lying on their backs. They are more prone to couping during warm showery weather in the weeks before clipping, when sunshine and shower set up an itch on the sheep's bodies, and when the fleece is at its heaviest. At that time of year we used to look our sheep three times daily, and of course were particularly anxious to get to them as early as possible in the morning. Hence the rule mostly adhered to of delaying the running off till after clipping, yet some flock masters insisted on shedders being started in early May in order to force the lambs on as soon as possible. In that case the shepherd had to leave the ewes shut in their pen, continue on his round and go back to let them out later. To run off the lambs made for a lot of extra work for the shepherds, especially if it was done twice a day, morning and evening, as was the practice on some farms; yet most herds accepted it cheerfully for they were as keen as their masters to have the lambs good for the sales. As I have already stated, summer feeding was regarded as a necessity on the poorer upland farms, as the bulk of the lamb crop was sold off at the earlier sales. It was also looked upon as a way of feeding the land. Maybe it was more beneficial and no more costly than the present day practice of lashing out on artificial fertilizer.

Spaining was done in late July and early August after the first sales were past. It was good policy to sell the first draws of lambs straight off their dams, to show them in the best of condition. Lambs usually lost a bit of bloom for a week or ten days after spaining. Spaining was effected by separating the lambs from the ewes, and shutting them in different fields out of earshot of each other. For the first night the din of their bleating would be deafening, but after about three days they would quieten and settle down. Well fenced fields and access to plenty of water were essential. One summer we had friends from the city to stay with us, and they arrived on the very day on which we spained the lambs. Kept awake that night by the incessant bleating they said next morning, 'So much for the peace and quiet of the countryside!'

Shepherds' wages were pretty low in the 1930s, though they were always a few shillings above those of the hinds. I myself had thirty-two shillings a week in 1930, rising by a shilling or two more by 1933, when I became twenty-one and qualified for the full man's rate. In 1936 in lieu of a rise of two shillings per week, I opted to get two sheep of my own, a mini pack as it were. The Wages Board recognised pack sheep as a perquisite, and fixed their value at one shilling per sheep off the weekly wage. I bought two ewes with single lambs apiece at three pounds a head at the May Day sale at Wooler. As I did not have a dog with me to drive them home, I asked a local contractor if he would have them transported home for me by lorry. He readily agreed and, to my surprise, refused to accept payment, for he had the reputation of being a hard man. Give a dog a bad name etc!

At the outbreak of war my wage was thirty-nine shillings per week, plus the keep of two ewes, the scheduled wage being forty-one shillings a week.

Sheep prices were never high between the wars apart from the short boom in 1918–20. In 1920 when lambs were making up to £5 per head and father got £7 each for his draft pack ewes prices reached their peak and fell steadily thereafter all through the twenties and early thirties, reaching rock bottom in 1932. In that year our draft ewes from North Doddington only realised thirty-one shillings each (£1.55), and inbye lambs were averaging twenty-five shillings or even less at the store sales. Prices improved slowly in the late thirties, 1937 being a good year, when things took an upturn, but they slumped again in 1938, and did not improve until after war broke out. From then on, prices rose every year, so that by 1945 they were double what they had been in 1932.

Before concluding this chapter I must make a few remarks about sheepdogs. The shepherd's dogs are at the same time his companions and his tools. Those Border collies are indispensable to the shepherd for his work; indeed it is no exaggeration to say that hill ground would be useless as grazing without them. They are justly famous for their intelligence and hardihood, and besides they are faithful and affectionate. If properly treated they will give cheerfully of their best, will follow their master and work till they drop. All they ask in return is a little kindness, a good feed and comfortable quarters. On the subject of quarters it always struck me as very unfair that shepherds should have to provide kennels for their dogs, for that was the norm on most places. After all, the hinds had stables for their horses, and gamekeepers had substantial kennels for their gundogs.

I never was what is called in everyday talk 'a great hand with dogs'. I always managed to get my dogs to do what was required, but beyond that I had little interest in handling dogs, and had little interest in sheepdog trials except as an occasional spectator. I confess I was always more interested in sheep than in dogs as such. Today sheepdog trials have become a way of life for many shepherds, and the breeding, rearing and training of collies is big business. Working dogs change hands at fabulous prices, and even pups can fetch up to twenty pounds each, which is a far cry from the days of my youth, when one could get a whelp from a neighbour herd or acquaintance for the asking. I remember the year I started herding I bought a pup for ten shillings, and a shepherd friend who was visiting us shortly afterwards was scandalised when I told him. 'D'ye mean tae tell me ye peyed ten shillings for a little dog?' he said.

During the years from 1927–1945 I had only about six different dogs through my hands, as we did not go in for more than one or two dogs apiece. In any case one had to have an exemption from licence for sheepdogs, exemption being granted for only two dogs over six months old to each shepherd.

Father and I did not breed our own pups, and seldom had a whelp to rear. The hinds' rows at Fogorig and Cortleferry, and in the middle of the village at Doddington, close beside neighbours, were not ideal places to rear pups, as they require a lot of freedom to run about when young. Outbye herds and inbye men who lived in houses by themselves, were better situated to breed and rear whelps.

When I was a young man someone once said to me, 'Herds are the maist miserable men on the face o the earth, they're aye lookin for what they dinna want tae see'. This was partly true of course, for we did spend a lot of time looking for trouble, but the job had its compensations, such as the open air life and a lack of monotony. For the ever-changing seasons brought their own different tasks, and fresh sights and sounds. Living close to nature one could not help being influenced by it. The weather ruled our lives to a great extent, and at an early age one absorbed the weather lore of one's elders, and soon learned to read for one's self the portents shown in the skies.

8

DROVING

Although the great days of droving had passed away with the advent of the railways, livestock had still to be shifted on the hoof. Until the development of road transport beginning in the 1920s, there was no other way of getting animals to the railhead, from one farm to another or from farm to market. Even when road transport became common in the inter war years, lorries were mainly used for the longer journeys where a railway was not available. Droving was a time-consuming business, for the average speed for driving sheep was a mile in a half hour, and for cattle about double that mileage. An old shepherd once remarked to me, 'If ye're bikin alang a road ye see a guid deal, if ye're walking ye see a lot mair, but if ye're following a drove o' a sheep there's no much that misses yer e'e'.

My earliest recollection of droving was watching the departure of father with a drove of sheep or lambs from Burnfoot to Kelso mart seven miles away. I would rise very early in the morning for the purpose of seeing him off. Both sheep and cattle were driven to the mart, except for very small numbers of fat sheep or lambs. It was more convenient to take these by horse and cart, as numbers below half a score were hard to keep together on a long journey. The cart used had temporary sides fixed on, and a hap over the top to prevent the animals from jumping out. A cart could accommodate half a dozen sheep, pigs or calves.

At Burnfoot we often saw shepherds out of the Kale and Bowmont valleys, going past with droves of sheep to and from the grass parks at Clifton Park. Grass parks have always played a part in the economy of Borders stock farming. They were let annually for grazing either by public roup or private bargain, for the period march to December. Farmers rented grass parks to gain additional grazing in summer and autumn, thus enabling them to keep more stock. In the case of the hill places just mentioned, the taking of grass parks was principally to get better grazing for the ewes with twin lambs, for which the ordinary hill ground was not adequate. A resident shepherd was provided to tend the stock at the parks, and this was a job often given to an elderly man, who would undertake estate work when the parks were empty. Clifton Park grazings were in Linton Parish and most of the farms in the parish, including Burnfoot, rented fields there.

It had been the custom for generations for the sheep from the Border valleys of Kale, Bowmont, Oxnam and College, to be sold at Rothbury mart at the other side of the Cheviots, a custom that was still going on when I was a boy. The hill men drove their sheep regularly across the Cheviot Hills, using well defined tracks and drove roads. They stopped overnight on the way at certain places in Upper Coquetdale, usually spending two nights on the road, Barrowburn, Quickening Cote and Harbottle were some of the stopping places. After the sale at Rothbury they walked all the way back home, getting food and a bed at some shepherd's house en route.

I remember a great annual adventure for me from the age of eight years was to accompany father to Kelso station on the Sunday morning that followed the Peebles ewe lambs sale. Mr Fraser always bought his Cheviot ewe lambs at Peebles which sale was on a Saturday. They were put on rail at Peebles after purchase and arrived at Kelso the following morning. Mr Fraser drove father and me in his car down to the station where we took the lambs off the waggon and drove them home. Both myself and the lambs were pretty footsore and thirsty ere we finished the journey, but for me it seemed well worth while.

From Roxburgh Newtown their sheep were mostly sent by rail to St Boswells mart some seven miles away, but sometimes Mr Bell would take it in his head to have them driven, especially the draft ewes. On some occasions father would have those to drive back home again, since the dealer who bought them would prevail on Mr Bell to take them back and keep them for another week or ten days. Dealers who bought ewes at St Boswells and other Border marts for resale at York a fortnight later used this dodge to get them kept in the interval. Farmers whose places were within handy driving distance – up to 8 miles – from a mart would agree to keep the ewes for a dealer who was a regular buyer. This was thought to be worth a shilling or two on the price of the sheep, or at least the help of a firm bidder at a future date. But the poor shepherd had to drive his ewes two ways in one day, and then back to the nearest station when the dealer required them. He would be lucky indeed should he get a tip for his pains.

I remember one year at Doddington, we were lumbered with fifty more ewes besides our own, brought back from Wooler mart, because our master had agreed to oblige a dealer.

One Saturday morning in 1924, when I was twelve years old, I got the job to help the byreman at Newtoun to fetch home a drove of cattle from Kirkton near Hawick. Mr Bell farmed Kirkton too, in partnership with his elder son, and he summered a good few cattle there, as it was a bigger place than Newtoun and more suited to cattle. The beasts were being brought to Newtoun in the autumn for fattening in the courts, and we were taken by car to Timpendean on the Kelso-Hawick road, where we met the Kirkton men and took over the drove. I was detailed to walk in front of the drove to steady them, and to guard any gaps or openings on the way. One had to wait at such spots until the cattle had passed, then hop over the hedge and run along the hedgeback to overtake them, clambering back on to the road in front of them once more, a fitting job for an agile boy. We brought the beasts home via Fairnington, and while passing a field on Rutherford Burnside land, the Burnside bull leapt the fence and joined our drove. At that time I had an almost paranoid fear

193

of bulls, so I was terrified and at a loss what to do. However the byreman managed to reassure me that the bull would not harm me, and after some delay we got it shed out and put back into its field.

It was a curious thing that when one was driving sheep along a road the sheep over the fence took little or no notice, but when cattle were being driven those in adjoining fields would come haring to the roadside, and would line up and stare at the drove, or scamper along the hedgeback uttering challenging moos and snorts.

Whilst we were at Fogorig we had a great deal of droving to do, as Mr Young rented grass parks in a big way, and had grazings all over the countryside. During our first summer there, he had most of the fields taken at Grindon, a very large farm down Norham way. This farm, which was wholly in grass then, was reputed to have had eighteen pairs of horses on it, and to have employed twenty women workers in its heyday of cultivation up till the end of the First World War. But the owner from then on had laid it down to grass and preferred to let the grazing.

We made several journeys to Grindon with sheep or were met halfway by the Grindon herds. One journey that stands out in my memory took place on the Saturday just after we had spained the ewes at Fogorig. We took a drove of ewes as far as Swinton, and I held them on the roadside on the Leitholm side of the village, while father proceeded along the village to meet the Grindon herd, who had brought a big drove of spained lambs from there to go to Fogorig. After the lambs had been counted past between the two men at the village green, father took charge of them and headed them up the Duns road, while the Grindon herd came and relieved me of the drove of ewes.

In the autumn of 1927 Mr Young had to vacate the fields at Grindon, for the farm was changing hands in November, and the new owner was not interested in letting the grass. We had to fetch the sheep stock belonging to Mr Young, all ewes, home to Fogorig. Father was taken to Swinton to meet them, and I remember he told me that on the homeward journey from Swinton, the ewes never stopped to graze or halted till they came to the first field gate on the Fogorig road. 'We've gotten hame', they seemed to say. Another group of fields Mr Young rented were at Fairnieside, near Burnmouth, which farm was also all in grass and let as parks by the owner. Fairnieside lay right on the coast, the fields stretching to the cliff tops. The first time I went here was to help dip the sheep. It was a foggy day, with a thick clammy haar on the coast, the foghorn on St Abbs Head nearby boomed incessantly, lending a sinister note to a gloomy scene.

Fairnieside was really too far away for sheep to be driven the whole way there, so they were sent by rail for part of the journey. A plan was evolved whereby sheep were trucked at Marchmont station for Chirnside station; we were taken by car to the latter station and took them off the train there, and drove them the five or six miles from Chirnside to Fairnieside. The process was repeated when they were fetched home; we went by car to Fairnieside, lifted the sheep there and drove them to Chirnside, where they were put on the train for Marchmont. Mr Young junior who did all the car driving met us at Chirnside and brought us home to Fogorig. Later that day we walked across to Marchmont and took the sheep off the train when it arrived. The object of all this palaver was to save the long drawn out and expensive journey by rail round by Reston Junction, to and from Burnmouth station, which was quite near to Fairnieside, but on the main line.

In connection with the Fairnieside saga, father once had an amusing experience at Chirnside, when droving through the village. It so happened that Mr Young had some hill farms in the Saline area of Fife. The Border Leicester rams off those places, numbering close on a couple of score, came to Fogorig to be wintered on turnips. In spring they were sent down to the grass at Fairnieside and father was duly given the job of driving them from Chirnside station. As he drove them up through the village one or two folk stopped to exchange a few words with him, making remarks such as, 'Yer yowes are looking raet weel', or 'Are ye taking them hame for the lambin?'

Now it was not every day that one saw a drove of Leicester tups on the road, and folk naturally assumed that being whitefaced and in quantity they must be ewes. Just after father had got clear of the village with his drove, he was accosted by a roadman who remarked, 'My, but ye've got a grand lot o yowes there!' Father could take no more of this so he said to the roadman, 'Ah could excuse thon toonfolk back there for no kennin better, but Ah'm surprised tae hear a *country* fella speakin like that. D'ye no see they're tups, man?'

Another incident on a poignant note, connected with the Fife farms, but not directly with droving had regard to a batch of Blackface feeding ewes we got from there. Feeding ewes are old sheep not in lamb, which are to be fattened for the market on turnips. Some of the ewes from Fife proved unexpectedly to be in lamb, due to some slip up on the part of the shepherds there. At the same time as some of them had lambs in the spring, others went missing and were found on different farms in the neighbourhood. True to the homing instinct of the Blackface sheep, they had broken out in an attempt to reach their home ground as their time to give birth drew near.

From Fogorig too sheep were sent to grass parks near Belford in Northumberland. Those were generally taken by train from Marchmont, but on more than one occasion they were driven to Little Swinton, where Mr Young also had two rented fields, and after resting overnight they were driven to Coldstream station and trucked there for Belford. I suppose the reason for this was that, going from Coldstream to Belford via Tweedmouth they could reach Belford on the same day, whereas in the journey from Marchmont to Belford via Reston, they would be in the waggon overnight.

One of the hardest drives we ever had was to take a drove of ewes with lambs about a month old from Little Swinton to Mindrum in Northumberland, a distance of eight or nine miles. The lambs were absolutely worn out by the time they got there, and it might have been kinder to have put them on the train at Coldstream for the station at Mindrum.

Mr Young had several fields at Leitholm for a couple of seasons, and as the fields were very small a drove of ewes and lambs had to be split up into batches of a dozen or so, depositing them in the various fields around the village. With all the droving we were called upon to do, we got to know the Berwickshire roads and lanes pretty well. We also knew the many openings where sheep could leave the road and get into a field, driveway or steading. Should work be going on in an arable field, it was a sign that open gates had to be looked for. Some of the roadside fields too were poorly fenced and the drove had to be on the alert lest a sheep dodge unseen through a gap.

At Fogorig we had little to do with the droving of cattle; that was usually done by the byreman, with the assistance of an orraman or a boy. Only on rare occasions was I called upon to go along. When we landed across the Border to herd, it was a different matter, for in Glendale all the cattle droving, except for fat beasts out of the cattle courts, was done by the shepherds. At Doddington however, we had much less droving to do, mainly from farm to mart or railway station, or maybe the very occasional drove of Irish beasts to fetch home off the train.

By the mid thirties motor traffic was growing thicker on the roads, and the driving of cattle especially could be something of an ordeal. Our home bred beasts reared as suckled calves were inclined to be wild, and should one break back when a drove was being manoeuvred past a motor vehicle, it was difficult to stop. Again, should a beast jump a fence into an adjoining field, the drover would be in a quandary, for he must needs leave the other beasts on the road while he recovered the stray, at times after it had mixed with other cattle. Irish cattle were not so hard to manage for they had become inured to handling during their journey from Ireland; moreover many of them had been reared on the pail on small family farms. The only Irish beasts I had any

A Shepherd Remembers

trouble with on the road was a batch of about thirty which I lifted one day at Wooler station. The minute I had got them out of the station yard and heading in the right direction along the road, they set off at a brisk trot, never halting until they reached an open part of a roadside ditch about a mile from the station, where they stopped to drink; they had been desperate for water. Luckily I had my bicycle with me and was able to keep contact with them and control them when traffic was encountered. Once their thirst had been assuaged they were quiet enough and ambled along at a steady walk, giving me no further trouble.

When driving either sheep or cattle it was handy to have a dog that would go in front of the drove, to steady them if they were inclined to move too fast, or to check them until a car was let past. There were not many dogs that would go in front, but one that would do so was looked upon as a great asset when on the road. Some dogs too were adept at locating and guarding an opening, when sent over the dyke or hedge and past the drove.

At certain times we did some droving between Doddington and Barmoor South Moor, which was then a led farm run in conjunction with North Doddington. The South Moor was wholly in grass, plus a large tract of heathery moor; it then carried a small sheep flock, and a large suckler herd. The lambs from the sheep flock, and the calves and cast cows from the herd were brought over to Doddington. For quite a few years it was the policy to wean the calves at home, and once they had quietened, to fetch them to Doddington. They were generally very wild and it was just as well that most of the way lay by Fenton Loaning, a fenced grassy track through Fenton Wood. The worst part of the drove was to get them across their home moor to the public road, and from there to the junction with the loaning near Roughting Linn, and at the Doddington end coping with the traffic on the main road and through the village. I was usually at the front of the drove, but sometimes we got hot skins when a calf or group of calves broke away from the main drove, and we had to run to help

198

the dogs to head them off. After a while a new shepherd came to the South Moor; he had the better idea of bringing the whole herd across to Doddington, weaning the calves there and driving the cows back home. There was some coming and going with sheep too between the two farms. I can remember once soon after spaining, we dipped a large batch of lambs, about fifteen score, one afternoon and father set off with them at dawn the following morning on the way to the South Moor. After delivering them he walked back, a round trip of eight miles and dipped sheep all day afterwards. Once the lambs had been a fortnight on the heather they were brought home, and the ewes were taken across for a few weeks. The spell on the heather was a splendid change for the ewes, and after they came to the clean pastures to be tupped we were assured of a good crop of lambs.

After Major Rea of Berrington took over North Doddington on the death of his father, there was quite a lot of traffic in livestock, principally cattle, between his two places. Berrington was a double herding too, a father and son, and it was usually the young herds who did any droving required. When I took a drove of cattle to Berrington I would be met by Willie Black, the young herd, and vice versa. We always brought our bikes with us on such occasions, for our respective shares of the journey would be at least four miles each way.

I remember once when fetching a drove home I had a frightening experience on the way. Traffic was scarce for it was fairly early on an Autumn morning, around seven thirty. Suddenly on an incline at Barmoor Red House, a large car came up behind me at a fair speed, ran straight past me and through amongst the cattle. The car was full of folk, a potato picking squad from Berwick on the way to work. Thinking the driver was trying to be smart, I shook my fist at the car in anger. The car halted a bit further on, and the driver got out and came back towards me. 'Oh gosh', I said to myself, 'he's ganna yoke on iz for shakin ma fist at 'um'. On the contrary the fellow was white in the face and badly shaken; he had come back to apologise for failing to stop, and to ascertain that the cattle were unhurt. His car brakes had momentarily failed on the incline and he had been unable to stop in time. Miraculously not one beast had been struck by the car.

We usually did our droving between farms as early in the morning as possible to avoid the traffic. Once I took a drove of cattle all the way to Berrington, landing there at eight o'clock in the morning. The kindly wife of the shepherd gave me a slap-up breakfast of ham and eggs. It was the done thing for herds' womenfolk to offer hospitality to anyone who came to lift or deliver droves of livestock. I remember one Sunday morning a drover from Berwick arrived with a bunch of stirks which had been bought at the market the previous day. He had his bike with him and a great big dog. We asked him into the house, where mother gave him a cup of coffee and a snack. Before he departed we were amused to see him bundle his huge dog into a bag, and strap it to the carrier of his bike.

For a few years Major Rea lent a couple of our grass fields to Mr Robinson of Tughall, Chathill, who then had the hill farm of Langleeford in the Cheviots. He put on some Irish cattle to graze, and sheep were brought down at intervals from the hill place. He also had a tenancy of Holburn Moor over the Belford way, and used the fields on North Dod-dington as a halfway house for keeping hill sheep overnight on their way from Langleeford, at such times as they were taken to Holburn Moor for a change. His shepherds fre-quently lodged with us for a night en route, to save them the journey from home next morning to pick up the sheep. In August they would fetch newly spained lambs, and in January separate hirsels of ewes in rotation from Langleeford Hope, to give them a change to the lower ground at Holburn.

The practice of changing hill sheep to lower ground was common then, and Mr Robinson was not the only hill farmer who rented low moorland for this purpose. I have been told that flockmasters in the upper reaches of Kale, Bowmont and other valleys where the hills were grassy, deemed it beneficial to their sheep to give them a spell on heather ground in

Droving

Rothbury Forest, the heathery moors surrounding Rothbury. They liked to spain the hill lambs on to low moor ground where possible. Going to church at Wooler by bus one Sunday morning in late July we encountered two herds from Cocklawfoot at the head of Bowmont Water, on their way back home after having left spained lambs at Roughtin Linn Moor. They had driven them down on the previous day and spent the night at Roughtin Linn. Men who had to stay overnight when droving always paid for their lodgings, recovering their expenses from their master afterhand.

The drove road and right of way to Ewart Parks from places on the east side of the river Till ran right through the North Doddington fields that lay beyond the river. Ewart Grass Parks had been in existence as such for many, many years before we went to Glendale, and are still being let at the present day. A fair amount of stock was driven to and from Ewart by the route mentioned. Most of the cattle were accompanied by men on horseback, which was a better way of controlling a herd, especially during the difficult drive through fields where cattle were grazing. Should I happen to be on the spot when a herd was going through, I lent help by holding back our cattle with my dogs until they got past.

Right up till 1940–41 driving stock to Wooler mart was no problem, and stock from Doddington, Nesbit, Fenton, Kimmerston and Wrangham were regularly driven there. But once the war was on the district was full of troops with their convoys of vehicles on the roads, which greatly added to the volume of traffic, and made it almost impossible to drive stock without having them unduly harassed. Although the farthest out of those places was no more than six miles from the mart, for the wellbeing of the animals, it was found to be better to have them transported by lorry.

Droving on the scale I have mentioned formed an integral part of the shepherds' work between the wars. But it was all done over and above one's regular job, for the sheep had to be looked morning and evening just the same.

Droving sheep was a slow tedious job and comparatively

easy in the days before motor traffic became excessive. If a sheep turned lame or ill it was usually pushed into someone's wayside fields, and recovered by cart the next day. No farmer would object to an animal being left from a passing drove provided he was informed about it. Much the same attitude was taken regarding cattle beasts. I can recall a complication which arose when a batch of Irish cattle were being driven to Doddington from Berwick, and the drover had to leave one which had gone lame somewhere on the way. Since Irish cattle were brought in under licence, the licence covering them had to accompany them to their destination, and the police notified of their arrival. They had then to be isolated from other cattle on the farm for fourteen days. When we notified the police of the arrival of this particular batch, we explained that one had had to be left at another place en route, but would be brought home by lorry the next day. In actual fact the drover had broken the law by leaving the beast at a place other than that designated on the licence, but the police agreed to overlook this under the circumstances, provided the beast was brought home as soon as possible.

At sales and markets the farmer was expected to pay a shepherd's expenses for at least the price of a meal. The sum given was usually half-a-crown or three shillings, but in those days a man could get a good meal out of that and a pint of beer forby.

9

THE SHEEP SALES

The sheep sales were always a highlight of the shepherd's year, for that was the time when the season's work was brought to fruition, more so on the breeding farms where the lamb crop was sold off as stores, to be finished off by those who bought them. On the farms where the lambs were all sold fat the special autumn sales were not so important, for the lambs were consigned to market numbers from June onward.

Before the general use of road transport there were many more auction marts in the borders than there are today. In my time I have seen the disappearance of marts at Kelso, Jedburgh, Duns, Cornhill and one of the two separate marts at Newtown St Boswells. Sales of both fat and store stock used to be held at all those centres, and in addition store lambs and ewes were sold at Belford, where sales are now confined to fat stock.

At the big store lamb sales featured at St Boswells, Hawick, Reston, Wooler etc. the lambs were sold in lots or pens of forty-five, fifty, ninety or a hundred, those numbers being based on the capacity of a railway waggon, eg medium (45 lambs), large (50 lambs); for although not all the lambs came to the sales by rail, nearly all of them left by rail after purchase. Farmers spoke of sending a waggon or a couple of waggons of lambs to such and such a sale.

The lamb sales started in the middle of July, and shepherds vied with each other as to who would have the best pens of lambs there, though of course much depended on the situation of the farm and the quality of its land. Another obvious factor was the quality of the sheep stock put in the shepherd's charge. No one could produce first class lambs from a second class stock. Unfortunately this latter consideration was sometimes overlooked when folk expressed their opinion on the various lots of lambs at a sale. If a lot was good the farmer got the credit, if it was middling the herd got the blame. The verdict of the pundits viewing a pen of lambs would run thus: 'The lambs off A- arena up tae much. He cannae be much o a hird that's yonder'. A favourite target for criticism was a farm that had once carried the palm for the quality of its lambs but was now on the slide. 'Aye they're missin auld Tam (a former shepherd) oure yonder at X; their lambs are no near as guid's they yased tae be'. No mention of the possibility that the flockmaster might be at fault.

At the first sale of lambs, those selected were usually sold straight off their mothers. This entailed a lot of work for the shepherd, for the lambs had to be drawn (selected), dressed and marked on the day before the sale, then returned to pasture with their dams. Early on the sale morning they were gathered, run off and fed in the field; then both ewes and lambs were brought into the faulds, and those for sale shed off, before being driven to the mart or the nearest railway station.

If two or more lots of lambs were being sold off the farm on the same day, one had to fetch in the sheep from more than one field, for it was only on the really big places that two pens of lambs might be drawn out of one field. A shedder was provided at the mart for those folk who had more than one lot of lambs to present for sale. The consignment from the farm could be divided up on the mart premises.

In the morning of the auction sales when I had sheep or lambs entered, I always experienced a feeling of excitement and anticipation. Yet they could be rather boring events if the sale was large and one's lot was far back in the catalogue. The catalogue or sale list was drawn by ballot and printed some days before the sale. At a very large sale, to be early on the ballot and sold near the beginning, or late in the ballot and sold near the end of the sale, could often mean getting a disappointing price, for the trade could swing up or down in the course of the day. One usually fared best in the middle of the catalogue.

In the early days of my herding career at Fogorig and Doddington, those were not store lamb producing places, the lambs being sold in the fat market for immediate slaughter. We would begin to sell in late May or June with the spring lambs, and it always made me sad to think of them going to be killed. Those lovely creatures one had lavished so much care on from birth seemed to be much more than mere animals. As I grew older of course I grew hardened to the situation, but through all my working life I never entirely overcame those qualms about sending the first of the season's lambs to slaughter. A short life and a merry one, I often reflected ruefully.

One of the most important lamb sales in the Borders, and of great interest to Border sheep men is the annual sale of Half Bred ewe lambs at St Boswells, on the first Saturday of August. This sale is now a mere shadow of its former self owing to the fall in demand for ewe lambs, consequent on the decline of Half Bred ewe stocks since the 1960s. Between the wars and for many years after the last war, this sale was the biggest in the country, attracting entries of twelve to fifteen thousand lambs each year.

In my earliest recollections of this event, there used to be a very strong Peeblesshire contingent among the lots, that county being then a veritable nursery for Half Bred sheep. A few years after the Great World War lambs from Kirkcudbrightshire made their appearance at St Boswells, and thenceforward they formed a large part of the lots catalogued. The advent and increase in numbers of those west country lambs, as we called them, may have contributed to the subsequent decline of the Peeblesshire entry over the years. Since St Boswells was the principal sale centre for Half Bred ewe lambs in Britain, buyers were attracted to it from all over the country, giving rise to the great popularity of Half Bred sheep in many parts of England.

A Shepherd Remembers

The draft ewe sales which took place in mid September were another source of the great interest, and important events in the sheepmen's calendar. Shepherds spent a lot of time trimming and preparing the ewes for the sales, this included blooming the ewes with soap and colouring in the same way as the lambs were treated. Some of the ewes would be bought by local farmers on low ground arable farms, where it was more convenient to keep a flying stock by buying in older ewes each year, instead of maintaining a permanent ewe flock of regular ages. The great majority of our Border draft ewes were, however, bought by dealers and farmers in the English counties of Yorkshire, Cumberland and Lancashire.

When the draft ewes were sold I always experienced a feeling of parting with old friends. At the sale itself one felt sorry for the poor beasts standing in the pens looking so bewildered, far removed from the familiar surroundings they had known for the past four or five years. I often pondered on what sort of home they would go to and whether they would be as well looked after as they had been by me. I was deeply moved at the draft ewes sale at St Boswells in September 1978, just a few months after I had retired from herding at Ladyrig. On approaching the pen where the ewes from Ladyrig were I recognised many of their faces, and when I spoke to them I could have sworn that they knew my voice, even though we had been parted since the month of May.

The farm displenishing sales which took place in the month of May, when farms happened to change hands, were important events in the rural scene. They drew large crowds of country folk, farmers and workers alike, some with the intention of buying, but most of them just as spectators. Should the outgoing tenant of a farm have been a while in the area, or be popular with his fellow farmers, his friends and neighbours bought items to help his sale, such as a few cattle, a work horse, a pen or two of sheep or some bits and pieces from among the implements. The result was that farm sales were generally dear places in which to buy. If the incoming

The Sheep Sales

tenant required to buy livestock and implements he usually had to pay sweetly for his purchases. The term 'farm roup' as applied to farm sales over much of Scotland, was not in use locally in the Borders, we just spoke of a 'ferm sale'. The official auctioneer's term was 'displenishing sale', the subjects sold being known as the 'plenishings' of the farm. Across the Border they used the curious term 'sale of live and dead farming stock'; the 'dead' part referred to the implements and other gear.

A lot of the work and organisation went into the farm sales. The implements, all newly furbished and painted, were displayed in lots in a field near the farm steading. Here too, were erected pens for the sheep with a temporary sale ring, and the ewes were shown in lots of ten and twenty with their lambs at foot. The cattle and the horses were sold in the farm yard, the latter all carefully groomed, and decked with ribbon on their manes and tails. With regard to the sheep, several neighbouring shepherds would be asked to come and help with the handling of the flock. The ewes and lambs were mothered off in batches in their respective fields, and driven in rotation to the pens where the auctioneer's staff numbered and penned them in the appropriate order of sale. Since all the sheep – ewes, hoggs and tups – had to be penned by ten o'clock in the forenoon, it meant an early start for the shepherd and his band of helpers. They were given breakfast in the farmhouse before gathering commenced, then lunch about noon before the sale of sheep at 1 o'clock. They were also allowed to drink at the seller's expense at the bar set up in the farm buildings by a firm of caterers hired in to provide refreshment for the crowd. At the day's end the helpers also received a sum of money at the going daily rate.

It was customary for the sheep to be returned to the fields after they were sold. From there they were lifted at the buyer's convenience sometime before the term day, being tended in the interim by the outgoing tenant's shepherd. The sale commenced in the forenoon with the implements, which included in some instances some household articles. After a break for lunch the sheep were sold, followed by the cattle and work horses.

Unless he was fetching all his own stock and plenishing from another farm, the incoming tenant was generally a prominent bidder. It could make a deal of difference to the sale were he not buying much. Should the shepherd be staying on at the farm with the new master, he often found himself with a good number of his old charges after the term. The same thing applied to the hinds with their horses, if they had been hired by the new tenant. In most cases, however, they would find that they had got a new pair to drive.

A certain number of farm sales took place every year, but in the early 1920s there was a spate of them, when more farms than was usual changed hands. This was due to some extent to the buy or quit policy operated by the lairds in the post-war period. They had become obliged to sell many of the farms on their estates to retrieve their declining fortunes, and gave the sitting tenants the option of buying their farms or quitting when the leases expired. Many tenants bought their farms, but there were others who would not or could not buy. Elderly tenants with no family to carry on into the future were faced with this dilemma, and one such was Mr Hogarth, the tenant of Linton Bankhead, who had occupied the farm and farmed it well for many years. I remember how outraged local opinion was when the laird presented him with a buy or quit ultimatum. The general view was that he ought to have been left undisturbed until his death or retiral. Some of the new owners and tenants of farms which changed hands in 1920 and 1921 lost a lot of money when prices slumped steeply toward the end of the latter year.

The first farm sale I ever attended was at Woodside, near Yetholm in 1920, when the Weir family went out of the farm and the Richardsons came in. Father took me there to see the well-known Cheviot flock disposed of; we walked the three or four miles from Burnfoot. Mr Weir had a small Border Leicester flock and bred Half Bred rams which he exhibited at shows and sales. I recall there was a single Half Bred ewe

The Sheep Sales

from the shepherd's pack with twin lambs at foot being sold, and father fancied it to add to his own pack. He tried to buy it but was outbid by Mr Bell the farmer of Primside, whom he approached after the sale, and managed to persuade to re-sell the ewes to him privately. The ewe was taken to Primside along with some other sheep that Mr Bell had bought, and was later delivered to father at the march by Willie Paterson the Primside shepherd, who incidentally was a great crony of father's. We there and then christened that sheep the 'Wudside yowe'.

Other farm sales I attended as a boy were Morebattle Mains in 1921, when the Smith family followed Mr Gownanlock into the farm, Kersknowe in 1922 when Captain Cowan from Shidlaw succeeded the Johnston family, and Linton Bankhead in 1924 when the Mitchells from the Tweedside area of Northumberland had bought the farm vacated by Mr Hogarth. Another sale held in 1921 was at Cherrytrees near Yetholm. Father went there to buy a young pig, walking all the way there and back from Burnfoot via Lochside. On the homeward journey he carried the piglet in a poke on his back.

Farm sales were occasions for drinking as there was always a refreshment bar set up in the steading. On occasions farmers and others imbibed too much and it was not unknown for fights to break out.

When we were herding in Glendale I was asked to assist at the farm sale at Nesbit in 1932, when Mr Logan was succeeded in the tenancy by Mr Robson from Crookhouse. I was one of the seven or eight shepherds from neighbouring farms taking part, three of us being under shepherds. It was usual for the young or second shepherds from double places to be sent to such events, the head shepherd stayed at home to see to the sheep, and came along later as a spectator. When a shepherd from a single hirsel was lent to help the farmer, steward or cattleman would give the sheep a look on that day. Another farm sale I helped at was West Weetwood in 1941, when the farm was vacated by Mr Mitchell, and the Turnbulls from Coupland moved in. The two shepherds there were Jock and Dod Wilson, two young single fellows who were special pals of mine. It was a bitterly cold day with squally showers of hail, for the day would usually be either nithering cold or pouring rain and sometimes a mixture of both.

The one supreme annual event for me was the Kelso Ram Sale, the Tup Fair as everyone called it, held on the second Friday of September. This event, the largest of its kind in the United Kingdom, aye, in the world, is still held at Kelso every year, and is now about twice the size it was between the wars. Since I was seven years old I have only missed it once, and in my schooldays I used to take a day off school to attend.

I remember vividly setting out with father in a farm cart, in the grey dawn of morning, on the way to my first Tup Fair. Needless to say I had been unable to sleep the night before, I had been so keyed up with excitement. He took the cart to fetch home any new tups that might be purchased. At the sale field the horse was unyoked, tied up loosely beside the cart and given some oats in a nosebag sometime during the day. The day turned out to be a very wet one, one of the wettest Tup Fairs ever known.

Sheltered in one of the tents for most of the time I did not really see much of the sale.

Out of the experience of that downpour came the idea to provide canvas roofs over the pens, that held the Border Leicester rams, paid for by the Breed Society. Other breed societies followed suit down through the years, so that today all but a few of the rams are penned under canvas.

At that time the Tup Fair was held in a field near the railway station, a site which had been used for generations. The rams from local breeders in the immediate neighbourhood were brought in on the sale morning by horse and cart, or more properly by a horse-drawn float which could hold about twenty rams; others a little further from Kelso came by rail. By rail too came large numbers of rams from other parts of the country, for two or three days before the sale. Those were housed and fed at nearby farms until the day of the sale, the main places where they were lodged being Spylaw, Wallace Neuk, Maisondieu, Ladyrig and Pinnaclehill. As one approached the sale site in the morning, one saw those rams coming in droves, attended by their respective shepherds, no dogs being used. One curious thing about the Tup Fair was that one never saw a dog, in direct contrast to all the other sales. The shepherds who looked after those rams from afar off found lodgings at the farms where their charges were, either with the shepherd there, or at a house in the row. Any flockmasters who accompanied their sheep stayed at the farmhouses or in the town of Kelso.

As the years passed the station field got built up with houses, so the Border Union Agricultural Society, under whose auspices the sale was held, changed the venue to Friars Haugh, where their summer show was held. I cannot remember the exact date when this move was made, but it certainly was sometime in the 1930s. Later the Society obtained Springwood Park, and ever since the show and Tup Fair have been staged there. By the time the Friars Haugh site came to be used, motor transport was available to ferry the rams in from their home places, from the railway station to the sale field, or from the farms at which they had been lodged.

Kelso district, situated as it was in the middle of sheep country, naturally became the home of many pedigree flocks producing rams of the various breeds. There are a host of places within a ten or twelve mile radius of the town, which have at one time or another sent rams to its famous Tup Fair. Many noted flockmasters in the area, both past and present, have attained the honour of topping the prices at the sale with their rams. Many noted shepherds too have shown their skill at bringing out the rams. When I was a youngster I cherished an ambition to turn out rams for Kelso sale. It was an ambition that I never achieved for I never had the luck to be in charge of a ram breeding flock. In any case by the time I reached manhood, I realised I had missed the chance of getting into what was really a specialised branch of shepherding.

Rams have always been consigned to Kelso from all over Britain; even in my young days they came from faraway places, and my youthful imagination was fired by the very romance of it. Oxford Down rams were sent from the Cotswold country, where the breed had its origins. A cluster of flocks was situated in the Fairford area, and others from near Oxford and from Wiltshire. Three large contingents came from places in Norfolk, and there was a large number of breeders in Co Durham, Cumberland and Yorkshire, as well as nearer home in Northumberland. Most of the Scots bred Oxford Downs were from the Borders and Lothians.

Suffolk Downs were sent from their home county and other parts of East Anglia. Ipswich was then the chief centre in Britain for sales of Suffolk sheep, but the Borders and other parts of Scotland were gaining ground as producers of rams of the breed, and since the war Scotland and the northern counties of England have completely eclipsed East Anglia as strongholds of the breed.

In the 1920s there were still a good few Half Bred rams exposed for sale at the Tup Fair, but their numbers dwindled year by year, until they were reduced to a mere couple or three pens, as more and more farmers came to prefer the first cross Half Bred ewes bred from Cheviot ewes, and Down rams for use in their flocks.

Hampshire Downs made their debut in 1924, under the auspices of their breed society, mostly coming out of Wiltshire, and have been brought to Kelso ever since, but their numbers have seldom exceeded a hundred in any given year. Other breeds which made an appearance at Kelso during the inter-war years were Lincoln Longwools, Kerry Hills from Wales, English Leicesters and Ryelands. None of those attained much popularity in the Borders as crossing sheep.

Though Oxford Down rams carried the palm for numbers at the Tup Fair, for many years right up till after the war Border Leicesters were always the main focus of attention, and invariably proved the top prices. In my earliest recollections of the sale, the number of Border Leicesters sold was usually around the thousand mark. They were sold in three rings and ring number 3 was the élite ring where the pick of the breed were on offer.

I was a great Border Leicester fan from boyhood upward, spending most of the day at Ring No 3, to watch the crack lots being sold. I well remember being at the ringside when the record price of £1100 was bid for a ram from the Mill of Marcus flock near Forfar. That was in the boom year of 1920, when prices for pedigree stock of all kinds were breaking former records, and I still remember the cheers from the onlookers when the auctioneer's hammer fell, for £1100 was an unheard of price for a ram at that time. The auctioneer was James Swan, the owner of the ram was Mr Alex Findlay, member of a noted family of Border Leicester breeders, and the buyer was Mr Cameron of Westside, Brechin, another well known breeder.

Some of the most famous Leicester flocks were in the Borders, notably that of Messrs Templeton, Sandyknowe, which topped the sale for several years in succession. Greenlawdean, Longcroft, Preston, Nisbet Hill, New Smailholm and Low Hedgeley were others which were often near the top. A group of crack lots came from the East Linton area of East Lothian, namely Deuchrie, Sunnyside, Papple and Phantassie. Another famous group of ram breeders who exhibited Border Leicesters were the Findlays from Angus: James at Craigeassie and Craigo, Alexander at Mill of Marcus and Hatton, and Harry at Myreton. Two long established flocks from Ayrshire which always did well, were that of Mr Cross of Knockdon and Mr Wallace, Auchenbrain, but the two oldest flocks which consigned Leicester rams at Kelso were Rock near Alnwick, and Spittal at Biggar. The former flock was the biggest consigner between the wars, sending a hundred rams regularly each year.

The shepherds in charge of the Border Leicester flocks near the top of the tree were no less renowned than the flockmasters, and though I only knew them by sight they were my boyhood heroes. Most of them remained in charge of the same flocks for many years and their names are worth recording. There was Wood at Deuchrie (I forget his first name), Wat Coltherd at Sunnyside, Eck Brown at Sandy-knowe and Wat Hall at Nisbet Hill, just to name a few.

Kelso Tup Fair was always unique, in that it was held in temporary premises in an open field, the rams being sold in separate rings according to breed, and by many different auctioneers. Those latter were commissioned by the sellers, and were drawn from all over the country. It was an education indeed to go round the sale ground, and listen to the different auctioneers, each with his own accent, gestures and form of patter.

When rams were bought for a farm, the shepherd accompanied his master round the sale, to share the responsibility of selecting them. In nine cases out of ten the flockmaster got his shepherd to help him to select rams for the flock and would often rely heavily on the shepherd's judgement.

Kelso Tup Fair is still going strong, and has greatly expanded in post-war years as regards the number of sheep sold, the variety of breeds presented for sale and the size of the crowd in attendance. There has always been a body in favour of scrapping the sale as an outdoor event, and holding it at Edinburgh, Lanark or some other auction mart centre, but such a move has always been opposed, on the grounds that it is a special day with an atmosphere all of its own. In 1966 because of an outbreak of foot and mouth disease, the sale was moved to the Highland Showground at Ingliston, near Edinburgh, but it was adjudged a dull affair with an air of unreality. A supplementary sale held later at Kelso after restrictions were lifted, for the benefit of those who could not get to Ingliston because of them, was really a wonderful event.

One great change I would like to mention regarding the ram sales of the present day is the large number of women and bairns to be found there. Between the wars it was almost entirely a man's day, with only a small sprinkling of ladies, but today it has become very much a social event and family outing.

In relation to sheep sales I have not mentioned any other Border marts save Kelso, St Boswells and Wooler, for between the wars my horizons were very limited, and those were the only marts I ever attended, though I was once at Cornhill with cattle. Any other marts I knew of only by hearsay, so they did not come within the range of my experience.

10

RURAL FROLICS

Before the advent of the Wages Board, which laid down statutory holidays for farm workers, the only holidays they got were specific days throughout the year. In the borders they were St James' Fair at Kelso, St Boswells' Fair on July 18, the agricultural shows and New Year's Day. The hiring fairs were allowed as days off, but only for those who were seeking a new situation. When I started work there were no half holiday on Saturdays, except for a few weeks during summer when the horses were at the grass.

For generations the St James' Fair at Kelso was a much looked forward to event in the rural calendar. The farm folk made their way to it from a wide area, some on bicycles and some in farm carts, before public transport became available. The fair was held in the Friars Haugh on the banks of the Tweed, the fairground being made more readily accessible for the townspeople of Kelso and others dwelling on the left bank of the river, by the erection of a temporary wooden bridge across from the Cobby. A small charge was levied for the use of the bridge.

Although it was held at Kelso, that town's dignitaries had no part in the proclamation of the fair. The right devolved upon the county town of Jedburgh, for it was the successor to the ancient county town of Roxburgh, under whose authority the fair had originally been held. The Jedburgh town crier proclaimed the opening of the fair, and listed all the rules and regulations governing it. I cannot recall the exact words of the full proclamation, but part of it ran as follows, 'In name and authority of the Provost and Baillies of the Royal Burgh of Jedburgh, and in name and authority of that High and Potent

Prince the Duke of Roxburghe . . .'. That last part always tickled me. Prince indeed! Surely that was stretching a point.

The main business of the fair centred on horse dealing, no other animals being up for sale. There were the usual booths, stalls and cheap jack vendors of crockery, textiles, watches and other trinkets. There were amusements on the fairground too, but the main roundabout, swingboats and such like were over in Kelso at the Knowes. There the young folk betook themselves in the evening, for further enjoyment after the fair was over. The chief horse dealer who brought strings of workhorses for sale was Mr Rush of Belmount near Eccles. Ponies were bought and sold by the many travelling people, or muggers, who congregated at the fair from different parts of the country. Both St James' Fair and St Boswells' Fair were traditional meeting places for them each year. One would see their carts and caravans strung out along the fairground, the camp fires surrounded by black haired sinister looking men and towsy headed women and bairns. I did not like the look of those folk when I was a boy, and had an uneasy feeling as I walked home through the line of tents and caravans. I suppose they were harmless enough though I did not realise that at the time.

My first visit to 'Jimses Fair' was from Roxburgh Newtown when I was eleven years old, for only then were we within easy walking distance from it. In subsequent years I cycled to it, both from Fogorig and Doddington.

Kelso's Fair of St James was discontinued many years ago, but the Border Union Agricultural Society's annual show, which used to be held on the same day in an adjacent field, is still going strong and is an event of some importance. This show, rather than the fair itself, was the main focus of interest for me and other farm men.

The show and the fair parted company sometime after the Second World War, because the date, August 5th, often clashed with the big annual ewe lamb sale at St Boswells, at which many of the show's exhibitors were also sellers of lambs. The date of the show was put forward to the last

A Shepherd Remembers

Saturday in July, and although the fair continued to be held for a few years after, interest and attendances fell away; the sale of horses ceased to take place since they were no longer required on the farms, or to draw the muggers' vehicles. Finally the proclamation ceremony was abandoned and the fair became just a memory.

From 1923 I attended the Border Union show regularly for many years, but after we removed to Glendale I did not get to it so often, for we were sometimes extra busy amongst the sheep on that particular week. Although there were good displays of cattle and Clydesdale horses, it was the sheep and the hunting horses that were of paramount interest. Though I never was an exhibitor myself there was always the excitement of finding out who the winners were. To get on to the prize list in such a strong display of sheep was counted no small honour by sheep men. I enjoyed the whole outing, not the least pleasant part being that of seeing kent faces, especially after we had left Scotland.

There was usually a pipe band in attendance at the show and, as I was very fond of bagpipe music, it was a delight to me to watch the band marching up and down and to listen to its strains. The various pipe tunes rang in my ears for days afterwards, among them such well known ones as 'The Barren Rocks of Aden' (familiar to us in parody as 'We're aa gawn tae the Tattie Field'), 'The KOSB'S Farewell to Meerut' and the 'Blue Bonnets'. A tune which particularly caught my fancy on one show day was 'The Glendaruel Highlanders'; for long that tune haunted me, but it was many years later ere I learned its title. That was told me by a pal of mine who went to be a soldier in the Argylls during the war. He explained that the tune was the march past of his battalion. Never a time when I hear any of the above pipe tunes played, but I am transported back to the Kelso shows of my youth. I see again the gay scene in the sunshine, the throng of folk round the pens of livestock and the industrial stands, the rows of Clydesdale horses on parade, bedecked with ribbons, shining harness and brasses, the country folk in holiday mood greeting each other in laughing, chattering groups, and maybe a bunch of young country chaps merry with beer, doing an impromptu dance beside the pipers.

In the period between the wars there were more local agricultural shows than there are now. Quite a few have disappeared but one that still survives, and of which I have many happy memories is the Yetholm Border Shepherds' Show. This show, held in the haugh at Yetholm on the first Saturday of October, is run by a committee of local shepherds and others, aided by folk from the village. The only animals shown are sheep, sheepdogs and terriers. The sheep consist of pack sheep, or others selected for show from their hirsels by the shepherds, and all are exhibited in the shepherds' names. In addition to the sheep, there is a sheepdog trial, a horticultural show, ladies' baking and needlework competitions, along with a programme of running and wrestling matches.

I remember clearly the first Yetholm show I attended in 1920, after it was revived following the Great War. I walked over with father from Burnfoot, and to me it was a never to be forgotten treat.

In the Borders we never referred to the hiring fair as 'feeing markets'; they were always called the 'hirins', and were held in various Border towns in the spring. As I pointed out in a previous chapter, hirings for shepherds and stewards were held earlier in the year, and were not such big events. The real hirings for the main body of farm workers were held in March. Earlston hirings, one of the most important, set the ball rolling on the last Monday of February, the rest following in quick succession during the fortnight after the first one. Each hiring catered for its own particular district, a relic of the days when folk were less mobile. The hinds tended to move around in certain orbits, a five or six mile radius of Kelso, Jedburgh, Hawick, Earlston and so on. The shepherds on the other hand, being fewer in number, would frequently take longer flits when they moved. My own family was a good example of this trend, for during his career father herded sheep in six different counties.

By the time I reached manhood the hirings were on the decline, as the local press played an ever increasing part in bringing employer and employed together through its columns of Situations Vacant. In the heyday of the hirings they were regarded with mixed feelings by farm workers. Some resented the idea of standing in the market place to be appraised by the farmers like so many cattle, but others accepted that custom dictated the need for this, as the only channel through which they could change jobs. The hirings also afforded them an opportunity to meet friends and cronies. For the young folk it was the chance of a night out, and enjoyment of the 'shows' which always accompanied the hirings.

To return to the subject of agricultural shows, from Doddington we went to the Glendale show at Wooler, and mother went along as well sometimes, if we could persuade her, for she was very much at stay-at-home person. Wooler show also had very strong sheep classes, with the prizes keenly contested for. It was held in a field behind the Cottage Hotel. The livestock pens etc. were at the top part of the field, and the horse sports and other afternoon events were conducted on the flat ground next to the auction mart, at the foot of a steep brae. This brae formed a marvellous natural grandstand from which to view the horse sports. The spectators either sat on the brae itself or stood along its top, all having an uninterrupted view of the proceedings. The last Wooler show I attended was held only a week before the outbreak of war. Like all other farm shows it was not held during the war years, and we had left the district ere it was resumed in the late 1940s.

Scotland's national farm show, the Royal Highland, used to be taken round the country, and held at a venue in a different district each year. There were eight separate districts which were visited in rotation. In 1926 after a lapse of twelve years since the show was at Hawick in 1914, it was again the turn of the Border district to play host to the 'Highland', and Kelso was chosen as the venue. The site was the Station Field where the ram sale was held annually, and the date was the last week in June.

I had never been to the Highland Show, but knew plenty about it, so I was fair cock-a-hoop at having the opportunity of seeing the Big Show on our own doorstep. Things were made easier by the fact that I was among the batch of senior schoolboys, chosen from various schools in the district, to act as runners from the judging rings and the secretary's tent on the opening day, and to sell catalogues and programmes on the ensuing three days. I thoroughly enjoyed the job, and after my stint of duty was over for the day, I had a good prowl round the stands and stock lines in the eventing, until it was time to catch a train back to Roxburgh. The weather on the first two days of the show was ideal, but following a hot sultry morning on the Thursday a violent thunderstorm broke in the afternoon, accompanied by a cloudburst. I had never before seen so much lightning nor such a downpour of rain and hailstones. Curiously enough that experience had the effect of sweeping away the dread of thunderstorms which I had harboured until then. It seemed to me, that having seen thunder and lightning at the very worst, I realised that there was nothing to be afraid of.

The storm played havoc with the progress of the show, for all the afternoon events had to be cancelled, trade stands and tents were flooded, and the whole evening was taken up with mopping up operations. However on the Friday, the last day of the show, the weather was kind again, and the show-yard, though muddy, was restored to normal. That was the day on which the show was visited by the Prince of Wales, later King Edward VIII. He stayed at Floors Castle as a guest of the Duke of Roxburghe, who was the Highland Show President for that year. A huge crowd of people turned out that day to get a glimpse of him, everyone saying how lucky it was that he had escaped the cloudburst of the previous day.

The next visit of the Highland Show to the Borders was in

1936, when it was staged at Melrose. A special excursion bus ran from Wooler, and father and I joined it. I have no special memories of that event, but I do recall that the Scots side of the Border was having a severe drought at the time, and all the pastures were brown and bare, in contrast to the greenery of Glendale.

In the year 1935 the Royal English Show came north to Newcastle in the course of its rounds of the country. We went to it on one of the days by a special train which was laid on from Coldstream station to Newcastle via Alnwick. Groups of country folk joined the train at every station en route as far as Alnwick. One or two of the local farmers, notably the Middleton Estates near Wooler, paid their workers' rail fare to the event. Not all of them sent to the show, as we gathered from the conversation of some farm lassies who came into our compartment on the return journey. They were from Middleton, and had used the free train journey to enjoy a day at the local metropolis.

In 1938 the Empire Exhibition was held at Bellahouston Park, Glasgow, and an excursion train was run from Alnwick and Berwick, a good crowd getting on at Wooler and other stations. My sister and I went with it and spent an enjoyable day. I remember we travelled across Glasgow by the Underground, a novel experience for most of us, but we found the noise deafening.

Our parents were strict teetotallers, therefore drink was never used in our home, and the evils of strong drink were dinned into us. Consequently we took no part in the New Year jollifications, first footing etc. though we did sit up to see the New Year in, drinking each other's health in homemade ginger wine. I followed father's footsteps in shunning strong drink for many years, though I did unbend a little through time, but I was thirty years of age before I ever entered a public house. Heavy drinking was not common among farm workers in my youth; some did get drink on Saturday nights, but that was only once a week, for folk just did not have the money to spend on drink. Women and girls of course never darkened the door of a public house.

New Year was the only time when hard drinking was indulged in, and some fellows who hardly touched a drop during the rest of the year would make fools of themselves on Hogmanay.

Weddings too were occasions for celebrations. When a girl from the row got married everyone on the place was invited. The ceremony was performed either at the kirk manse or in the bride's home, the best man and best maid acting as witnesses. The custom of being married in the house or at the manse was deep-seated among the farm worker community, and we never saw a church wedding until we crossed the Border and then only in the Church of England. The same applied to christening, all the bairns were christened at home before a gathering of friends and relations.

After the wedding ceremony there was usually a dance in the bride's home, in the nearest village hall, or quite often in the granary in the farm steading, kindly lent by the farmer. I remember my sister and I were invited along with our parents to a wedding at Roxburgh Newtown. The family involved had been lent the granary for the wedding supper and dance. It was a big affair for those days, with tea, plenty to eat and both soft and alcoholic drinks. Some of the guests ended up the worse for drink, and that was the first time that we youngsters had seen anyone in that state.

Some farmers were reluctant to allow such events within their farm buildings, for they were much afraid of fire from the careless use of cigarettes and matches by guests who had imbibed too freely. I have been told of one farmer who granted the use of his granary for a wedding, on the strict understanding that no smoking was to be allowed in the farm buildings. He happened to come across some chaps smoking in the course of the evening, so he put a stop to the celebrations there and then, and cleared everyone out of the steading. This was a drastic step and naturally caused some resentment, but with the buildings full of grain, straw, cattle and

A Shepherd Remembers

horses, could one really blame him for his action? I imagine some of the ill feeling would fasten on the culprits who had 'spoiled things for other folk'. How often that phrase cropped up in local parlance, with regard to the abuse of some concession or privilege by certain persons, which led to such concessions by an employer being withdrawn. A striking example was of a large farmer, the owner-occupier of his farm, who gave his workers leave to enter the woodlands and help themselves to fallen trees and dead branches, until someone went secretly to fell and carry out small live trees. The offender was caught and sacked, but from then on access to the woods was forbidden to the rest of the workers.

Many border farmers gave a kirn or harvest home to their employees. The kirn was held in the granary or loft, which was gaily decorated for the occasion, hung round with streamers and lighted with a row of hurricane lamps slung from the rafters. All the workers and their families were invited, and each worker was allowed to bring along a couple of friends. The evening started with a supper, followed by all-night dancing to the music of two or three fiddlers. Beer and lemonade were provided in the way of refreshment. Dancing was carried on till three or four o'clock in the morning, and the next day was proclaimed a holiday.

At the dance the proceedings started with the Grand March followed by the dance called Triumph, led off by the farmer himself with the steward's wife for partner. They were followed by the steward partnering the farmer's wife, the shepherd came next with the farmer's daughter, then the farmer's son and the shepherd's wife. The programme was a hefty one and included set dances like the Lancers, the Quadrilles, the Eightsome Reel, Circassian Circle, Drops o' Brandy, Petronella, Corn Rigs etc. interspersed with various types of waltzes and the polka. Foxtrots and other newer dances were introduced sparingly.

Later in the evening the farmer would make a speech thanking the workers for their efforts during the year, and the steward would reply in suitable terms, thanking the 'maister an mistress' on behalf of the workers, for the very fine kirn they had given. On Border farms the farmer's spouse was always referred to as the 'mistress'. Songs and recitations were rendered at intervals between dances. Some of the items would be humorous, some slightly ribald but not outrageously so. Favourite songs were the 'Lea Rig', 'When you and I were young Maggie' and others with a Scots flavour. Popular songs were sung too; I remember one girl sang 'Peggy O'Neil' and right well she did it too. Some of the young men, after much prodding and prompting, would stand up and launch into a song, only to flounder after a verse or two, either because of stage fright or because they had forgotten the words and had to sit down amid a chorus of laughter and jeers.

Emigrant songs of the nostalgic type were still very popular with the farm folk in my youth, for there were few families who did not have relatives 'far owre the sea'. At kirns ditties like 'There's a wee bit land far across the sea', 'Scotland ever braw', and 'Rolling home to bonnie Scotland' were sung with feeling and gusto.

Most of the relatives of farm workers who had emigrated were engaged in farming in Canada or Australia. What a sense of freedom they must have felt, those emigrants of the nineteenth and early twentieth centuries, having their own land, doing their own thing and working for themselves, free from the tyranny of farmer employers and in the case of small farmers who had emigrated to better themselves, free from the petty restrictions imposed by lairds. The privations, the heartache and homesickness, that many of them suffered ere they got their feet in the new land, seem eminently worthwhile. Our own father had three brothers and two uncles who went out to Saskatchewan, the former in 1912 and the latter in 1890s.

I can still recall at least one kirn I attended at Burnfoot, and one at Roxburgh Newtown. At the latter event my young sister and I, fresh from our dancing classes, were eager to try out our steps, but alas we soon found ourselves out of our

225

depths in no time, discovering that the sedate atmosphere of the dancing school was a far cry from the exuberance of the kirn.

Since kirns were fairly common events; in late autumn some of the young folk would, by invitation, get the chance to enjoy more than one during the season. The farmers too would have their own party of invited guests at their kirns, and for once those would mix freely with the ordinary folk.

Two occasions which afforded us a deal of fun and entertainment before the war, were the celebrations to mark King George V's silver jubilee in 1935, and the coronation of King George VI in 1937. Both functions fell in the month of May and were the subject of concerts, dances, feasts and bonfires in all the towns and villages. At the jubilee celebrations I attended three all-night dances in one week.

I was very fond of dancing and thoroughly enjoyed myself whenever there was a good mixed programme of old fashioned and modern dances. By modern I mean of course quick steps, fox trots, slow waltzes, tangos and the like. When it came to the set dances we country chaps would doff our jackets, roll up our shirt sleeves and wade into the Lancers, Eightsome Reel, Drops o' Brandy, Spanish Waltz and so forth, hoochin with enthusiasm. The girls were lively, leaping about like mad things, skirlin and clapping. To those unused to such rustic spectacles our antics must have seemed odd, to say the least. One lad from southern England, who was footman in the big house, was amazed at the exhibition of 'tribal dancing' as he termed it, when he was at a dance in our village hall at Doddington. The more sedate 'modern' dances gave us a breather in between hectic country numbers.

At the village dances the girls all sat on one side of the room, and the lads on the opposite side. When the Master of Ceremonies called out the dance, and the band struck up, one had to nip across the floor at speed, if the dance a popular one, to lift the girl of one's choice before someone else got her. It was considered bad manners on a girl's part to get up to dance with someone else after she had already refused a fellow the dance. If she refused to dance with the first person who asked her, she was expected to sit out that dance, which was really rather unfair. There were other small points of etiquette which were sometimes breached, such as the fellows who danced the local girls at the beginning of the evening, only to ignore them completely when the more glamorous birds from farther afield arrived on the scene later. For the set dance it was the Master of Ceremonies' duty to get the sets arranged, exhorting fellows still seated or standing around to get hold of a partner to complete a set where it was necessary. At our late night dances which went on from 8 pm till two in the morning, a buffet supper would be laid on at a small charge per head. Lemonade was on sale, also, but there never was a bar at dances, not even at events in towns such as Kelso and Wooler. Alcohol was banned inside most halls, but chaps used to plunk bottles outside and run out and in all night for a swig of beer or whisky. Admission to late night dances was usually eighteen pence (7½p) for men and a shilling (5p) for ladies. A whist drive followed by a dance would cost half-a-crown (12½p), and for the dance alone one and six and a shilling. A Saturday night dance from 8 till 11.30 pm cost a shilling or sometimes it was just a sixpenny hop.

Young folk cycled long distances to and from dances, though in the late 1930s it became common for a few to club together and hire a taxi for the journey. Men with motor bikes were at a tactical advantage for bringing girls to dances or taking them home. Should a fellow just have a push bike it meant walking the girl home if she lived near the dance hall, or if she was cycling, accompanying her home maybe for several miles in the opposite direction from one's own route home.

It was really great to cycle to a dance on an autumn or winter evening, little heed being taken of the state of the weather, one was so primed for excitement and anticipation. If it were stormy our elders would shake their heads and say that we were daft to brave the elements. They forgot, of course, that they had done exactly the same when they were young. It did seem daft cycling home in the small hours, the shirt sticking to one's back with sweat, and one's eyes heavy with lack of sleep, but it always seemed worth it. It did not deter us either that we had to go to work at seven that same day.

Between the wars it was customary for both lads and lassies to carry their dancing shoes with them to the dances. The roads were generally pretty muddy in the dark months, and heavier footwear was necessary for travelling. The use of dancing pumps made for cleaner and lighter feet on the dance floor; the floor itself was carefully swept ere dancing commenced, and soap flakes or some brand of floor dressing sprinkled on to make it slippy.

I conclude this chapter with two true stories about travel to and from dances. The first concerns a chap who owned a motorbike, on which he took a girl he fancied to a dance some miles away. Having got there the girl chose to ignore him and danced with other lads all night. Greatly disgruntled by this, her escort left her to walk home after the dance was over. My second tale is of a chap who went to a dance about twelve miles distant with a taxi party. At the end of the dance he was nowhere to be found, and after waiting some considerable time without him turning up, the other members of the party went off without him. The bold boy had been seeing a girl home and when he returned to the dance hall he found the taxi and his companions gone, and he was left with no alternative but to hoof it home twelve weary miles.

11

THE FARM WORKERS

When I was young everyone took it for granted that the farm workers should live on the farm, either in the hinds' row, or in the case of the steward and shepherd in two semi-detached houses or in a house by themselves. The house was free and went with the job, also a garden, a pig stye and a stall for the cow in the workers' byre. From the time that the layout of the farms had been planned during the 'improvements' period, roughly 1780–1820, in which the old runrig system was swept away and individual farms established, no other system of housing workers would have been convenient, given the scattered nature of the farmsteads on both sides of the Border. Even in those instances where the farmsteads formed part of a village the farm cottages were tied to the farm.

Yearly engagements were the order of the day, the renewal of the yearly bargain was called 'speakin time', which took place about a week before the first hiring fairs, which were held in the first week of March. In the case of the shepherds and stewards who were hired earlier in the year, it was customary for them to be 'spoken to', and a new bargain struck in the middle of December. The man would be asked if he intended to stay for another year, or would be told that the farmer wanted a change. Farmers mostly set a great deal of store on those two key men, and would not part with them lightly, but when either party wanted a change it was usually accepted amicably. In some cases there was a tacit understanding between a shepherd or steward and his employer that, whichever of them wanted a change, the one would intimate his intention to the other. This was called a 'first tired tells' agreement, and was fairly common between farmers and their key men.

There were certain employers, when wishing to be rid of a herd or steward, who would not have the decency to tell the man to his face, but would send him a letter to tell him that his services would not be required after the May term, or, worse still, would put an advert in the local press for a herd or steward, leaving the person concerned to draw his own conclusions. A neighbour herd of ours, who had been twelve years with his employer, and had had no quarrel with him, was treated in this manner. He had no inkling that he had been sacked until he saw his place advertised in the morning paper and was absolutely stunned. The under shepherd, a single man, was served in the same fashion. The farmer's excuse was that the two herds, head and second man, had not been pulling too well together, and he wished to replace them with a father and son. He could of course have told both men openly that he wanted to change and why.

The 'speakin time' for hinds and other workers was on a different basis. Those who were to be given the chance to renew their bargain for another year were summoned to the farmhouse one after another on a set evening, and interviewed there by the farmer and his steward. If a bargain was struck they were 'bidin on' after the May term, but if not they were 'leavin'. It often happened that workers whom a farmer would have been willing to hire again had no intention of staying on. This fact they would indicate by not answering the summons to the 'big house' to be 'spoken to'. In some instances, where really good workers were concerned, the steward would be told by his employer to approach them and try to persuade them to change their minds. Such cases, however, were extremely rare in those days of a plentiful labour supply.

Those workers not summoned to the farmhouse to be 'spoken to' were more or less sacked, though of course they worked on till the May term, fulfilling what remained of their current bargain. Such persons might have no idea that they were not wanted until they found out next day that their neighbours had been 'spoken to' the previous night and were 'bidin on'. It was a crude underhand way of concluding affairs, but was generally accepted as normal practice. The unwanted householder then hired him to the hiring to try his luck elsewhere. In many cases of course the person thus dismissed would have known what was coming, for they would have differed with the steward or farmer sometimes during the past year. Causes for sacking varied: unsatisfactory work, insubordination, being a troublemaker by speaking out about grievances relating to working conditions, housing etc. are examples. If a man expressed himself too plainly in criticism of farmer or steward to his fellow workers, there was always a sneak amongst them, ready and willing to carry tales about him to headquarters.

There was a widespread belief among outsiders that farm workers in the old days kept shifting around year by year and moved from farm to farm in an aimless sort of drift. This was not entirely true, for the majority of workers did not flit any oftener than they could help. Certainly folk were always looking for a chance to better themselves either financially or in relation to housing, and if that meant flitting, well that was that. The majority of moves were made for family reasons, since members of a family were hired together under the same contract. A move could be caused by a son or daughter marrying and leaving home, school leavers needing jobs, or youngsters seeking promotion as they grew older.

There was of course a minority who were semi-nomads and who flitted regularly every year. Among those were the lazy and shiftless who could not hold down a job; the hasty tempered who found it difficult to get on with people, and who were ever ready to take offence at a real or fancied slight; the proud independent spirits ever in search of El Dorado, which was impossible to find, for everywhere one went there would be a 'bubbly jock at the door', i.e. a snag of some sort. One byreman, a real good worker, confessed to my parents that he had flitted every year as regularly as the clock, since he had married and set up house. He just could not settle long in the one place. One side effect of such continual flitting was the disruption of the bairns' schooling.

In contrast to the annual flitters there were families who stayed at the same farm for many years, sometimes for generations. The reason for this was a real fondness for the place, coupled with a good master and working conditions. Amongst all the turmoil of workers moving around there stood out a solid core of those who earned medals for long service of thirty years and upwards. It must be said too that juveniles from such families acquired priority over others regarding vacancies and promotions among the staff, other families having to shift to make way for them over the years. A certain amount of cynical comment was sometimes directed by other workers anent those 'established' families. One heard such snide remarks as, 'Oh, thaim, they're a pairt o the lease!' or 'Farmers come and farmers go but they go on for ever!' The latter saying was literally true for some folk served under a succession of farmers at the same place.

For as long as the yearly engagements were in vogue it was a very rare thing for anyone to flit between the terms. On the worker's side he would grin and bear a lot rather than put himself and his family at risk of breaking his bargain, although a man I know only stayed a month at his new situation, so disgusted was he by certain conditions he found there. When asked by the steward why he had broken his bargain he said, 'If Ah'd kent it was ganna be like this, Ah'd nivver hae been here'. Another example was a shepherd who had a violent quarrel with the boss halfway through the year and walked out. One big snag for such folk was getting a house somewhere, and surviving on casual work for the rest of the year. On the employer's part only a very serious offence would justify summary dismissal, perhaps a case of assault or flagrant theft. I can only recall one instance in which a householder had to leave a farm where I lived, between terms. That was a man who was jailed for indecent offences against schoolgirls, his wife and child having to quit the house. Should a worker be dismissed between terms he could, under certain circumstances, sue his employer in a court of law for what was called wrongous dismissal. I have no personal knowledge of such cases, but they did appear in the newspapers from time to time.

During a working life spent on farms I never came across an instance, except the one mentioned above, of a family being put out on the road from a tied house. Even in the case of the death or chronic illness of a worker, he or his dependants were usually allowed to occupy the house until the May term, the farmer meantime filling the job with whoever he could get hold of, and doing his best to get alternative accommodation for those he'd have to move.

The population of the farms between the wars was almost wholly indigenous, natives of the Borders, whose forefathers had been there for generations back. There were of course families of incomers like our parents, but those too were bona fide farm folk, bred from generations of such in their home area. The position today is much different for all sorts and conditions of folk inhabit farm cottages. Many farm employees are outsiders from far away places, some of them without roots in agriculture at all. The native Border farm workers were descended from those who tilled the land here from time immemorial. We often hear it said of some laird or farmer that he belongs to an old and noted family. But what of us, the workers? Are not our roots as deeply sunk in the land, as those of the folk who lord it over us? History tells of the exploits of the improving lairds and their farming tenants of yore, who changed the whole aspect of our Scots landscape. But what would have become of their plans without the toil and sweat of the 'lower classes' as they were pleased to call them? I maintain that the farm folk are the lineal descendants of the cottars, portioners, aye and bonnet lairds, who were displaced by the Agricultural Revolution and turned into landless labourers. Was their role in agriculture any less vital down through the years because of that?

The atmosphere on the farm towns was generally good,

and the folk lived together peaceably enough for most of the time, though there were occasional squabbles and intrigues. Friction was generally more marked on the larger farms, where cliques formed among the households in the big hinds' rows. At times genuine friendships would develop between folk living next door to each other, friendships that lasted for years, after the parties had become separated having left the particular place where they met each other. Again, a couple of families would get awful 'thick wi other' on a more superficial basis, and they would be constantly in and out of each others' houses, prying deeply into each others' concerns. This state of affairs was viewed with scepticism by the other neighbours, who would observe, 'Aye, thur awfu thrang the noo, but there'll be a big stink when the pattie brecks.' Meaning, that when they fell out the quarrel would be all the more bitter.

Dominant personalities were found among the housewives in many a hinds' row – women who sought to involve themselves in the affairs of their neighbours if given a chance to do so. Inevitably if other stouter types resented their interference, clashes and ill feeling arose. In extreme cases men have been shown the road at the term, solely because their wives were troublemakers. 'I must have peace in the camp', was the maxim of one farmer, who had been plagued with rows on the doors, and had had to take the above drastic action.

A common cause of friction amongst farm staff was the charge of favouritism, either real or imaginary, levelled against the steward. This person had to be very careful not to show partiality in his dealings with the workers, for it gave rise to jealousy if he favoured one more than the other. Most stewards had wit enough to avoid such pitfalls, but as they were only human and had their likes and dislikes, cases arose in which a steward got his 'horns into' some particular worker or family and took an 'ill will at them'. When that happened that person or family's days at the farm were numbered, and 'their name would be Walker come the term'.

The Farm Workers

It was no use for them to appeal to the farmer, for few of those would go over the steward's head and have dealings directly with the workers. The steward had full authority and it was up to him to exercise that fairly. The farmer did not care as long as the work was going well.

Shepherds and their womenfolk led a life slightly apart from the rest, more especially if their house was not in the row, which frequently happened. I remember our mother was a bit apprehensive about going to live in the big row of cottages at Fogorig, after many years of living in a semi-detached house. She expressed her fears to a friend, who advised her, 'Jist keep tae yersell and keep yer een open, an yer bound tae see somebody worth making freends wi', and so it turned out.

There was always much speculation about any new families who might be moving into a place at the term. 'D'ye ken whase comin in tae Broon's hoose?' one would say to another after the hirings were past, 'Weel, it's the Scotts frae Upperton Mains, oo neebur't thum at Littleton Rig a wheen year back'. It was seldom that the newcomers would be strangers to all the folk in the row, and no matter where one went there was someone who knew you or knew about you. When I was at school there was always a sprinkling of new bairns after the May term, and some kent faces would disappear.

When we arrived at a new situation, we were generally accosted by at least one new neighbour, who proceeded to give us a thumbnail sketch of everybody else on the place. We never took much notice of this, but just made everyone alike, and took folk as we found them. It was not always the gushy forritsome ones who made the best neighbours ultimately.

I remember when we lived at Doddington a certain new family were hired to come at the term, whose reputation went before them. They got the name of being tarry-fingered, and we were advised before the term by those who already knew them, to keep all our belongings under lock and key. On the strength of this advice, father even went to the trouble of buying padlocks for the doors of our outhouses, a thing we had never had up till then. When the new folk came, however, he just had not the heart to fix the padlocks, as it seemed to him a mean sort of thing not to trust one's neighbours. The new family proved to be quite decent neighbours, and we never had anything go missing while they were beside us.

All the same it would be idle to pretend that there was not a light-fingered minority among farm folk. A lot depended on the character of a place and the class of folk who were hired to it. Some had no scruples about pilfering from their neighbours in a sly way hard to prove. Our own trust in neighbours was severely tested after we moved from Doddington, and we felt the need for padlocks and keys. Suspected offenders against neighbours were sent to Coventry when discovered. Stealing from the steading was not unknown either; the main acts were the appropriation of small tools or other articles from the farm, or filching food from the barn for the pig or cow, and for hens. When caught red-handed the thief could be dismissed on the spot, though he was more likely to be ordered to leave at the term under a cloud.

Although all was not sweetness and light among farm workers' families all the time, there was a strong sense of neighbourliness, almost a community spirit one might say. Everybody stuck in and lent a hand at pig killings, firewood carting and other such jobs that required communal effort. In times of trouble and sickness they would stand by each other. It was a different story, though, to get folk to stick together to air a grievance they had against the farmer. Many a bold wight who tried to organise a protest about some grievance found himself holding the baby when it came to the crunch, the fear of the term and the master having proved too strong for the rest. For example on a certain farm there was a strong feeling among the workers that their cows were not getting proper treatment in winter time. It was agreed to air this grievance to the master, the shepherd agreeing to act as spokesman. When he put their case to the master, the latter was greatly displeased and denied their allegations. He straightway went and tackled the other men on the subject. They reneged on their stand, and weakly conceded that the cows were not being unfairly treated after all. The poor shepherd found himself the 'bad yin', and though he was not asked to leave, he was so disgusted with the other men that he quitted at the term.

We were all more or less on the same level as regards our standard of living. There was little evidence of the 'Joneses' mentality, for none of us possessed a great deal of this world's goods, and to be clean, tidy and neighbourly was enough. Indeed anyone who put on airs was quickly cut down to size. 'Aye, she'd fain be up, if her backside wad let her', would be said of a wife, who thought herself better than anyone else. On the other hand, such attitudes could be positively stifling for any who was, or tried to be different, for they were at once suspected of uppishness. Women, especially, who through marriage came from another background to live in a hinds' row, found the atmosphere hard to thole until they became inured to it.

Certainly all the folk were not alike in character. There were the well doing and thrifty who were in the majority, and the shiftless or what we now call 'problem families'. The latter tended to be found at the less desirable places, where the houses were inferior or the farmer had the reputation of being a bad master. Such farms were well known and were shunned where possible by the general run of workers. Farmers who advertised their situations in the farming papers, rather than in the local Border newspapers, where they were too well known, came into this category. Many a family from outside the district first arrived in the Borders to work for these problem farmers, but once they had had their eyes opened they soon left for something better. Those unfortunate local men, who, because of poor health, lack of skill or bad social habits, had difficulty in finding a job, had perforce to hire themselves to such farms.

Wages were very low between the wars and living was not

easy for folk with young families. It was amazing how the majority of households managed to feed and clothe their bairns and keep them respectable. The garden produce was a help, and all farm men cultivated their gardens well, for it was looked upon as an affront to have an untidy or neglected garden. Each garden was allowed a load of muck from the cattle courts, which helped to maintain the humus content. In addition most workers managed to come by some of the artificial manure used in the fields. The crops grown were pretty varied, but on traditional lines such as potatoes, onions, leeks, shallots, peas, cabbage, cauliflower, brussels sprouts, curly greens and turnips. A few of the more enterprising grew various other items such as parsnips, radishes, broad beans and runner beans. Carrots were seldom grown owing to the prevalence of pests, and it was not till derris dust, DDT and other insecticides were introduced after the war that they could be grown satisfactorily.

Casual workers who for some reason or another could not bind themselves to regular employment, were not too well off. They could maybe get plenty of seasonal work where competition was not too keen, but there were inevitable gaps between seasons when they had to be idle. Their seasonal jobs were turnip singling in June, followed by haymaking in July, and then harvest from August till October. In October, too, there was the potato lifting which was only important on a few farms in the Borders for, prior to the war, large acreages of potatoes were not grown in the area. The late autumn and winter provided a fair amount of work at threshings and the shawing of root crops. From New Year till June casual labour was not much needed for the regular staffs could mostly cope.

The pigs kept by nearly every household were a valuable source of food, and made for a 'rough hoose', where there was a family to be fed. The trouble was that there tended to be a glut of meat and by-products at the time when the pig was killed and for two or three weeks after. There were collops and liver for frying, spare ribs for roasting, mealie puddings, black puddings, potted head, sausages and so forth, but in the absence of a freezer such items had to be consumed within a certain time. The cured hams certainly were a long term insurance of food for the family, and their presence suspended from hooks on the ceiling was regarded as a very fine picture to adorn a cottage! The pig fat rendered into lard was another valuable asset.

The pigs were put in as weaners and bought at the local auction mart or privately from some local farm where brood sows were kept. From the latter, word would get round when young pigs were ready to lift. Some workers' wives went to the mart to buy a young pig since their husbands could not always get time off to go. If the shepherd or byreman was at the market with fatstock, he would be asked to buy a pig for a neighbour and fetch it home. Everyone kept at least one pig at a time, and some families had two killed in a season. The killing season extended from October till April, for the successful curing of hams outside that period was regarded as tricky. ·As I have already pointed out the slaughter and cutting up of the pig was regarded as a job for the shepherd, and it was only seldom that a butcher was employed. In some parts of rural England a person called the pig killer went around doing the job, but I never heard of any such operating in the Border country. Father was a very good pig killer, but I did not relish the job and never attempted to learn it, although I was always on the spot with the other men to lend a hand.

On the pig killing day the neighbours helped each other, the menfolk with the actual deed, and the womenfolk boiled water for each other to scald the carcase, and enable the hair to be scraped off. They filled their big iron washing pots, which were hung over the fire on washing days, and boiled them for this other occasion. The pig was killed, scraped, hung up and disembowelled during the dinner hour. To hang up the carcase a tripod called 'the shear legs' was used complete with pulley, and where a tripod was not available the pig would be suspended from a long ladder leant against the gable end of the house. After the job was done the men helping were given refreshment by whoever the pig belonged to, before departing to the stable for yoking time. This took the form of a glass of whisky before the operation, to steady their nerves. In the afternoon the women would help one another with the 'reddin o', i.e. the sorting out and cleaning of the entrails, for use in the making of mealie puddings and sausages. In the evening once the pig's carcase had cooled sufficiently it was carried into the house and cut up on the kitchen table. The head and trotters were put by to make potted head, spare ribs were cut up into handy sized pieces for roasting, or as 'tilies' for those who had helped. The head was singed with a red hot poker to remove any stray hairs, cut open and thoroughly cleaned before being boiled to make the delicious and much prized 'pottit heid'. The trotters were also singed and boiled along with the head, but some people ate them by themselves as a delicacy.

The farm women took a great pride in their pigs, and fed them three times daily on a mixture of boiled chat potatoes and barley meal. A by-product of the milled barley, called 'barley dust' or 'pig's dust' was much favoured. It was a common sight to see the potfuls of pigs' potatoes sitting outside the doors to cool. As bairns we often slyly pinched a potato when no one was looking. Household scraps went into the pig's trough as well, 'It's no lost what a freend gets', was a humorous remark often made when leavings from the table were consigned to the pig's pail. As an occasional variation of diet, green garden produce, sods of grass and such like were thrown into the stye, and our mother used to pull nettles and scald them to stir into the pig's food There was a tendency to feed pigs too fat, for it was generally referred to as the 'soo', even when it happened to be a hog pig; another Border name for the pig was the 'guffy', a form of grumphy. Our pigs did not 'grunt', they grumphed.

The 'soo craves', as we called the pig sties, were stone built in a row, generally a short distance from the cottages, and were a favourite rendezvous for the wives to meet and have a blether, at the same time comparing the progress of each other's pigs.

Sometimes pigs took ill, a very serious event for a household. The main ailments were stomach troubles and 'soo measles'. The latter disease sometimes proved fatal, but when a pig recovered, its skin would slough off in patches. In hot weather sunburn could harm the pig, and a canopy of sorts was put over the outside part of the stye as a preventative. The vet was seldom called in to deal with pigs, and again it was the shepherd whose help was enlisted, as he had a smattering of knowledge of sick animals. When physic had to be given to a pig the method of administering it was to cut a hole in the toe of an old shoe and pour the stuff through it over the pig's throat.

The white breed of pigs were most in evidence, but a number of different types and crosses were kept, such as black pigs, redhaired pigs and spotted pigs. As bairns we used to do the rounds of the 'soocriffs' to note the various shapes and sizes.

When so many young folk lived and worked on the farms it was inevitable that lads and lasses would be attracted to each other. Their courtship would start at some farm where they both worked, and when one or other moved away to a different place, the chap would still go to see his lass, wherever she might be. Fellows often cycled a fair distance thrice a week to see their lasses. A chap I knew cycled ten mile each way thrice a week, a total of sixty miles a week! It happened too of course that a friendship would fizzle out after the couple were parted by the flitting, and new attachments formed in their new surroundings.

Couples met, too, at dances, kirns and in town on a Saturday night. During the thirties, when the cinema became all the rage, lads took their lasses to the pictures in the same way as their urban counterparts. The traditional wenching nights were Sunday, Wednesday and Saturday, when the pair would meet and go for a walk together. To ask a lass if she would go for a walk with you on a wenching night, was the equivalent of today's term 'dating a girl.'. At first the couple would tryst privately, but once the romance developed on serious lines, the chap would go to the girl's house to collect her, and eventually he was invited into her home. When that happened his mates would tease him about 'getting his feet under the table'.

A sharp look was kept for budding romances by the other workers, the young ones involved coming in for a lot of 'renking'. If a lad was keen on a lass and was seen by his fellows talking to her mother, they would say to him, 'Aye, that's right Jock, keep in wi 'er mother. Mind, ye've got tae clap the auld soo afore ye lift the pig!' Girls who were in service in farmhouse, mansion house and whatever, were generally allowed to have their lads to visit them at their place of work. If they lived locally they would cycle home on their day off, and their beaux would convey them back to their lodgings in the evening.

Occasionally it happened that young folk from two families on the doors who were not on friendly terms would take up with each other and meet in spite of this coolness. This did not please their parents, especially the mothers. One such case was a pal of mine at Fogorig, who wooed a girl from along the doors, of whom his mother did not approve. In spite of parental opposition, and hammerings from his brothers who waylaid him when he was out with her, Jock stuck to his girl and eventually married her.

Unmarried mothers were sorely looked down upon. No matter if many a couple had to have a shotgun wedding with a birth following shortly afterwards, folk thought it was all right so long as the girl had got her man. It would be a 'speak' at the time but soon forgotten. But for the unfortunate lass who was left holding the baby because some wight had declined to marry her, or because she had bestowed her favours somewhat freely and could not pin the blame on any one fellow, life thereafter was a bleak prospect. Paternity suits were frequently brought before the local courts and some restitution was gained, but even that did not remove the stigma of single parenthood. A number of those girls did get married later to someone else, and the earlier love child would be brought up by her parents as one of their own. In some instances parents would endure the shame of their daughter being an unmarried mother, rather than have her marry a rake, even though he was willing to do so. 'Ah'd raither see ma lassie deid than mairrit tae yon wastrel', as one father put it. On the other side of the coin, a fellow sometimes found himself trapped into marriage by an unscrupulous girl, who was out to get a man by any means, and used her sexy wiles to ensnare some decent honest lad whom she knew would stand by her, even though there might be doubt whether he was the father of the child she had conceived. One mother who was loudly lamenting about her son being trapped into marriage, was told, 'Ach weel, if he hadna been among the craws, he wadna have been shot at'.

For most of the period between the wars, the hinds yoked at 6am except during the darkest part of the winter, when yoking time was at daylight. They had to rise at five to get to the stable to feed, muck and groom their horses before yoking. They had a short break for breakfast about eight, this meal being a few slices of bread and a flask of tea, carried about with them in a tea bag, which was either a satchel or a bag with draw strings. The forenoon 'yokin' stretched till eleven o'clock, when they lowsed for dinner, yoking again at 1pm. It was well known of course that this long break of two hours at dinner time was instituted, not for the hinds' sake, but to rest the horses. The afternoon yoking was from 1pm till 5pm or till dark in winter, a break being given for a snack at 3pm. The men returned to the stable later in the evening to bed, supper and groom their horses. On Sundays they attended to the horses morning and evening. The time spent in the stable at night was looked upon as a social hour, enlivened by crack, music and song.

The other workers such as spademen and women workers had the same hours as the hinds, except for the stable tasks; they yoked at six and lowsed at 5pm with the same breaks for dinner etc. The byre folk attending cattle beasts worked somewhat similar hours, except that they had to give the beasts a look over before bedtime.

In this day and age when all farm work has been mechanised to the nth degree, it is hard to believe that up till little over thirty years ago, every farm task was carried out by manpower and horsepower alone. Farm implements were all horse drawn and were made to last a lifetime, or at the very least for the space of the average farm lease of nineteen years. Many of the tasks performed by hand were hard indeed. For example the filling of dung into carts by hand graip in the cattle courts, and the graiping of it out of the carts on to a muck midden and the spreading of dung on stubble or in drills for potatoes or turnips, were all jobs requiring strength, knack and staying power. The handling and carrying of sacks of grain was another heavy job. The bagging of grain was all based on the bushel measure, four bushels to a bag. Since the weight of a bushel of the different types of grain varied, it meant that oats were in twelve-stone bags at three stones to a bushel; barley at four stones to the bushel was in sixteen-stone bags; and wheat, the heaviest of all at four-and-a-half stones to the bushel, produced bags of eighteen stones weight. No wonder that the carrying of such burdens, often upstairs to a granary loft, taxed the strength and stamina of men to the limit.

In general, the emphasis on all aspects of farm work in my youth was on expertise and efficiency on the part of the staff. Woe betide anyone who was slow, clumsy or slovenly at work, for he or she would only be tolerated for a year. A person had to be good at his or her job to survive. Employers and their stewards were quick to find fault, and berate anyone whose performance was not up to standard.

Looking back today one tends to wonder what all the fuss was about, all the insistence on perfection, efficiency, economy. I wonder what those oldtime farmers and stewards would say, should they return to view the present farming scene, with its appalling hashiness and waste. Hashiness and

The Farm Workers

waste was not perpetrated by a band of folk earning a few miserable shillings each, but by expensive machines costing many thousands of pounds. What price the lumps of hay left behind the baler, the grain spilled from the combine harvester, the potatoes left in the soil by the lifting machine, the turnips bruised and battered by the turnip harvester, the handfuls of loose wool scattered about the clipping shed.

Excluding the shepherds, there was an established pecking order on the large and medium-sized farms, with the steward at the top. This person's role on the farm varied greatly according to the size of the place. It varied from that of being virtual manager where he had a large staff under him, to that of mere messenger who carried the farmer's orders to the other workers on the smaller places tenanted by working farmers. Ideally the steward had to hold a balance between farmer and workers, he had to get the work done, but might have to deflect the farmer from some course which he knew would antagonise the staff and give rise to grievances. Some stewards were good at the balancing act and maintaining harmony, but others leant too much to the employer's side, driving the folk on to please the master. A man of the latter type could be the cause of a clean sweep at flitting time when everybody would leave a place rather than stay on to endure tyranny. By contrast a steward who was too soft with the workers, would soon find himself being taken advantage of. 'The better ye are tae folk, the waur they're tae you', was a remark made by a farm steward who had tried the soft option.

A right steward had to keep his place and not get too familiar with those under him. If he fraternized too much with them he lost their respect. On farms where relations between the steward and the shepherd were good, which was regrettably rare, they would treat each other as confidants and companions. All too often, however, jealousy and rivalry soured their relationship.

The worst thing an employer could do was to have dealings with, or give orders to the workers behind the steward's back, thus undermining his position. Should a steward have any of his own sons or daughters working under him, as likely as not he would be more strict with them in the field, to avoid showing favouritism or merely because he wished his own to excel the others at work.

Next to the steward came the ploughman steward, who drove the first pair. It was his job to dole out the corn to the other hinds for their horses from the corn kist in the stable. He kept the time and set the pace for the others during work in the field. At yoking time in the stable he cried 'bridle' as the signal for harnessing up, and woe betide any hind who put harness on horse before the ploughman steward spoke, his ears would be made to ring with invective. The same precedence for the ploughman steward was followed out in the field, he was first to move off from the headrig when ploughing, and first to unyoke his horses and leave the field at lowsing time.

In the event of the steward being off ill, the ploughman steward was left in charge, and frequently when a steward left a farm the ploughman steward was promoted in his place. Anyone aspiring to a stewardship usually did so from this, the second highest step in the ladder.

Next in line to the ploughman steward came the second, third and fourth hind etc, down to the odd laddie. The spademen or orramen were men of all work except that they did not have charge of horses. If they could clip sheep, as most of them could, they were sent to help on those farms where professional clippers were not engaged. Every farm had at least one spademan and the larger farms employed three or four. They were mostly middle aged or elderly men, who had given up driving horses, and maybe had grown up sons hinding or daughters as women workers.

The women workers were led by the first woman, who got her orders from the steward. In former times men called 'women stewards' were in charge of the band of women, but that office had died out in the Borders before my day. The forewoman took precedence in all the field jobs allotted to the female staff, and when turnip singling was in progress, with all the farm staff on the hoe, the forewoman and her band of women workers led the field.

The byreman or byrewoman were in a category of their own, at least when the courts were full of cattle during the winter and spring. At other times a byreman worked with the spademen and a byrewoman with the rest of the women, except that they had to attend to the farmhouse cows morning and evening. The milking of these cows was done either by a woman hired for the job, who was a householder in her own right, or by one of the worker's wives. The dairymaid, to give her her proper title, also doubled up as henwife.

On large farms where a lot of cattle were kept in the courts, the byreman had a girl assistant. Byrewomen were frequently in charge of the beasts on medium-sized or small farms. 'Byrin the beasts' as the duties were called, was an arduous task in the period of which I write, even though those engaged in it were not so much exposed to the elements. The turnips had all to be cut by hand, and the hay and straw was carried to the hecks on their backs with burden rope – there were no bales, then, as the hay was fed loose, also the oat straw for fodder. The barley straw for bedding was in bunches, i.e. trusses. The sliced turnips were carried in creels to the troughs from the turnip shed, and feeding stuff, cake and meal mixture were all mixed by hand, and carried to the cattle in bags.

Before the advent of the Wages Boards there were no overtime payments for farm workers to cover the extra hours worked at busy seasons. The kirn was supposed to recompense them for that. A cash payment of £1, called the 'harvest pound', was given to cover extra hours worked during the corn harvest, plus a bottle of beer and a bap every day for lunch. The bap was a large bread roll made especially for harvest time by the local bakers.

Before mechanisation Irishmen played an important part in the labour side of Borders farming. They came over in large numbers for seasonal work such as turnip singling, haymaking, harvest, potato lifting and the shawing of sugar beet and turnips. They were accommodated in bothies, and in various hole-and-corner spots in the farmstead, some of which were not fit to house a dog.

Some farmers favoured Irish labour, but others never employed them. In my calf country the Scotts of Frogden, Cessford and Spylaw were always extensive employers of Irishmen, and I can remember as a boy a large company of them could be met with on the road from Frogden to Morebattle on Saturday and Sunday evenings. Berwickshire too was a favourite haunt of the Irish, for nearly all the big farms there employed them. They arrived in the early summer, just after the term, when they could be seen tramping the roads from one farm town to another seeking turnip singling. Some of them disappeared after the singling, maybe going back home or to Glasgow. They returned for the corn harvest, and stayed till the potatoes were lifted, and the beet and turnip shawing completed. Some Irishmen came back to the same farm year after year; in this category were the Currans, father and two sons, along with a relative called Frank Dougan, who came regularly from Donegal to Fogorig. Curiously, the majority of those who frequented Berwickshire were Donegallers. The Currans came over in June and stayed all summer and back-end till nearly the New Year. They did singling and shawing on piece work, but at harvest and potato lifting they were on day's wage. Whilst on piecework they bought their own food and lived very frugally, but at other times food was provided for them and they demanded that it be good and plentiful. At Fogorig accommodation for them was pretty rough, but better than on some places, and they got free coal for their fire.

On one particular year when we were at Roxburgh Newtown, 1924 I think it was, the crops were badly laid and the harvest was late. Mr Bell, who did not normally employ Irishmen, hired a gang of them to shear a field of oats by hand on piecework. I recall that they fell out amongst themselves – for the Irish were very quarrelsome – and had a fight which was so bad the police had to be called. Brawls between rival groups of Irishmen were not unknown in the Border towns on Saturday nights. More than once Danny Curran, the old man, paraded a keeker when he set off for mass on Sunday mornings. The Currans resented the presence of another family group, who had been hired as extras for the harvest, and arguments leading to fisticuffs arose in the bothy. The elder of the strangers told us that the Currans even went so far as to dowse the fire with water after they had cooked their own meal, to spite the other men. Eventually the 'interlopers' were housed in other accommodation that was rigged up for them in the steading.

The farm folk of the Borders at that time despised and disliked the Irish. The reasons for this were varied. Firstly there was the question of religion, and the antipathy of the Lowland Scot to Roman Catholics and Irish Catholics in particular; secondly there was their dirty appearance and the fact that they would put up with living conditions that no self respecting Borderer would tolerate. However the main factor which caused their resentment was competition for work, for the Irish were engaged for seasonal work that the local farm folk not in regular employment could have performed. There had always been a fairish pool of casual labour in the Borders, which the Irish were seen to supplant. The fact that the Irishmen were paid the same harvest wages as the hinds, plus their food and coals, did not endear them to the folk of the farm towns. During the war years their presence in this country was resented more than ever because of Eire's neutrality, and in addition their ability to dodge income tax, when farm wages rose and became taxable.

12

RURAL HOUSING

The standard of housing on Border farms varied a great deal according to whose estate they belonged to, for different estates had different styles and qualities of cottages. The tenant farmer usually had with the responsibility of keeping the cottages on his farm wind- and waterproof, but this depended on the terms of his lease. When they came to view a farm with intent to rent it, few perspective tenants bothered to look over the cottages housing the workers. This neglect often caused them bother once they had occupied the farm, for if the housing was poor they had difficulty in keeping workers, or in obtaining the best class of workers.

By the time I came into this world, rural houses had improved some since my parents were bairns, but they still left a lot to be desired. Sanitation was poor, with dry outside closets or none at all, and 'ash middens' just behind or beside the cottages. There was no inside water supply, and the water was got from a tap on the doors, a nearby pump from a well or running water from a pipe which led from a spring. The state of houses on some places was a disgrace, even in my time, and we used to hear harrowing tales of damp running down the interior walls, leaking roofs and rats in the skirting boards. Fortunately for us we never encountered such horrors, nor did we have trouble with poor soundproofing, whereby next door neighbours could hear each other through the walls.

Most farm cottages had cement floors in the kitchen, back kitchen and milk house. Except for homemade clouty rugs laid down here and there, the floor of the kitchen, as the living room was universally called, was bare and scrubbed regularly by the womenfolk. Linoleum or waxcloth, as we called it, just started to be used on farm cottage floors as I was growing up.

The room or ben-the-hoose usually had a wooden floor. This apartment was used as a spare bedroom. Where the family was not large, it was also used occasionally as a sitting room. The room was furnished with the best that folk could afford, chairs with horsehair seats, a sofa, a dropside table and the floor was covered by fancy rugs or maybe a carpet. Here were housed the family portraits, prized ornaments such as wally dugs, small statuettes etc. and the 'gless press'. In the case of our family, there was a bookcase as well for we were always book lovers. Nearly everybody had a double bed in the kitchen in which the parents slept. Where there were a lot of bairns, a couple of beds was quite common. Box beds were unknown in Borders farm cottages. The kitchen furniture consisted of a large square or oblong table, chairs, stools, an armchair and sofa, also a large dresser for dishes, cutlery, tablecloths and other household necessities.

At Burnfoot, my birthplace, the houses were owned by the Clifton Park estate, an estate which had a collection of farm cottages well above the prevailing standard. Those at Burnfoot had been built in the 1880s to replace older ones, by the then laird, R. H. Elliot of grassland improvement fame. The houses were of the conventional two-storey type, comprising kitchen-cum-living room, ben-the-hoose or parlour, back kitchen and milkhouse on the ground floor, and two separate bedrooms upstairs. There was a cupboard under the stairs which mother nicknamed 'Lab's Hole', though other folk called theirs the 'Glory Hole'. I have never been able to ascertain the reason for those names. The room and the bedrooms had small fireplaces, and in the kitchen the fireplace had an oven on one side, and a small hot water tank with a tap on the other. The swee from which the kettle and hanging pots were suspended, was a fixture as were the cleeks and fire irons. There were still places, even in my boyhood, where the swee, cleeks and fire irons were not fixtures, a relic of the days when a householder had to carry his own from place to place, but such places were fast disappearing. The houses in the hinds' row at Burnfoot were built on the same lines as ours, except that they had back doors, which ours and that of the steward lacked.

The water for our house came from a 'pant' or pump set on the roadside across from the house. This pump was an iron edifice about three feet high, with the top part in the form of a lion's face, and the water came out of its mouth when one turned a knob resembling a door handle at the side of the image. When there were severe frosts the pump had to be thawed out by burning a bunch of straw around it. The dry closets were built beside the pig sties quite a distance away at the other side of the road from the cottages. Both closets and pig sties were set in the runs of what had been the original herds' and stewards' houses. It was no fun going to the 'duffy' in the dark, down steps, across the road, then up some more steps to get there. In severe weather it was something of a hazard to carry water up the slippery steps from the pant, or a pail of pig food up and down two sets of slippery steps to the soo crave. The folk at the row got their water from a pipe of running water led from a spring in a wood nearby. It had to be carried in buckets fifty yards or more.

At Roxburgh Newtown, which was on the Duke of Roxburghe's estate, the houses were tolerably good, ours having two apartments upstairs and two downstairs, plus back kitchen and milkhouse. Only one of the upstairs rooms was partitioned off, the other one was just open from the stair head. I cannot remember whether or not the upstairs apartments had fireplaces. The kitchen and room were of conventional style, with a small fireplace in the latter. The kitchen fireplace had the usual swee, cleeks and fire irons, and there was a good oven at one side but no water tank. We had no back door, and the dry closet was built on to the end of the house, and abutted the coalhouse. Our water came from a tap on the doors, which was an improvement on the Burnfoot set up.

Rural Housing

When we went to Fogorig we found that the house was built on somewhat the same lines, two up and two downstairs, with back kitchen and milkhouse, but no back door. The kitchen grate had no oven or water heater, just the bare jambs without even a hob, though it did have a swee and fire irons. Mother missed the oven very much, as her only means of baking had to be a girdle. Eventually our parents decided to invest in a small oil stove with oven attached. Oil stoves came to be used more widely by housewives in farm cottages as the 1930s advanced. This was partly to make up for the lack of proper kitchen ranges as at Fogorig, and partly because they could be housed in back kitchens. Paraffin stoves were popular right up till electricity was installed in farm cottages. There were no back doors in any of the houses in the row, and access to the outhouses etc. was by two vennels. As I mentioned before, water was pumped by hand from a well behind the houses.

In the upstairs section, the shepherd's house at Fogorig was the only one in the row to have a partitioned bedroom; all the rest just had the open loft, and folk with mixed grown-up families had to make do with curtains between sleeping quarters of the sexes.

The upstairs partition in our house had been erected at his own expense by a previous shepherd, who had left in 1922 after only one year after a stormy sojourn. He had been branded as a troublemaker, because he had spoken out about housing conditions and sanitation. When father went there to plant the garden and was shown over the house he was taken aback when told by the outgoing shepherd that the partition belonged to him, and that he (father) would have to pay him for it, since he had had to buy it from the man who had erected it. After he came home father wrote to Mr Young, his prospective employer, pointing out that when he was hired he did not expect to be charged for taking over part of the house! Mr Young wrote back to say that he had looked into the matter and would pay for the partition, so that was that.

A Shepherd Remembers

The farm cottages on the Charterhall estate, including Fogorig, were all pretty scruffy at that time, little having been done for them over the years in the way of improvements, but a move was made in the direction just before we left.

In the 1920s a scheme to upgrade rural housing in Scotland was set afoot by the Government and local authorities. Landowners were to be compelled to bring the cottages on their estates up to a certain standard, chiefly regarding sanitation and water supply. They were offered a grant of £100 per house (a respectable sum at that time) to improve farm cottages, the main object being the installation of an indoor water supply and water closets, but the grant covered other improvements as well. The Border lairds and owner-occupiers of farms took advantage of the grant, and a general improvement of housing took place during the thirties. Many estate owners installed baths in their cottages as well, and wrought other improvements. It was not until after the Second World War, however, that both hot and cold water, baths and electricity were installed in most farm cottages. Even before 1930 however, one or two farmers had their own generators to supply electricity, and gave their employees electric light at a small charge. A notable example was Bogend Farm in Fogo parish.

It was the practice when large scale improvements were carried out on farm cottages, to keep one house in the row empty, to which the occupants of each cottage under repair could be moved in rotation. When the row at Fogorig came to be sorted later in the year 1930, this was not done, and the folk just had to stay put in their homes and endure the upheaval. Much as our parents would have welcomed the new amenities, they were relieved that they had already left and were spared that ordeal.

At Doddington the farm workers' houses were not in two compact rows, one for each farm, but were scattered about the village. At the North side there were two rows of four houses at different locations, then the steward's house stood

254

by itself opposite the steading. The groom and gardener lived in two houses built together farther down the road. Our house was the end one in one of the two rows.

Once again we had a four apartment house, with two separate bedrooms upstairs minus fireplaces, and access to one bedroom was through the other, for the stair went up at the side of the living room, rather than by the usual route opposite the front door. The 'room' downstairs had a fireplace, and in the kitchen there was a big old fashioned English fireplace, with an oven on one side and a boiler on the other; the mantelpiece was high and broad. We had a fair sized back kitchen plus pantry and milkhouse. The back kitchen was large enough to accommodate the washtub on washing days, an advance on what mother had been used to, for the washing had always to be done in the kitchen-cum-living room. Some farms had washhouses adjoining the cottages, but these were very rare. With regard to the washtub in the middle of the kitchen floor, I am reminded of a neighbour's wife who used to rise very early in the morning on wash days, and would be busy at her washtub even before her husband was up. He, poor man, was still abed and enveloped in clouds of steam!

At Doddington we also had both a front door and a back door, with coalhouse and dry closet just beyond the back door. Water was obtained from a tap on the doors, shared by the four cottages.

Outhouse facilities attached to workers' cottages varied from farm to farm. Most places had stone built coalhouses, and, where they were big enough, those housed firewood as well as coal, and bicycles, garden tools etc. But in too many instances the lack of adequate outhouse room meant that workers had to erect sheds for themselves with slabwood, and roof them with corrugated iron. When a family left a farm they were entitled to dismantle this temporary shed and take it with them. At Fogorig outhouses were somewhat skimpy, except for the steward and shepherd who had access to parts of old cottages for outhouses. Most of the other folk kept potatoes and bicycles upstairs in the houses. One snowy night the sons of our next door neighbour took their snow covered bikes upstairs with them when they came home. During the night, water from the melting snow trickled down through the ceiling on to the parents sleeping in the livingroom below.

The house at Cortleferry I described in another chapter was of the traditional four apartment type and had been improved by the installation of an inside water supply. There was a water closet, and taps, sinks and a wash boiler in the back kitchen, amenities appreciated by mother. The rest of the house had not been touched by improvements at all, and was not so good as we had been led to believe.

The provision of kennels for shepherds' dogs seems to have been a matter that never entered the heads of landowners and farmers. This was disgraceful when one saw the fine elaborate kennels provided for the gamekeepers' gun dogs. Even at the present day there are few inbye farms where accommodation is provided for sheep dogs.

At Burnfoot father's dogs were housed in a part of the sheep shed partitioned off for the purpose. At Newtown the previous herds had turned the privy into a kennel for their dogs, but this would not do for my parents, and the closet must needs be put to its proper use, so father got some slabwood and erected a kennel, roofed with felt. We had a kennel for our dogs at Fogorig in what had been the outhouse attached to an old empty cottage behind our house. This ancient cottage was one of a pair; my folk had the use of one as a coalhouse, washhouse and general outhouse combined, and the other was used as a bothy for the Irishmen.

There was a proper dog kennel at North Doddington, which had been erected by the shepherd we succeeded. It was well built of wood, had a cement floor and wooden bench for the dogs to lie on, and it was easy to muck out and keep clean.

In contrast to the rather mediocre housing provided for the farm workers, the 'big houses', as the farmhouses were called, were much more substantial. On the large farms these resembled mansions and had all the amenities then in vogue, with tennis lawns and spacious gardens and grounds. Folk were prone to ask what was so special about the farmers and their womenfolk, that they had to be provided with such grand accommodation. To be fair though, one must understand that, substantial though the buildings themselves were to begin with, many of the frills were added by the tenants themselves out of their own pockets throughout their long leases.

For the most part the occupants of farm cottages took a pride in keeping their humble dwellings clean and tidy, even though they might be in them just for one year. There were exceptions of course, and new tenants of a farm cottage sometimes found it left in a filthy state by the outgoing family, and would have to put in a lot of hard work and expense getting it clean and to their liking. Should any of the fittings be missing or broken, the employer was expected to come good for the damage, even though he might be ignorant of what had been going on, but such cases were exceptions, for most housewives were jealous of their reputations, and few relished the idea of being accused of leaving a dirty house behind them when they left a place. At the flitting time there was a general scrubbing of floors and sweeping down of walls by those who valued their reputation for cleanliness.

13

THE FARMERS

The shepherds had a man to man relationship with the farmers, which led, under the right circumstances, to a sort of partnership in the management of the sheep flock. The shepherd with his expertise was allowed a good deal of rope in this respect, once his employer was aware that he had the welfare of the flock at heart and could be trusted. It took at least a year for a shepherd to get the feel of a new place, and about the same time for the employer to test his merits, so that shepherds tended to stay longer in one situation. The more years they stayed the better their relationship grew with the master. Overall the Border shepherds were a set of dedicated men, and fully justified the reliance put upon them by the farmers. But there were employers who could never bring themselves to trust the shepherd. This sort earned for themselves a bad name amongst the herding fraternity and it was with reluctance that any but yes-men would go to serve them. One shepherd who served for many years with a flockmaster of the masterful type, was asked how he managed to get on so well with him since nobody else could, 'Weel, he thinks he's clever an Ah jist let um think sae', was the cunning reply.

Shepherds were jealous for the welfare of their flocks, and were quick to spring to the defence of their charges, when they thought that the sheep were being unfairly treated compared with the other farm stock. It often happened that arguments arose between shepherd and farmer, concerning shortage of turnips or of feeding stuffs, poor grazing or any other matter regarded as unfair to the sheep.

Apart from his man to man contact with the steward and

The Farmers

shepherd, the farmer's attitude to his workers varied according to his social position. By and large the farmers regarded the workers as inferior beings, and this attitude became more marked the higher up the social scale an employer happened to be.

There were many social strata amongst the farmers, but three main categories could be defined. First there were the gentleman farmers who were either owner occupiers or tenants of big farms, of say six hundred to a thousand acres or more. This class had sprung form generations of wealthy farmers, or if their farming was of more recent origin, they had well-to-do antecedents. They lived like gentry in the large mansion-like farmhouses provided for them, they dined at night and rose to hounds, they shot and fished in their leisure hours, and occupied a high status in the neighbourhood. Their offspring were sent to expensive boarding schools. They maintained a fairish establishment, having a groom who doubled up as chauffeur, a gardener and two or three maids in the house. The gulf between such farmers and their work folk was very wide indeed. They stood on their dignity, expecting along with their wives a measure of deference from the 'cottage people' and their families. Indeed, one farmer's dame to my knowledge even went as far as to demand that the bairns from the row should touch their caps and curtsy to her when she met them. The youngsters from such farming households were not allowed to mix and play with the cottage bairns when they were small, and later when they were on vacation from their fancy schools, they expected to be treated as young ladies and gentlemen.

The workers on their part made fun of the masters and other 'big hoose' folk behind their backs. Many were the stories that circulated round the countryside regarding the eccentricities of this or that farmer or his wife and brood. 'She's a right pup thon', would be the verdict on some stuck up wife or daughter, 'She looks at folk as if they wur dirt', 'It's a peety she pees when it's sae common', was another quip one would hear. Some tales were hilariously funny, others downright bawdy. One circulated about a certain gentleman farmer's wife, an imperious haughty young dame, was that when she and her husband were in bed enjoying conjugal union, she remarked to him 'Do the cottage women get this as well?' 'I suppose they do', her husband replied. 'Oh no!' she protested, 'It is far too good for them!'. Such was the working folk's way of repaying the arrogant disdain with which they were treated by their 'betters'.

On the other hand there were gentlemen farmers and their ladies who, in their own patronising way, showed a real interest in their employees, and were genuinely liked and respected by them. Anyone needing help in time of trouble or illness was not ignored.

One drawback under the big farmers was their paternalism and interference with the workers' everyday lives, by laying down petty restrictions, rules of behaviour etc. 'Ye canna dae that here', 'It's as much as yer place is worth tae dae such and such', 'Yer no supposed tae dae this or that', and so on, were remarks made to newcomers by employees who already knew the ropes.

It could be a stifling experience for folk of independent spirit to undergo, and some folk deeply resented restrictions imposed upon them which bore no relation to their job. It was an offence for bairns or young folk to be found haunting the avenue approaching the farmhouse or near the front of the house itself. When I was a boy I was checked by a farmer's wife for daring to take a short cut from the back door of the farmhouse to the lambing field, with bottles of milk for the lambs. In my haste I passed by the front door and was told, 'the way through the steading is the place for you'. My father was incensed when I told him, and complained to the farmer about it. The latter just laughed it off, as he was more easy going than his prim, prideful spouse.

At another farm the women of the row were forbidden to hang out their washing in the gardens in front of the houses beside the public road, and had to dry them in an enclosed space behind the houses out of sight. The lady of the farmhouse could not bear to see washing hung out in public. I suppose the underlying motive for such rules and regulations was the preservation of their privacy, and an effort to prevent any lowering of the tone of the farm.

Apart from the sheep, the running of the farm was largely delegated by the gentleman farmer to his steward, who enjoyed a measure of power and independence.

The second type of farmer I now describe was the middle class sort of person, who could either be a tenant or owner occupier, mostly the former. He and his family lived in a plainer sort of fashion in a less pretentious mansion. His bairns were sent away to a boarding school, but of a less expensive sort. He exercised a bigger say in the day to day running of the farm, giving the two key men their place certainly, but keeping a watchful eye on things, ready to prod them on or question their judgement. This type of farmer was, in certain circumstances, a bane to the really conscientious shepherd or steward, for he was often querulous and hard to please. Of one such man a shepherd was heard to say, 'Ye could gaun on a' day an a' night an he'd never say, Ye've dune plenty'. A steward complained of another 'Yin canna wheel a barra across the road, without him askin what yer daein'.

Farm households of this rank had one resident maid, and a girl or woman from the row who came in daily. The middle class type of farmers and their wives generally showed a more tolerant attitude to the working folk they employed. Some of them had forebears who had sprung from the ranks of the farmworkers, others were shopkeepers, millers, tradesmen and the like who had made their pile in other walks of life and then had ventured into farming. A few had come from middle class backgrounds of various kinds, and had entered farming from being mud students at agricultural colleges. It was common for farmers to have mud students living in with them, and paying for the privilege of learning to farm. Mud students were welcomed as potential husbands for farmers' daughters.

A Shepherd Remembers

Again there were many of the womenfolk of middle class farmers, who took a kindly interest in the workers' families; they visited the wives in their homes and proffered help and advice in time of trouble.

Quite a few of the middle class of farmers followed the hounds, and were horsy minded, especially those in the hill and upland areas. Those types could be a nuisance to the shepherds and the sheep, for at lambing time all the nicely sheltered fields near the farmstead would be taken up with their hunting horses and ponies.

The next rung on the farming ladder was occupied by the working farmers, who had graduated by sheer hard work and thrift from smaller farms, or whose fathers or grandfathers had done so. This class of farmers was really the backbone of the industry, and a boon to the countryside; they were usually hard working themselves and hard men to serve, for with them every minute and every penny was a prisoner. They lived plainly but well, their wives and daughters often worked hard too at poultry keeping, calf rearing etc., but still considered themselves above the hired workers. One such farmer's wife who had a large brood of daughters forbade them to fraternize with the young herds and hinds at dances and such like. The sons too were discouraged from consorting with bondagers or farm kitchen girls, but sometimes one would fall by the wayside, and would even go as far to marry such a girl. More often the wretched girl who aspired to become a future farmer's wife would be left in the lurch. Working farmers' bairns attended the village school which they left at the age of fourteen or sometimes from the age of twelve they went to the local high school for a year or two.

Unless they had come of shepherding stock, few of the working farmers had a deep interest in sheep. They kept a ewe flock of course, for sheep were then regarded as essential on all but the smallest Border farms. The sheep were usually tended by the farmers themselves or by one of their sons if they had any. Quite often the steward had a dual role under the working farmer, acting as both steward and shepherd. A

The Farmers

steward serving this type of farmer, if one was kept at all, was a mere messenger carrying the orders to the rest of the staff, and acting as leader of the men in the field work.

Working farmers tenanted places in the two hundred to four hundred acres bracket, carrying two or three pairs of horses, and ten to fifteen score of ewes. They were ambitious men who had their eyes on the higher rungs of the ladder, eager to expand their activities and rent a larger farm, either for themselves or their sons. Although only a generation or two back their forebears had been hired workers, they had little sympathy with their employees, and screwed them down to the last penny in wages. By the same token they expected maximum effort from their workers, although the latter had not the incentive to slave on as they themselves did. One young working farmer, on reaching the field of work with a gang of workers, doffed his jacket and cried, 'Ony bugger that canna keep up wi me (at the work) let um gaun intae the hoose!'

At the foot of the farming ladder were the small farmers and smallholders. Smallholders was the specific name given to those who occupied the smallholdings that had been formed after the First World War by splitting up large farms here and there. Many of these holdings were situated on poorish land, and some of them were too small to be viable unless they were devoted to dairying, pig or poultry farming. Apart form the 'new' holdings, there was, in my young days, a sprinkling of small places worked by the tenant and his family. But such places were all too scarce in the Borders, and were keenly sought after by the shepherds, stewards or hinds who had managed to gather a bit of money, and aspired to become their own masters. Because of the demand and the limited supply, rents were rather higher in proportion for small farms. Another factor governing supply was the practice of leasing those little farms to big farmers as led places, who used them for some branch or other of their farming activities, keeping a man or men there to do the work.

Few of those workers aspiring to the small farms could go

it alone or rent a farm with their own resources, and it was usual for them to obtain financial backing from a larger farmer or from some other source. It is only fair to say, therefore, that many big farmers were ready and willing to help working men into farms.

One good feature of the landlord-tenant system was that it afforded a chance for farm workers to get into farming on their own account, and for small farmers, where they were able, to rent bigger farms. In my youth a large proportion of Border farmers, or their immediate forebears, had come into farming by this door, a door that has now been closed for ever.

Throughout all the various types of farmers, a great deal depended on the character of the men themselves, as to how their workers fared under them. Many were mean and grasping, greedy for money and selfish in outlook. Some pithy remarks were coined around such men, and here are a few examples: 'He wad skin a louse for its tallow', 'He wadna pairt wi the reek o his fart if he could help it', 'I'd like fine tae drive the hearse at Auld X's funeral, I'd gie um a right hurl, for he was aye hurryin folk on, whan he was leevin'.

By contrast some were good enough at heart, but shortage of money kept them from being as open handed or generous as they might have been. One would hear it said regarding a certain farmer, 'Aye, he wad be a richt guid maister if he had plenty money'. Such attributes were shown more clearly by those farmers who bought their farms in the early 1920s and found themselves caught up in the depression years of the next decade. A curious story was once related to me, which illustrated the benign streak to be found in farmers. Two Border farmers had words about a certain thowless man that the one had recommended to the other at the hirings. Shortly after the term farmer A accosted farmer B saying 'What did ye mean be gie'in yon Jock Thamson sic a guid character tae me at the hirin? Man his useless!' 'Weel', says farmer B 'the pur fella hez tae leeve, an if Ah gie um a job for an 'ear, an you gie um a job for an 'ear, it'll help the pur fella tae git by!'

The Farmers

A change of generation at the helm could make a difference to a farm and its workers – a niggard or martinet of a father might be succeeded by a more benign and generous son. Or again a well liked man who had treated his men fairly could be followed by a son, a young man in a hurry, who tended to ride roughshod over everybody in pursuit of his aims.

The better sort of employer would pay the highest wages that he thought he could afford, but he had to be careful not to incur the wrath of his colleagues should he be found out paying more than the going rate. Before Wages Boards came into being, there existed an unwritten code or level of wages, governed by custom and demand, known as the current rates of pay. Those were loosely agreed amongst the farmers, and the workers had just to try to make the best of them. The forty shillings a week rate, common in 1919, had dwindled to a norm of twenty-eight shillings by 1932.

Following the Great War, out of which the farmers had done very well financially, most farmers acquired motor cars, which were dubbed 'war memorials' by the cynical among farm workers and those outside agriculture. Having been used to horses and traps, some farmers found the new contraptions difficult to handle. Much mirth was caused by stories current at the time regarding farmers and their motoring experiences, especially those addicted to a dram. They found the motor car to be a different animal from the docile nag that had hitherto transported them home from market or carousal. One farmer in the Morebattle area who was something of a dandy and playboy was on his way home from a ball at Kelso in the small hours, when his car failed to take a bend at Kersknowe and went through the hedge into a field. The farmer escaped unhurt, but had to foot it for the four miles to his home, in his tails and evening shoes. Another man who tried to stop his car from going through the hedge forgot that it was not a horse he was driving. 'Like a damned fuil', he said, relating his experience afterwards, 'I cried whoa! and stelled ma feet again the boards, as if I was haudin back a horse by the reens. I forgot

265

A Shepherd Remembers

I was strampin on the throttle an jist making the bluidy thing gaun faster'.

During the period between wars, the farming scene in the Borders became very fluid, as old families died out or sold off, giving way to an influx of incomers from other districts, particularly from west Scotland, Fife and the Scottish Midlands. The dairy farmers of Lanarkshire, Ayrshire and Galloway, keen to expand, saw that good sized farms were to be had in the east country, at cheap buying prices and low rents. The men from the west came from family farms which maybe employed just a single man or two besides the members of the family, so that the Border scene with its large staffs presided over by stewards was new to them. True they had less of the class distinctions evinced by the native farmers, but they had little use for the protocol and pecking order that existed among the hinds. Moreover they drove the workers harder than the Border men, being accustomed to working at all hours, and in all sorts of conditions on the family farms at home. One related to me how he and his brothers had ruckled corn by moonlight in Ayrshire. They were deeply resented by the Border farm workers, who miscalled them bitterly. The Fifers and others from north of the Forth were somewhat different in character, but were still pretty hard taskmasters.

Many of the west countrymen got their new farms equipped to carry on dairying. Dairy farms, a rare feature of Border farming up till then, sprang into being wherever those men from the west had settled. They also brought in families of workers from the western counties and Galloway to work their dairies, thus adding a fresh element to the ranks of the Border farm workers. Some of those immigrants used to irk us by holding forth in praise of their home country, its ways and its inhabitants. We felt like asking them why on earth they ever left it. Precious few of them ever returned there anyway.

With regard to the shepherds and the sheep, the Fifers and such were tolerable enough, since they had some interest in sheep and beef cattle. The men from the west cared little for sheep, and a generation was to pass ere they became of any use as flockmasters. Yet they were longheaded enough to perceive that the ewe flock had its place in the farming picture, and grudgingly accepted it as part of their farming policy. They and the shepherds mixed about as easily as oil and water, just tolerating each other and that was all. The farmers needed the herds to look after the ewes, and the herds needed the jobs. A shepherd was asked by a crony at the mart, who had not seen him for some years, whereabouts he was now working, and gave as his reply, 'Oh, Ah'm at Hillside Mains, wi yin o thon soor dook men'.

There can be no doubt that the big tenants and richer farmers were the best men to work for from a shepherd's point of view. They had the resources to provide one with good sheep stock to take charge of, and plenty of material to work with. The best of them gave the shepherd a pretty free hand in planning and carrying out his work; moreover they were purse proud and spared no expense to have the sheep good, for they were as jealous of the flock's reputation in the sale ring as was the shepherd.

I end this chapter with the tale of a very revealing conversation between a working farmer and his gentleman farmer counterpart, who was also a noted breeder of Border Leicester sheep.

'Man', said the gentleman, 'I often lie awake at night, and try to count up how many of my Border Leicester I know by sight'.

'Ye're lucky', was the other's reply, 'I often lie waken at night wonderin hoo I'm gaun tae pey my rent'.

14

CRAFTSMEN AND LAIRDS

The country craftsmen played an important part in rural life, and there were still plenty of them around at the time of which I write, 1918–1945. The blacksmith and joiner were the two most prominent, and every parish had at least one of each, and some parishes had two of both. The smith and joiner were also smallholders and had fields on the outskirts of the village, and kept a cow, pigs and some poultry. The blacksmith got plenty of work shoeing horses and mending farm implements. The smithy was a meeting place in the evenings, where the hinds came during the ploughing season to get their plough socks 'laid', as the act of reinforcing the worn point was called. When we were bairns we used to frequent the smithies at Linton and Roxburgh in the school dinner hour, fascinated by the clang of hammers on the anvil, the roar of the fire under the impact of the bellows, and the hiss of steam as the glowing iron was plunged into the cooling vat.

Apart from the routine job of horse shoeing, the smiths were kept extra busy at tasks at certain times of the year such as 'laying' or reinforcing the teeth of harrows for the spring cultivation, and cobbling up various implements when they were required for some seasonal task. It was just too much to expect of farmers to think of having implements overhauled and any repairs done a few weeks before the season for their use became due. Of course breakages did occur during field operations, and the smith would be expected to drop everything and come to the aid of a disabled implement, either at his shop or out on the farm. At such times the smith would be rushed off his feet, and had a hard task to keep everybody sweet. Besides the horse shoeing and implement work, the blacksmiths were skilled at making all sorts of metal appliances, from runners for a bairn's sledge to wrought iron gates. Village blacksmith businesses were usually on a family basis, a father and son or two brothers, with an apprentice employed as well. Most farms of any size had a smithy building of their own, to which the local smith came once a week to do any horse shoeing that was needed. The work was done on the horses while the hinds were lowsed for dinner.

The joiner's shop usually stood next to the smithy, for the two craftsmen were complimentary to each other in such tasks as providing wheels and shafts for farm carts, shanks for hand tools etc, anything requiring both metalwork and woodwork combined. The joiner's shop smelt of paint, putty and wood shavings, just as that of the smith smelt of singed hoof parings, cinders and steam. In addition to jobs involving buildings, cart frames, tools and such like, the joiners undertook repairs to furniture and other wooden household appliances, but in this respect they were terribly dilatory, and sometimes an article would lie in their shop for weeks or even months ere they got round to sorting it. A family at Burnfoot had an armchair which had lain at the joiner's shop awaiting repair for nearly a year, when they found they were leaving the district at the term, and had to retrieve it unmended in time for flitting. There was a good living for country joiners in those days, for the farms and smaller estates were always needing joiner work done. The big estates of course had their own tradesmen. I should mention that the smithy and joiner's shop and any land attached to them belonged to the laird and were rented by those tradesmen.

Although most farmers employed their spademen for repairing burst drains, there were a few professional drainers scattered about the countryside between the wars. They usually lived in villages or had rented houses on farms or estates. Often they would be attached to an estate, and could pick up any other draining work that came their way. Very little field draining on a large scale was done at this period, but I can remember that a gang of drainers was employed laying a new set of tiles in a field at North Doddington in 1930. Two noted drainers lived in the vicinity, one at Ewart and one at Doddington. They were much sought after for repairing burst drains on the farms round about, and for organizing gangs on any drainage scheme that was afoot. Field draining was all done by hand with pick and spade. On the Scots side of the Border, farmers often employed Irishmen to sort choked or burst drains in the winter and spring. Some Irishmen were good at it and returned annually to Scotland to undertake the job.

Drystone dykers had become thin on the ground by the 1920s and 1930s, for there was very little incentive for men to take up the job. Very little dyking was done during that era of acute agricultural depression. When dykes became too broken down to be effective, wire fences were erected alongside them rather than rebuild them anew. It was not until after the war that an attempt was made, quite successfully, to revive the craft. There were drystone dykers in Morebattle, and the Roxburghe Estates employed dykers who lived in Roxburgh village.

The horse breaker was an important man in the rural scene, who was much in demand for breaking in young work hoses. This was done when the horses were about three years old. Mr Fox at Rutherford Mill was a well known horse breaker when I was a boy; he broke in riding and carriage horses as well as farm horses. In Glendale there was a professional horse breaker who lived at Crookham, whose name I cannot recall. Quite a few of the big farms reared and broke-in their own young horses, the task being assigned to one of the hinds who had a flair for the job. Once the horses were broken in to harness and cart they became part of a pair, going along with a steady mature horse. In some cases the horse-breaker's good work was undone by hashy, inconsiderate horsemen who mistreated them, and some horses were even spoiled altogether. Bad horsemen were in the minority but they did exist.

I have already mentioned the rabbit catchers in a previous chapter, but omitted to say that there was a class of rabbit catchers, whom one might call master rabbit catchers, who also employed others to kill rabbits for them, and paid them on a percentage of the catch basis. Such men occupied a small piece of ground with house and buildings attached from which they carried on their craft, catching rabbits themselves as well and engaging in the usual seasonal work.

Mole catching and rabbit catching went hand in hand, rabbit catchers frequently doing both jobs. The professional molecatcher carried out the job on farms and estates at an agreed fee related to the acreage involved. The more places he could get to catch over, the more he could earn, making a visit to each place at intervals during the year.

Last but not least in the rural world came the lairds and their households. Although shorn of much of their former glory and affluence after the Great War when taxation began to weigh heavily on them, the lairds still wielded much power and influence in the countryside.

Each parish had its laird and mansion house. At Linton there was Clifton Park, the property of the Elliot family. In Roxburgh parish all the land between the River Teviot and Tweed was on the Duke of Roxburghe's estate, with the exception of the estate of Fairnington in the western end, which was owned by the Rutherfurds. In that part of Roxburgh on the south side of the river Teviot, the land was divided roughly between Colonel Scott-Ker's Sunlaws estate, and the Springwood property of Sir George Douglas Bart. The Edinburgh Merchant Company owned two farms in this area as well, but with no mansion house or parkland attached.

At Fogo the farms belonged to the Charterhall estate owned by Colonel Trotter, while at Doddington there was no laird as such, both farms in the parish being owner occupied. However there was Fenton estate nearby, with Fenton House a seat of the Earl of Durham.

All those lairds named kept full staffs of both indoor and outdoor workers, contributing substantially to the life and economy of the countryside. Each estate had its home farm with a farm manger and complement of workers on the home farm; the other outdoor staffs on the estates were considerable, each department having its head. There were a good many gardeners and foresters, also gamekeepers, coachmen (later chauffeurs) and grooms.

The foresters undertook fencing, hedging and suchlike tasks on the various farms. Although the requirements of farm leases made the tenants responsible for the upkeep of fences, any large fencing jobs were undertaken by the laird's men, the tenant sharing the cost. The same applied to farm buildings and houses. On certain estates, however, the terms of the farm leases provided that the estate foresters undertook all fencing repairs and the farmer footed the bill. The rule could be awkward at times, should livestock damage a fence and break out, for the farmer was not supposed to lift a hand to repair the fence, but had to send for the foresters to do it.

In the big house itself there was a veritable army of servants, both male and female, each with their own specified jobs and place in the pecking order.

The lairds and their families kept themselves to themselves very much aloof from the local folk. Occasionally they would condescend to open some village function or preside at a concert. To us farm folk their posh English accents were all but unintelligible, and, be it said, an object for mockery. On their part they looked down on us as a very inferior species. The main thing we disliked about the gentry was their arrogance and exclusiveness; their extensive grounds and policies were considered to be strictly private and sacrosanct. For anyone to venture into the woods for firewood was considered a crime, and even to gather fragments of branches from the wayside hedgerows or woodland fringes was

Craftsmen and Lairds

frowned upon. Carving their initials or names on trees was a pastime carried out by young rustics of both sexes. One laird was incensed when he discovered that a village chap had entered his woods and carved his name on a tree trunk. 'How dare he carve his filthy name on my tree', raged the laird. But that same lad was later to be killed in the war, fighting for his country and the laird's land. The woodland laws, if we might call them such, were rigorously enforced by the gamekeepers, who were persons of some power even as late as the 1930s. Some were more officious than others, of course, depending on how much pressure they were under from their game preserving masters, the gentry. After all they were only carrying out their duty of guarding the game birds.

Most of the country gentry were shooting mad from childhood upwards. A keeper once explained to me how they were taught, graduating from the catapult and air rifle to the small bore shotgun. Once they were old enough to handle a double barrelled shotgun, they roamed the estate when they were home on vacation from boarding school or college, blattering at everything that moved. I vividly remember one wanton act which took place when I was very small. One day the laird's daughter, a young lady of about twenty, was passing by Burnfoot, watched by us bairns and our mothers. Gun in hand as usual, she spied a heron standing on the banks of a stream in an adjoining field. She stopped on the roadside and fired a shot at it, killing it on the spot. Such senseless killing of an inoffensive creature made a lasting impression on me, and I disliked shooting and guns ever after. When I was a boy I pitied the poor partridges and pheasants driven over the guns on the days when the laird and his party had a shoot. The thud of the guns filled me with fear, and I was glad when the shooters moved on from near our house. Those shooting days were always big occasions, and the older schoolboys were often recruited as beaters; they got a sum of money and their food.

Young fellows from the farms used to frequent the big houses to court the maids. In most mansion houses 'followers', as the swains were called, were allowed in the servants' hall, and romances flourished between farm and village chaps and the servant girls. At the farmhouses and other establishments where maids were employed, they too were allowed to have their lads in the kitchen of an evening, but in some houses followers were forbidden, and many were the tricks resorted to by the maids and their lads to circumvent the rules.

One despicable practice employed in mansion houses to test the honesty of young girls and new servants was to leave money and valuables lying around. Farmers' wives and other persons who employed maids, including, alas! some ladies of the manse, used the same methods. Naturally this caused resentment on the part of the girls' parents when they were told about it. Some made protest by recalling their girl from the job, but most folk just tholed it, for they were glad to see their offspring in a job at all. The general idea of such bait-laying on the employers part was that the 'lower orders', as they termed us, were tarry fingered and presumed to be guilty until proved innocent. On the working folks' part, the inference to be drawn from such conduct by employers was that they themselves must be dishonest, seeing they suspected other people.

With all their faults, there is no doubt that the decline of the lairds, of their mansion houses and estates, and in many cases their disappearance from the scene altogether, left a vacuum in the countryside. They employed a large number of folk, even though those might not be highly paid. The numerous estate workers kept the environment tidy. Incidentally persons who worked on an estate were reckoned to be a cut above the ordinary farm workers.

One thing to the credit of the lairds was the manner in which past generations of them had beautified the landscape, by causing woods and hedgerow trees to be planted. This fact is brought home to anyone who stands at a vantage point and views the inbye Border scene. Very few of the owner occupiers of farms, who succeeded the lairds with the break up of

Craftsmen and Lairds

many estates after the First War, had much interest in tree planting. Frequently they got the woods felled and sold timber, leaving the spaces derelict, or turned the ground into fields for crop growing or pasture.

Epilogue

The year 1944 was a watershed in my life, for my father retired, and I was obliged to strike out on my own as a shepherd, after sharing with him a partnership of seventeen years' duration. During the subsequent nine years I worked as shepherd on three different farms. Some of that time I spent in lodgings but I had a house of my own for a brief period of two years. I sampled hill shepherding in two separate spells, and for eighteen months I even quit shepherding. For a short time I tried working to my own hand at seasonal work, and for another eight months I went to work on a dairy farm in Ayrshire. Eventually I got married and settled down as shepherd at the farm of Ladyrig, on the Heiton side of Roxburgh parish, where I spent twenty-five happy and fruitful years until my retirement in 1978.

The end of the war in 1945 marked the end of an era for the countryside as well. From then on occurred the period of change which has been called the Second Agricultural Revolution, and which has left its mark on the rural scene and obliterated much of what had gone before.

But it is the years between the wars which were the main theme of my present narrative. The record of events during the years since 1945 might one day become the subject of another book.

GLOSSARY OF SCOTS WORDS AND FARMING TERMS

a' all
ablow below
a'body everybody
aboot about
afore before
agin against
ah I
ahint behind
ain own
aipple apple
airm arm
airt place, area, direction
allooed allowed
an' and
anns beards
arles engagement or earnest
  money
as than
a'thegither, allthegether
  altogether
a'thing everything
atween between
auld old
awa' away
awfa', awfu', awfy awful
aye yes, still, always
bade stayed, remained
baith both
baits boots
barrae barrow
becis because
ben through

besom, bisom a difficult or
  disagreeable woman
bide stay, remain
bile boil
bits boots
blawin' blowing
boaught, bowght bought
borrae borrow
bowie a broad shallow dish
brat a coarse apron
braw fine
breid bread
brocht brought
brogglin' finding the way
broon brown
burds birds
ca', ca'ed call, called
cairry carry
cairt cart
caff, calf chaff
cannae can't
cauld cold
caun'les candles
cheen chain
chinae china
chinges changes
claes clothes
clapped burrowed
clatchy muddy
coo cow
cornins feeding stuffs
couldnae couldn't

277

A Shepherd Remembers

cowp overturn
cowpit overturned
crabbit crabbed
craive pigsty
cried called, named
dae do
daist just
daurnae daren't
deese dais, shelf
deid died, dead
dicks ducks
didnae didn't
din done
dinnae don't
div do
dizen dozen
dooked ducked
doon down
drapped dropped
dreel drill, row
drugget coarse woollen cloth
Edinbury Edinburgh
ee you
een eyes
eer your
efter after
efternin afternoon
erles arles, earnest money
et ate
faimly family
faither, fither father
faur far
feared afraid
feenish finish
fellae fellow
ferms farms
fit foot, feet
flair floor
flooer flour, flower
forbye besides
forrit forward
fower four

frae from
fu' full
gairden garden
Galae Galashiels
gang go
gaun go, going
gether gather
gey quite
gie give
gied gave
gi'en gave, giving
gin go
gird a child's hoop
greet weep
gress grass
guddle catching fish by hand
guid good
ha' have, hall
hae have
hale whole
hame home
handfae, handfu' handful
hap cover
harrae harrow
hei he
heid head
helpit helped
hervest harvest
het hot
hevin' having
hey hay
hind a married ploughman
hingin' hanging
hissel' himself
hoo how
hoor hour
hoose house
hows, howes hoes
hunder hundred
i' in
inby near the farm or steading
ingans onions

278

Glossary of Scots Words and Farming Terms

ight eight
ither either
iz me, us
jaist, jist, jeest just
jamb stanes upright stones at the side of the fireplace
Jeddart, Jedbury Jedburgh
jeely jelly
joukin' ducking, twisting
ken know
kent knew
kirn a celebration at the end of harvest
K.O.S.B. King's Own Scottish Borderers regiment
kye cows
kyles small heaps of hay
lang long
leid lead
lest last
lowse loosen, unbind; stop work
luggie a wooden milking pail
ma my
masel' myself
mair more
mairried, merried married
maist most
meenute, meenit minute
mony many
morn, the tomorrow
muckle big
nae no
naethin', nithin' nothing
nane none
neebour neighbour
nicht night
no' not
noo now
noob nob
o' of
ony any
or until, unless, if

orra, orrie spare, extra
oo we, us
oor our
oorsels ourselves
oot out
ootbye outlying
ower over
pant a public well
pawkies mittens
peenie apron
peerie a child's spinning top
peevers hopscotch
pert part
pey pay
pickle, puckle little
picturs cinema
pints points
ploogh plough
plotted scalded with boiling water
polisman policeman
pooder powder
Portybelly Portobello
pownd pond
pu'ed pulled
puir poor
putten put
raw row
reest to refuse to move
richt right
rin run
rither rather
roond round
row'ed rolled
sae so
saicond second
sate seat
schule school
scrogs crab-apples
seeven seven
selt sold
shair sure

A Shepherd Remembers

shawin' cutting off shaws from turnips
shouldnae shouldn't
shovelfaes shovelfuls
sic, sich such
sin, sinner soon, sooner
sma' small
soop sweep
sowl soul
speelin' climbing
stane stone
stent stint
stert start
stookin' setting up sheaves
strae straw
stripit striped
strip the cows draw off the last drops of milk by hand
sue in to turn to, buckle in
swee a hinged horizontal iron bar on which pots or kettles can be hung over a fire
sweir swear
syne ago
tae to, too
ta'en taken, taking
tatties, taetties, taitties potatoes
telt told
thae those
thame them
thegether, thegither together
theirsels themselves
thir these
thoaught, thocht, thowght thought
threshin' thrashing
trait treated

traivel travel
tumblin' tam a horse-drawn implement for gathering hay
twa, twae two
twal' twelve
wa' wall
wad would
waeter water
weel well
weemen women
weir, weer wear
wey way
werenae weren't
wha, whae who
whirly night a night for the fireside
whupper-in school attendance officer
wi' with
wid would, wood
widden wooden
widnae, wouldnae wouldn't
wight weight
windae window
wir were, our
wirsel' ourselves
wis was
wummin, wuman woman
yae one
yaise use
yaised, yaist, yist used
ye you
yellaes yellows
yersel' yourself
yin one
yince once